LIVING BLACK IN WHITE AMERICA

Books by Jay David

THE KENNEDY READER
THE FLYING SAUCER READER
GROWING UP BLACK
GROWING UP JEWISH
LIVING BLACK IN WHITE AMERICA (with Elaine Crane)

Edited by Mel Watkins and Jay David
TO BE A BLACK WOMAN

LIVING **BLACK** IN WHITE AMERICA

Edited by JAY DAVID
and ELAINE CRANE

With a Foreword by David L. Lewis

WILLIAM MORROW AND COMPANY, INC.
New York 1971

Contents

Foreword

IT has been no closely guarded secret that it has always been difficult to live as a black person in white America. Whites have known it, although most have minimized and many have denied the fact. Blacks (at least all but a very few) have been so preoccupied with survival that the experience has and continues to affect every aspect of personal and collective expression. The analogy of the concentration camp only *appears* to be extravagant to those whose knowledge of black history is distorted or fragmentary. It is an exact parallel, nevertheless, for like the Jewish death brigades at Dachau and Treblinka, the surviving generations of American blacks have been compelled to observe and to assist, actively or passively, in the systematic psychological and physical butchery of their kin. Moreover, the analogy stretches to the majority of whites who, like the "good" Germans of Hitler's Reich, have professed not to know precisely about or to bear, individually, responsibility for their country's treatment of its largest ethnic minority.

Perhaps (after all, there is no statistical research yet available) the great majority of whites has never known the awful details, the inhuman particulars of racial prejudice as they weigh upon and suffocate the great majority of black Americans. It is one thing to appreciate abstractly that the lot of a group of people is not a happy one; quite another to know intimately and empathetically that that lot is almost unbearable because, historically, neither talent nor money, neither education nor cultural assimilation, neither compliance nor militancy, neither legal victories nor government policy has ameliorated (for more than a small mi-

nority) the disabilities of pariah status. But if whites have
known only that it was indubitably not an advantage to be
black in white America without knowing precisely how
much a disadvantage—indeed, the word "disadvantage" is
exaggeratedly euphemistic!—this, too, had to be a self-serving concomitant of rascism, an ideological need *not* know.

The extravagant analogy becomes altogether reasonable
as one reads the foregoing excerpts selected by the editors of
Living Black in White America. I found myself thinking
of the recently published autobiography of Hitler's chief
architect and, later, armaments minister, Albert Speer, *Inside the Third Reich*. It was no closely guarded secret to
Albert Speer that European Jewry was dying in Nazi Germany; and there were, of course, thousands of politically
powerful Germans like Speer believing themselves to be
fundamentally humane and cosmopolitan (each with many
Jewish friends and each compromising official policy to
help his own Jewish coterie) but all of them willfully blind
to the total picture of genocide. Not once, Speer tells us, in
all those interminable evenings with Hitler at Obersalzberg,
did the gangsters who ran Germany after 1933 discuss the
Jewish question and the "final solution." Indeed, it was
never discussed in the salons of the Third *Reich*. The lesson
is obvious: For the butchers—those with the callousness of
their convictions—the matter was *res judicata*; for the politically genteel and the morally squeamish the raising or the
discussing of the question would have been far too painful.
Not only do the good die young, they usually receive gratuitous assistance from the good who survive.

The embarrassed colonel (an acquaintance of James Weldon Johnson) whose soldiers nearly killed Johnson and his
female companion and whose apology for the "incident" is
clearly sincere (described in *Along This Way*) exemplifies
this point. Then there is the incredible party Sammy Davis,

Jr., attends in his honor at which dozens of good Americans—none of them prejudiced, of course—behave in a manner which is, without knowing it, racially scandalous. "The worst thing in the world," Sammy tells his manager, "is when you're up against people *who don't know they're prejudiced.*" This species of punitive white "liberalism" and its companion outlook of determined indifference about the racial problem assault the reader in Ellen Tarry's *The Third Door.* Too white for anybody to suppose her black and too proud to permit an interview for a job (in the teeth of the Depression) to end on a note of beneficial mistaken racial identity, Miss Tarry discovered that her beauty, poise, and intelligence were universally appreciated by her would-be and temporary employers (all honorable men) even though she was black, and even though ("Now don't get me wrong. I have nothing against colored people") she was not hired or was summarily fired when the truth was revealed. Good Germans and good white Americans, how they suffered when they were prevented from acting decently!

For the sake of *leitmotiv* the editors, Jay David and Elaine Crane, have chosen to arrange their materials so that what is properly the middle portion ("Living Black in White America") begins the book while the appropriate beginning ("The Seeds of Bitterness") follows. People in the history trade are likely to regret this, as I did, in the few seconds required to scan the table of contents. This is a quibble, however, for once beyond the contents and into the text (and reading *Living Black in White America* straight through in one sitting as I did) the cumulative effect of these twenty-two selections is—and I intentionally use the word—staggering.

When any group of people begins to slug its way up from the bottom of the heap, it suffers, is victimized and victimizes, fights valiantly and ignobly and is fought against in like manner. The works of Dos Passos and Willa Cather in literature, Oscar Handlin and Marcus Hansen in social history are random citations of excellent treatments of aspects of this phenomenon. To know a little bit about blacks in American history has become *de rigueur* of late. Milton Meltzer's *In Their Own Words,* Joanne Grant's *Black Protest, Black Nationalism in America* edited by John Bracey, August Meier, and Elliott Rudwick are several of the still not so many well-conceived anthologies depicting black survival, growth, and assertiveness in America. *Living Black in White America* will be another.

Perspective is always a problem in history. It is especially problematical in what has come to be called black history because, in reacting to the decades of willful distortion and neglect by white society and its white historians, black history tends to be compensatorily strident, propagandist, and self-serving. And, also, because distressingly little is exactly known about the subject, either by blacks or whites. The traditional approach to historical interpretation by most white academics has not been altogether satisfactory because, far too often, the methodical sifting and arranging of "the facts"—even reasonably interpreted—have fallen short of presenting the truth for want of empathy and imagination. Conversely, the history that the "militants" are writing is all too frequently cavalier about accuracy and *too* imaginative and *too* empathetic. The writing of good history in a given area or field is, after all, dependent upon its own history of good historical writing. The research and writing of black history lacks this didactic and mature tradition. The problem of perspective will be with us for a very long time, I suspect.

The great utility of the David-Crane work is that it enhances our perspective considerably. With remarkable appropriateness it selects from the troubled stream of black

consciousness testimonials that appear to satisfy the pre-
conditions of an authentic record of the black experience.
The authors' policy of quite brief prefatory notes to each of
the selections, limited to name, predicament, and era, is
suited to an anthology intended for general readers. The
selections are sufficiently vivid to make their own points
within the context of the general theme.

The pathos is there in *Living Black in White America;* we
read it in Saunders Redding's *On Being Negro in America.*
The ghastliness is there; Charles Ball's *Fifty Years in Chains*
is an horrific personal distillation of the grotesqueries of
slavery. The acrid humor is there; it was only her superior
humor that permitted Billie Holiday's unique talent to
thrive in a world of racial troglodytes. Billie was undaunted
by the mean sheriffs and sallow-complexioned waitresses,
deeply wise about the hotshot liberalism of Artie Shaw and
his band members, and beautifully forbearing when, at the
end, opportunity knocked and knocked her right out of the
picture. Then there is the sophisticated irony of Langston
Hughes: George Gershwin's, Carl Van Vechten's and Heywood Broun's passion for Negroes, along with the nocturnal
white inundations of Harlem in the twenties, were hothouse
passions which all the brilliance of the Harlem Renaissance
writers and all the booze of Madame J. C. Walker's daughter's
salon could not perpetuate. Then there are the mulatto and
upper class tragedies contained in the James Weldon Johnson, Ellen Tarry, and Bob Teague selections.

There is much more in *Living Black.* What counts most,
I think, is the passion and sincerity of those who have
lived black in white America. Just as one cannot write a
useful history of modern Europe without particular attention paid to victimized and decimated Jewry, in the same
way American history henceforth is impermissibly inaccu-
rate and impoverished to the extent that the treatment of the

Negro is unexplored or distorted. If the American Negro
is not special because of his sufferings, certainly his sufferings are unique because of him. The awesome challenge, of
course, is to be able to digest this eruptive mass, to make
sense of it all but without depersonalizing its essence, to
interpret and to retain the intractably existential and par-
ticularistic.

The temptation to forswear analysis for passion is great.
The slice of keening hypocrisy Sammy Davis, Jr., serves us
is simply indigestible. The caviar and southern fried chick-
en and the unobtrusive plate of gefilte fish for Sammy's
manager at the far end of the buffet table, the bizarre com-
pliments—"He's only the finest performer in the business,
that's all. . . . Let me get you a drink, Sambo"—induce
nausea. What Jesse Owens experienced as a boy growing up
in Alabama (the lynch scene he recounts) pushes us to the
precipice of maddened revulsion. And in a podunk town in
Humphreys County, Mississippi, one Gus Courts is determined to vote. Only a fool would want to vote in that town
and Gus Courts, the avowed president of the local NAACP
chapter, is that kind of fool. The whites try to ruin his business, to bribe him; a local minister is shotgunned to death
and the sheriff refuses to investigate, saying that the lead in
his neck and jaw might well have come from "fillings in his
teeth." Still Gus perseveres. He, too, is shotgunned. Ultimately, he votes.

There must be a better way of living black in white
America, one thinks. Out of these twenty-two representative
pieces only Jesse Owens' *Blackthink* (Booker T. Washington is absent here) is truly optimistic in the traditional American sense of expressing the firm conviction that so much has
become so much better that most of the other inequities and
injustices will vanish within a tolerable period of time. Although the reader will admire the man Owens, he may very

well feel compelled by the sheer weight of the other entries to doubt the relevance of Owens' views. Of course, black racism is as reprehensible as white racism, and undoubtedly the majority of black militants today would collapse in shock before the feudal savagery of white racism of nearly fifty years ago. Nevertheless, Jesse Owens' *Blackthink* is an uncomfortable *apologia*. If he were not who he is black readers might call him an Uncle Tom. Frederick Douglass' remarks to Sojourner Truth appear to be far more apposite: "Because God is not dead, slavery can only end in blood." Servitude in its myriad contemporary guises is likely to result in massacres notwithstanding the straightforward optimism of a Jesse Owens and his fine example of manhood.

And so how does one remain "balanced," how does one incorporate the saga of black survival into the sober lineaments of a national history? American history is revolutionary only in the sense of having brought off a rejection of a quaint and quite inappropriate species of political sovereignty. The social side of our revolution, an American 1871 (the Paris Commune and all that), has not come to pass. And it is the American black by and large who is the alienated fourth estate, the incipiently politicized proletariat.

Many black readers will be convinced by the implications embodied in Bobby Seale's *Seize the Time*. They will allow themselves to believe that living black in this country in the future will entail the heroic risk of willingness to die. Of course, to some extent this is true. Moreover, the threat and the example of violence and even nihilism are healthy catalysts in the process of sluggish social change. But violence— however attractive, purifying, and schematized in the manner of John Brown—is only a partial and highly risky antidote, a cure easily more deadly than the malady. One turns the pages back to the fascinating session between the venerable John Brown and Frederick Douglass for counsel and conviction at this point. If unconvinced still, then one should turn again to Martin Luther King's nonviolent advice towards the end of this anthology.

This must be the ultimate and authentic service of this anthology. It compels the attention by lighting up some of the awful and awesome burdens a people has somehow borne for a long time. It compels attention because it instructs us how far we have come in almost one generation during which a class of professionally impressive Bob Teagues has emerged. It compels attention also because it instructs us how far American society has gone backwards in that same generation with the emergence of an impressive class of professional militants of the Bobby Seale stamp. Staggered, we are obliged—we ought be—to make some sense of all this. We probably will not be able to for a while yet. We need more anthologies of this caliber to provide the emotional backing to the "facts" being uncovered by the growing army of researchers in black history. Eventually, when the inside and the outside of history come together, we will understand the American past better because we will understand better the crucial role of blacks in that past. It cannot be demonstrated that the study and knowledge of the past has ever once precluded a specific disaster in history. Conversely, it is assuredly beyond debate that ignorance of the past is a certain guarantee of future collective idiocy and injustice.

DAVID L. LEWIS

Introduction

Living Black in White America is *Growing Up Black* grown up. The latter recorded the childhood reminiscences of nineteen black Americans over the past two centuries, and in so doing became a history as well. *Living Black in White America* is a natural sequel to that book. It is an autobiographical journey through two hundred years of adult black experience; it too is rightly called an historical narrative. In addition, however, *Living Black in White America* takes on a more pointed focus of its own. It not only recalls the mental and physical suffering of twenty-two Negro Americans, but confronts us with the staggering *effects* of this experience on the American social scene—ever-increasing alienation, mistrust, and frustration.*

The autobiographies in this book also enable us to understand in a personal way why and how the American dream bypassed 10 percent of America's people. Each selection illustrates a different aspect of the humiliation and subjugation the black man has been forced to endure as a fourth-class American. Together they present a remarkably accurate and human account of the Negro in America. Gustavus Vassa's tale of his voyage across the ocean in chains, Jesse Owens' story of his parents who were the first generation of American Negroes freed of chains, Ellen Tarry's recollections of the difficulties she encountered in her job-hunting days of the 1930s, James Baldwin's account that illuminates the psychological bonds borne by all black men and women—

*Of the twenty-two black Americans who recount their adult experiences in *Living Black in White America*, only four also appear in *Growing Up Black*.

these and other narratives make the disaffection so many
blacks hold for America comprehensible. What is surprising
is the affection and hope that many black people still express
for this country.

While the first and second parts of *Living Black in White
America* focus on the heritage of white racism and the effect
it had on the nation's black people, the third part concen-
trates on the consequent movements of protest and militancy.
The seeds of bitterness sown some 350 years ago and culti-
vated by ensuing generations have yielded an angry harvest.

JAY DAVID
ELAINE CRANE

LIVING BLACK IN WHITE AMERICA

ALL of the following episodes took place at various times during twentieth-century America. They are so filled with anguish that the reader almost feels he is intruding upon these narrators, who have had to withstand indignity and who have suffered the most barbaric acts. These moments, extended through time and multiplied by similar experiences of millions of people, have produced the racial turbulence of two centuries and the spreading militant protest of the 1960s and 1970s.

1

FROM

On Being Negro in America

by Saunders Redding
(1906–   )

As a native of the upper South, Redding keenly felt the everyday symptoms of discrimination, but it did not approach the anguish he suffered as a father trying to comfort his eight-year-old son who had been told that he was not as good as his friend because he was black.

Born in Washington, Delaware, of college-educated parents, Redding lived in a predominantly white neighborhood. He attended Lincoln University in Pennsylvania, but transferred after one year to Brown University in Rhode Island. There he felt the pressure of racial tensions. By his senior year he was the only black student, and it seemed to him that he was "fighting the whole white world" singlehandedly.

Author of several books, among them the widely acclaimed No Day of Triumph, *Redding is a professor at George Washington University in Washington, D. C.*

PERHAPS I make too much of this, and perhaps I am overwrought and unreasonable about it. I must confess that there flit across my mind, like stones skipped on the surface

21

of water (only to sink into it), thoughts of my sons. There are moments when I am sentimental enough to hope that history is a necessary progress toward better things and that frustrations of the human spirit grow less and less. I know better. But I have such hopes when my sons are involved, and I am inclined to support them intemperately.

It does not serve merely to shrug one's shoulders and carp about the psychic traumas that bedevil American man. At least it did not do seven years ago, when my older son was eight and my younger not yet born. And now that my younger is himself almost seven, it still will not do. Argument does not exactly serve either, although I think I argue for something eminently sane. It is simplicity. I argue the substitution of spontaneous, instinctive responses for the deliberate responses based, as I have said above, on unchanging ideas and ideals. It seems to me that the old rules— evoked as they were out of the utmost confusion of morality and social expedience, and deliberate ignorance—are not only unnecessarily complicated for modern times and people, but that they are progressively unsuitable to modern ways of living, to the advance of knowledge, to technology, and (surely everyone will allow this) to one-worldness. Make the rules simple enough and we can play the hardest game.

What happened to my older son (and also to my younger son just recently, though not in circumstances so distressing nor in details so graphic) was that while he was playing the game with all the exuberance of an eight-year-old, somebody "complicated up" the rules. I remember distinctly how it happened.

For several weeks while my wife was with child it was my unaccustomed duty to "make the marketing," as it is so quaintly put in the upper South. Our market was a co-op on the highway just outside town, in the heart of one of those neat and monotonous residential communities that seemed to spring up everywhere in the 1940s. My wife loved the place. It was convenient; its stock was excellent; and its prices generally somewhat lower than in the chain groceries. Besides, it had a Negro (a colleague and friend) on its board of directors, and, as a second novel attraction, it employed several Negroes—at least one as clerk and another as butcher. The co-op's atmosphere, unlike that of the chain's, was friendly, warm, leisurely. My wife supposed it was because of the neighborhood—a better-than-average middle-class neighborhood, segregated of course, of aircraft designers, engineers and other technological experts and a scattering of armed-service personnel (no one lower than a lieutenant in the Navy or a captain in the Army, it seemed) from the various military installations close by. As one of the charter stockholders, I was determined to love the place too.

Friday was market day. Until her condition prevented her going, my wife's eager companion on these expeditions was our son. Sometime in the spring he had struck up a friendship at the co-op and he anticipated its weekly renewal with pleasurable excitement. The first time I took him there I saw the revival of the fraternity with quickened heart. My son burst through the door ahead of me, stopped, looked down the first aisle (fresh fruits and vegetables), ran to the second and looked, and then suddenly let out an Indian whoop—"Reggie!"—and got one for an answer—"Conway!" And then I saw a handsome dark-haired, dark-eyed boy of about Conway's age break from the side of a young Negro girl and come bursting up the aisle between the high-stacked shelves of brightly packaged foods toward my son. They stood looking at each other for a moment, then they came together, each with arm around the shoulders of the other, and exploded off to play outside among the cars until market was made. I looked at the uniformed Negro girl and she smiled and I smiled, and that was that.

It was that way for four or five weeks—Conway and Reggie met each other with what seemed the force of projectiles
and went skyrocketing off. Leaving the market, I would find
them outside, hot and happy playing at some impossible
game.

Then one Friday, Reggie (we never learned his last name)
was not there with the Negro maid. His guardian this time
was a man—a tall, handsome person, about forty, I judged,
who in spite of the Phi Beta Kappa key slung across his flat
stomach, looked outdoorsy and virile. The boys came together as usual and went outside as usual, but the man's
marketing must have been nearly done, for before I could
finish picking out the heaviest, juiciest oranges, Conway
was back with me again. "Where's Reggie?" I asked him.
"He had to go," he said. "His daddy was in a hurry." But
already he was looking forward to the next week.

The uniformed maid was with Reggie again the next
week, but this time when Conway let out his customary
whoop, there was no vocal answer. Reggie turned, it seemed
to me with momentary eagerness, but there was no yell and
rush. He approached very slowly. He was smiling weakly,
but that smile died as he came. Perhaps sensing that something was wrong, Conway himself now hesitated. "What's
the matter?" he asked Reggie. "Come on, man, let's go. Don't
you want to play?"

"I can't play with you," Reggie said.

"What's the matter, are you sick?" Conway wanted to
know.

"I just can't play with you any more," Reggie said.

Conway moved a fraction closer to me, clutched the handle of the food cart I was pushing. The maid stood at some
distance, pretending not to watch. The pleasant-voiced,
pleasant-faced shoppers of the neighborhood flowed around
us. Other children, younger, skittered and yelled up and
down the aisles. The compacted odors of fresh pastry, of

ground coffee, of fruits and vegetables, and the colors of all these were as ever. But a chill was beginning to form around my heart. Before Conway asked the next question, I knew the answer that was coming. I did not know the words of it, but I knew the feel—the iron that he would not be prepared for; the corrosive rust that it would make in his blood and that, unless I was skillful—as my father was not—I could never draw off. At that moment—no, before the moment of the answer I wanted to pick Conway up and hold him hard against me and ward off the demoralizing blow that might be struck for a lifetime. But I could not forfend it even by grasping my son by the hand and walking off in another direction. I was transfixed.

"Why?"

Reggie scowled then, a grimace that was not really ugly yet, because it was associated only with words and not with feeling. That would come later, and the word would be made flesh, and the flesh would be his forever. Now the scowl was only imitation.

"Because you're a nigger, that's why." Reggie said.

Conway looked at me wonderingly, not feeling hurt, as they say a man knowing himself shot but still without pain will look with surprise.

"I'm better than you," Reggie said, " 'cause my father said so."

"You are not," Conway said, but I thought he shrank a little against me.

"No, son, he isn't," I said.

"I am so, too," Reggie said, looking at both of us. Words were beginning to arouse emotion and link with emotion. The sneer was no longer imitation. He stood bearing his weight on his left foot, his hands in the pockets of his khaki shorts, the whiteness of him showing in a streak just below the hairline, the rest of him—bare trunk, bare legs—tanned almost to the color of my son.

"No, son," I said, as much to the one as to the other. I think I felt sorry for Reggie too. I do now at any rate, thinking back.

"You are not," Conway said, and straightened. "My daddy says you aren't."

"You don't go to my school, you don't go to my church, you don't go to the movies I go to. I bet you've never even seen Tim Holt," he put in parenthetically, "and that's because you're not good enough. Yah-yah!" Reggie said. "Niggers work for us, niggers work for us, you're a nigger and Trixie's a nigger and Trixie works for us." It was a shrilling singsong. "Yah-yah nigger nigger, go peddle your papers, nigger!" With this he ran off, back, I suppose, to Trixie, who worked for him because she was a nigger.

Conway did not cry, but in his eyes was the look of a wound, and I knew how it could grow, become infected and pump its poison to every tissue, to every brain cell. He stayed close to me while I made market. On the way home, he said savagely, "I hate this car!"

It did not seem like any kind of entree to what I knew I must talk about, and the sooner the better. When what happened to him happens it makes a nasty wound which demands immediate attention. You want a knife to do the job quickly, deftly, cleanly, but the only instruments in the surgery kit are words.

So when I wanted to know what was wrong with the car and why he hated it, and he said, "Why can't we have a good car, a new one with a radio, and a bigger one—like Reggie's?" I tried to explain to him that it was wartime, that cars were scarce and prices high, and that in order to get a new car you had to do something a little underhanded, something that was not much different from stealing or cheating.

"Did Reggie's father steal?"

"I wouldn't say that," I said, "but I wouldn't put it past him. He's not a good man."

"How do you know? You don't know him, do you?"

"No," I said, "but I don't have to know him to know he's not a good man." I put it as simply as I could. I told him that parents are frequently reflected in their children. I made him laugh a little by reminding him of the time, when he was six, he had acutely embarrassed his mother and me by telling one of our friends, "I think you have store-bought teeth," which was exactly what he had heard me say about the friend.

"Those things Reggie said today, his father said to him. That's how I know Reggie's father is not a good man."

"He wasn't telling the truth, was he?"

"No," I said, shaking my head.

"I mean about him being better?"

"No," I answered.

"Then why can't I go to his school and to his movies?"

This was the deepest infection, and I did not know how to deal with it. Words were poultices to seal the infection in. I could recall them from my own childhood in answer to a "why?". For children are not born with answers. Words spoken by my parents, my teachers, my friends. Words could seal in the infection and seal in also the self that might never break through again except with extreme luck. But I had no choice save to use them. I told him about prejudice. No one has ever made the anatomy of prejudice simple enough for children.

"And the reason you don't go to Reggie's school," I remember saying, "is because there are people like Reggie's father."

"It's all complicated up," Conway answered.

It was a relief to laugh at his child's expression, but I noticed he was not laughing, and at home some minutes later, when I had finished storing the groceries in the pantry, I found him pressed against his mother's rounded bosom crying without restraint. But even that did not end it.

"He cried it all out," his mother said. She was wrong.

Seven years afterward, in the late spring of 1950, we had a letter from the headmaster of Conway's New England preparatory school: "We have been unable to reach him . . . . He seems to prefer to be alone and will not participate even in those activities for which he has undoubted talents. Naturally this attitude has given us serious concern, for an important part of our educational program is training in citizenship and cooperative living . . ."

Perhaps there is only a slight connection, but I would be hard to convince.

2

FROM

Along This Way

by James Weldon Johnson
(1871–1938)

Racism not only struck at children but insulted the manhood and womanhood of each black person. The sexual overtones of discrimination are all too evident in the laws against miscegenation and the types of punishment—such as castration—meted out to blacks for various crimes.

   This selection, which takes place in Florida in the very early 1900s, portrays both the debasement of black Americans and the absurdity of a system which prohibits the association of a black man with a white woman, but permits this same association if the woman has a white skin but is legally a Negro.

   James Weldon Johnson was the first Negro to pass the Florida bar examination, but he did not spend much time practicing law. Instead he became an important figure in the development of Negro-American literature and culture. He was also an eager participant in the earliest civil-rights movements, as well as a teacher and diplomat. Johnson is

29

perhaps best known for his novel The Autobiography of
an Ex-Colored Man. *In* Along This Way *Johnson tells the
story of his life.*

THERE was a lady from New York who was an occasional
contributor to various papers and magazines visiting in
Jacksonville at the time of the fire. A very handsome woman
she was, with eyes and hair so dark that they blanched the
whiteness of her face. One afternoon she came to the com-
missary depot where I was engaged and told me that she
had written an article on the fire, dealing especially with
its effects on the Negro population, which she would like to
have me read over before she sent it off. I readily consented
to read the article, but told her I couldn't possibly do so
until after four o'clock, when the depot closed. It was a
sweltering afternoon, and I was hot and tired; so I suggested
that after closing time we might take a street car and ride out
to Riverside Park, where we could sit and go over the article
leisurely and in comfort. She decided that instead of waiting
around for me to close she would go out to the park and wait
there.

At four o'clock I washed up and boarded a car. I had not
yet been to this new Riverside Park; in fact, it was not yet
quite a park. There was an old Riverside Park that I knew
very well; but the city had recently acquired a large oak and
pine covered tract on the bank of the river, a few miles farther out, which it was converting into a new park. I was,
perhaps, more interested in seeing how this work had progressed than I was in reading the lady's article. When I
reached the end of the car-line, I noticed a rustic waiting-
pavilion near the edge of the river. I made my way to it, expecting to find the lady there. She was not there, and I looked
about but saw no sign of her. I judged that she had grown
tired of waiting and had returned to the city. I walked back

to the car-line. The car I had come out on was still there.
The conductor and motorman were standing on the ground
near the rear end. I waited until they were about ready to
start, then got aboard. The car was empty, except for me,
and I took a seat near the center—there were then no "Jim
Crow" street car laws in Jacksonville. As I settled in my seat
and glanced out of the window I saw a woman approaching
across a little rustic bridge a hundred or so feet away whom
I at once recognized by her dress and the black and white
parasol she carried to be the lady I was to meet. I jumped
off the car and walked over to join her. We went back
across the bridge, then along some newly laid out paths
until we came to a little clearing on the other side of which
was a barbed wire fence. I helped her through the fence and
followed. We then walked through the trees until we came
to the bank of the river, where we found a bench and sat
down. She read the article to me, and I offered one or two
suggestions.

We sat talking. The sun was still bright, but was prepar-
ing for his plunge under the horizon, which he makes more
precipitantly in the far south than he does in the north. At
the point where we were sitting the St. Johns River is several
miles wide. Across the water the sun began cutting a bril-
liant swath that constantly changed and deepened in color
until it became a flaming road between us and the dark line
of trees on the opposing bank. The scene was one of perfect
semi-tropical beauty. Watching it, I became conscious of
an uneasiness, an uneasiness that, no doubt, had been struggling the while to get up and through from my subconscious.
I·became aware of noises, of growing, alarming noises; of
men hallooing back and forth, and of dogs responding with
the bay of bloodhounds. One thought, that they might be
hunters, flashed through my mind; but even so, there was
danger of a stray shot. And yet, what men would hunt with

such noises, unless they were beating the bush to trap a
wild, ferocious beast? I rose to go, and my companion followed. We threaded our way back. The noises grew more
ominous. They seemed to be closing in. My pulse beat faster
and my senses became more alert. I glanced at my companion; she showed no outward sign of alarm. Suddenly we
reached the barbed wire fence. There we stopped. On the
other side of the fence death was standing. Death turned and
looked at me and I looked at death. In the instant I knew that
the lowering of an eyelash meant the end.

Just across the fence in the little clearing were eight or
ten militiamen in khaki with rifles and bayonets. The abrupt
appearance of me and my companion seemed to have transfixed them. They stood as under a spell. Quick as a flash of
light the series of occurrences that had taken place ran
through my mind: The conductor and motorman saw me
leave the street car and join the woman; they saw us go back
into the park; they rushed to the city with a maddening tale
of a Negro and white woman meeting in the woods; there
is no civil authority; the military have sent out a detach-
ment of troops with guns and dogs to get me.

I lose self-control. But a deeper self springs up and takes
command; I follow orders. I take my companion's parasol
from her hand; I raise the loose strand of fence wire and
gently pass her through; I follow and step into the group.
The spell is instantly broken. They surge round me. They
seize me. They tear my clothes and bruise my body; all the
while calling to their comrades, "Come on, we've got 'im!
Come on, we've got 'im!" And from all directions these
comrades rush, shouting, "Kill the damned nigger! Kill the
black son of a bitch!" I catch a glimpse of my companion;
it seems that the blood, the life is gone out of her. There is
the truth; but there is no chance to state it; nor would it be
believed. As the rushing crowd comes yelling and cursing, I

feel that death is bearing in upon me. Not death of the empty sockets, but death with the blazing eyes of a frenzied brute. And still, I am not terror-stricken, I am carrying out the chief command that has been given me, "Show no sign of fear; if you do you are lost." Among the men rushing to reach me is a slender young man clad in a white uniform. He breaks through the men who have hold of me. We look at each other; and I feel that a quivering message from intelligence to intelligence has been interchanged. He claps his hand on my shoulder and says, "You are my prisoner." I ask him, "What is the charge?" He answers, "Being out here with a white woman." I question once more, "Before whom do I answer this charge?" "Before Major B—, the provost marshal," he replies. At that, I answer nothing beyond "I am your prisoner."

The eternity between stepping through the barbed wire fence and the officer's words putting me under arrest passed, I judge, in less than sixty seconds. As soon as the lieutenant put his hand on me and declared me his prisoner, the howling mob of men became soldiers under discipline. Two lines were formed, with my companion and me between them, and marched to the street car. The soldiers filled the seats, jammed the aisle, and packed the platforms, and still some of them, with two men in civilian clothes holding the dogs in leash, were left over for the next car. As we began nearing the city my companion had the reactions natural to a sensitive woman. Both of us were now fairly confident that the danger of physical violence was passed, but it was easy to see that she was anxious; perhaps, about the probable notoriety; perhaps, about the opportunity for malicious tongues. I assured her as best I could that everything would come out all right. I said to her, "I know Major B—, the provost marshal, very well; he is a member of the Jacksonville bar." On the way in, the car stopped at the electric power house.

It was met by a crowd of conductors, motormen, and other employees, who hailed our car with cries of, "Have you got 'em?" "Yes, we've got 'em," the soldiers cried back.

Before the car left the power house, the young lieutenant, whom I had hardly been able to see after we left the park, made his way to our seat. Again I felt the waves of mental affinity. In the midst of the brutishness that surrounded us I felt that between him and me there was somewhere a meeting place for reason. He leaned over and said, "I'm going to put these men off the car here and take you in myself." He ordered the men off. Of course, they obeyed, but they were openly a disappointed and disgruntled lot. The car moved across the aqueduct and into the heart of the city. I was thankful for the lieutenant's action; because, for reason or no reason, I did not want to be paraded through the streets of Jacksonville as a prisoner under guard of a company of soldiers. In my gratitude I was tempted to tell him what I did not have a chance to tell before I was put under arrest. But I was now comparatively light-hearted. I was already anticipating the burlesque finale to this melodrama—melodrama that might have been tragedy—and I disliked spoiling any of the effects. However, I did say to him, "The lady with me *is* white, but not legally so." He looked at her curiously, but made no comment; instead he said to me, "You know where the provost headquarters are, don't you?" I answered that I did. He continued, "When you get off the car you walk on ahead; I'll follow behind, and nobody will know you are under arrest." I thanked him again. We got off and walked to the provost headquarters, passing numbers of people, colored and white, who knew me. We went into the provost marshal's tent, followed by the lieutenant, who turned his prisoners over.

Major B— showed astonishment and some embarrassment when he recognized me. I said to him, "Major,

here I am. What is the charge?" He repeated the charge the
lieutenant had made. "Major," I went on, "I know there
is no use in discussing law or my rights on any such basis
as, 'Suppose the lady *is* white?' so I tell you at once that according to the customs and, possibly, the laws of Florida,
she *is not* white." In spite of appearances, he, of course,
knew that I spoke the truth. He was apologetic and anxious
to dismiss us and the matter. He spoke of the report that
had been brought in, of his duty as commanding officer of
the provost guard, of how he never even dreamed what the
actual facts were. In answering, I told him that I appreciated
how he felt about it personally but that did not balance the
jeopardy in which my life had been put. I added, "You know
as well as I do, if I had turned my back once on that crowd
or taken a single step in retreat, I'd now be a dead man."
He agreed with me and said he was as glad as I that nothing
of the kind had happened. At this point my companion began to speak. She spoke slowly and deliberately at first;
then the words came in torrents. She laid on the Major's
head the sins of his fathers and his fathers' fathers. She
charged him that they were the ones responsible for what
had happened. As we left, the Major was flushed and flus-
tered. I felt relieved and satisfied, especially over the actually minor outcome of the avoidance of any notoriety
for my companion. It was now dark, and I took her to her
stopping place, The Boyland Home, a school for colored
girls supported by northern philanthropy.

I did not get the nervous reaction from my experience
until I reached home. The quick turn taken by fate had
buoyed me up. When I went into the provost marshal's tent
my sense of relief had mounted almost to gaiety. Now, the
weight of all the circumstances in the event came down and
carried me under. My brother was the only one of the family
to whom I confided what had taken place. He was terrified

over what might have happened; I never mentioned it to my parents. For weeks and months the episode with all of its implications preyed on my mind and disturbed me in my sleep. I would wake often in the night-time, after living through again those few frightful seconds, exhausted by the nightmare of a struggle with a band of murderous, blood-thirsty men in khaki, with loaded rifles and fixed bayonets. It was not until twenty years after, through work I was then engaged in, that I was able to liberate myself completely from this horror complex.

Through it all I discerned one clear and certain truth: in the core of the heart of the American race problem the sex factor is rooted; rooted so deeply that it is not always recognized when it shows at the surface. Other factors are obvious and are the ones we dare to deal with; but, regardless of how we deal with these, the race situation will continue to be acute as long as the sex factor persists. Taken alone, it furnishes a sufficient mainspring for the rationalization of all the complexes of white racial superiority. It may be innate; I do not know. But I do know that it is strong and bitter; and that its strength and bitterness are magnified and intensified by the white man's perception, more or less, of the Negro complex of sexual superiority.

3

FROM

Yes I Can

by Sammy Davis, Jr.
(1925–   )

*Racial discrimination has been an American social problem
for so long that even an honest attempt to bridge the gap
between the races, as Sammy Davis explains, can turn into
an embarrassing situation.*

*One of the great entertainers of our time, Sammy Davis,
Jr., was born into a show-business family while the 1920s
roared around him. He was on the road by the time he was
three, and virtually never left it. Shielded by his father and
uncle from the realities of black-white relations in America,
Sammy found it very difficult to adjust to the fact that
people could hate him solely on the basis of the color of
his skin. He could not accept this blind bigotry, yet he did
not know how to cope with it. Out of his frustration came
the desire to become "so big, so strong, so important" that
those people and their prejudice could never touch him.
Unfortunately, no matter how big, strong, and important*

he became, the acceptance he so passionately sought as an
individual, rather than as a black man, continued to elude
him.

I SPOTTED the doorman from a block away: another Concentration Camp Gerhardt, in full dress uniform. I let
myself get caught on a traffic light and watched the cars
headed the other way, down Park Avenue. I was tempted to
make a U-turn and go back to the hotel.

"I'll take care of it for you, Mr. Davis." He was smiling
as he opened the car door. He rushed ahead of us and held
open the front door, then he ran ahead and bowed me
toward the elevator. I smiled, "Thank you."

He turned to the elevator man. "Mr. Davis and this other
gentleman are going to the penthouse."

I hadn't said where I was going. He hadn't recognized me
and been courteous out of respect, he'd been expecting me,
I was getting "safe conduct"; someone had warned him,
"Sammy Davis, Jr. is coming here. He's colored. Watch for
him and don't embarrass him."

There was only one apartment on the floor and the party
sounds floated through the open door. The host hurried
over. "Sammy, welcome, welcome, welcome." His eyes
tensed. "You didn't have any trouble . . . finding us, did
you?"

"The number was right on the building. This is George
Gilbert, my producer."

"Glad you could make it, George." He put his arm
around my shoulder. "Come on in, Sammy, everyone's
dying to meet you." He walked me around the living
room introducing me to attractive people who were smiling,
being courteous. A group formed around me. Somebody
said, "I saw *Mr. Wonderful* and you really are. You were
just marvelous."

My host said, "He's only the finest performer in the business, that's all." He put his arm around my shoulder. "Let
me get you a drink, Sambo. What'll it be?"

I took out a cigarette. "I'll have a coke, thanks." Before
I could reach for my lighter somebody had one flaring in
front of me. "Thank you very much."

"My privilege. I'll light your cigarettes any time. I wish
I knew where you learned to dance the way you do."

A woman interrupted. "Oh, Biffy, don't be ridiculous.
No one *learns* to dance like that. Some people are . . ."

There was a death pause and I tried to take them off the
hook. I smiled. "Well, you know what they say about colored
people having rhythm."

Biffy wouldn't take the out. He was looking at me blankly.
He couldn't imagine what I was talking about. Not the
foggiest. "Oh? I'm surprised I never heard that."

I shrugged. "It's just an old cliché."

"Say, that's very interesting. I mean, do you think there's
anything to that? I mean, about colored people . . . do you
think that the Negro people"—he lowered his voice as he
said the words "colored" and "Negro"—really do have
rhythm? I mean, now that I think of it I do recall hearing
something about the background of jungle life. Naturally
I'm referring to centuries ago . . ."

George mumbled, "I *hope* so," and wandered off to the
bar.

"Uh, what I'm trying to get across is . . ." He was staring
into my eyes, afraid I'd think he was looking at my skin,
talking like a man struggling to get out of quicksand. Beads
of perspiration were forming around his forehead.

The merciful thing was to play it straight. "I doubt it. I
know some Negroes who can't dance the foxtrot. On the
other hand there are people like Fred Astaire, Gene Kelly,
Donald O'Connor . . ."

Someone said, "I'm going to look at the buffet table."
I smiled. "But don't eat anything. Just look!" They roared, relieved, the pressure released.

A man with a plate in his hand said, "Sammy, my name's Endley. Funny that I should meet you. My kid goes to school with Ralph Bunche's son."

"I haven't had the pleasure of meeting Dr. Bunche."

"Well, neither have I, actually. But his son's a fine lad. I've never exactly met him but I hear nothing but the finest things about him . . . the finest things."

It was a dead end. I excused myself and walked over to the buffet table. It was beautifully laid out. There was a large silver chafing dish of Lobster Newburg, something elegant looking like pâté de foie gras, a tin of caviar resting on shaved ice, and a platter of fried chicken.

The hostess came over to me. "I do hope you can find something you like. I didn't know . . . I wasn't sure what you like to eat."

I smiled. "Anybody who can't find something to eat here just plain ain't hungry."

She picked up a chicken leg between two fingers and smiled. "I adore this. Just adore it."

Her husband came by. "Come on, Sam, I'll give you the fifty-cent tour."

He took me from room to room. "Sammy, c'mon and say hello to our cook. It'll be the biggest kick in the world for her." He brought me into the kitchen. "Sarah, I guess you know who this is, don't you?" He stood back beaming at us.

She smiled and wiped her hand on a towel. "I'm glad to meet you, Sammy," and shook hands. Harry Host put his arm around her, elaborately. "Sarah's a member of the family, aren't you, Sarah?"

She nodded and smiled. "Yes, sir."

As we left the kitchen he said, "Great woman."

His wife joined us and we went upstairs. I said, "This is a fantastic setup. I wish I had something like it myself."

The wife said, "Uh, well—uh, maybe there's something available in the building—we can check if you're interested . . . ." She was rushing on, trying to convince me she hadn't noticed I'm colored. Her husband said, "Of course vacancies are pretty rare . . ."

"Look, I was only talking. I've got a home on the coast that I haven't spent a full week in, and I'm usually not in New York enough to make it worth while."

She leaped for the out. "Believe me, you're just as well off. The city's ruined . . ." Oh, God, she'd done it again. She tried frantically to recover. "It's those damned *spicks*. Ever since *they* started coming over here . . ."

The car doors slammed shut, first one then the other, sealing us off safely from the rest of the city. I rested giddily against the soft leather seat. "George, if you ever wondered how come colored people's hair is kinky—it's from going to parties like that one."

"Did something happen I don't know about?"

"Nothing special." I turned the key and started the engine. "But before I accept another of those invitations it's a definite half-gainer into the river."

I sat behind my bar grinning at George as if somebody were rubbing my back. "Baby, your star is home from the wars and he ain't about to leave this room unless someone yells fire."

"Have you forgotten that Jane and Burt and Michael and Chita are going to be meeting us at Danny's in an hour?"

"A great star never forgets." I called Danny. "This is your old buddy Sammy Davis, Jr., known to his close friends

as just plain Mr. Wonderful. . . . No, baby, I'm dead on my
feet, but the buddies'll be looking for me in about an hour.
Will you tell them there's been a change in plan and there'll
be a Carey car for them and to just get in it and come over to
the Gorham? And, Danny, give them a couple of jugs of
spaghetti and some of that veal-pajamas and maybe a little
shrimp marinara . . ."

George was puzzled. "I still don't understand what happened. I admit the people were a little square . . ."

"Hey. Hold it. You know I've never put anyone down
'cause they're square." He was waiting. I sat back against
the curve of the bar, lit a cigarette, blew the smoke out and
looked up. "George, did you happen to notice the platter of
fried chicken?"

"Well, yes . . ."

"Do you think they serve that at all their parties? With
the caviar?"

"Well . . ." He took a slug of his scotch. "They were trying to be nice."

"Baby, I'm not saying they weren't trying. And I love
fried chicken, I could eat it all night. But I also eat other
food—like anybody else. It's not like they invited a rabbit
so they had to have a head of lettuce on the table for him.
Let me put it this way: how would you like to be the only
Jewish cat invited to a party and you look at the food and
it's lovely and then over in a corner of the table you see
they've got a little side order of gefilte fish for you?"

"Well, now that you mention it"—he couldn't resist
smiling—"I did wonder when they were going to start your
crap game."

"You see? You did catch it."

"Well . . ."

I leaned across the bar. "Listen, y'know the old cliché
'Some of my best friends are colored'? It's been updated.

Now it's 'My kid goes to school with Ralph Bunche's son.' "

He smiled slightly, holding back, knowing that his complete reaction would only steam me. He shrugged, trying to minimize it. "Well, I don't want to do a cliché, too, but you've got to remember that to most people," he made a face, "particularly that crowd today, you're the first Negro they ever met socially and they just don't know how to handle it."

"Baby, if that's the case, and it probably is, then they'll have to get somebody else to practice on. Let them go out and hire some colored kid who needs the dough. Let them sit down and talk to *him* 'cause I've had it with running classes for learners."

"Well, I can understand that it's not exactly kicks, but at least you know their intentions are good. You know how they feel about you. They certainly wouldn't be throwing parties in your honor if they were prejudiced or anything."

"I know exactly how they feel about me. The trouble is *they* don't know how they feel about me. Let's not celebrate National Brotherhood Week just because a woman throws a party for me instead of keeping me out of school. They wanted to show off to their friends that they know Sammy Davis, Jr. Fine. I'm only flattered. But let's carry it a little further: here's a woman who adores herself for being a liberal and having 'a colored man' to her apartment, right? But do you want to do about ten minutes on what a shake-up it would have been if instead of you I'd brought Charley Head with me? Or any colored guy who dresses well, who makes a lot of dough and has been around—but isn't famous. I'd have set back her personal integration movement by fifty years. There'd be lorgnettes dropping all over the place, with mumbling, 'Well, we like *him* but did he have to bring his friends?' "

"I don't know why I'm defending her, but as long as

I'm involved, how can you be so sure she'd react like that?
Okay, they tried to do something they weren't experienced
at and they blew it, but that doesn't mean . . ."

I came out from behind the bar. "Look, you're talking
to Charley Optimist. I don't just casually jump to the conclusion that people are prejudiced. I'm hoping and praying
I won't see it. Further, if I expect people to give me the
benefit of the doubt then obviously I've got to give *them* the
benefit of the doubt. But when a woman says to me, 'I like
the colored people. It's the spicks I hate,' *this* is a prejudiced
woman. Here's an educated, presumably intelligent person
lumping a whole group of people together—millions of
them in one swoop—and judging them. It doesn't occur to
her that if her Negro maid didn't come in one day you
don't go around saying Ralph Bunche, Sidney Poitier, and
Thurgood Marshall are unreliable. By the same token there
is nobody justified in hating all the Puerto Ricans 'cause
nobody has *met* all the Puerto Ricans. But this woman
wants to believe that she prejudges one group without pre-
judging another. Impossible. Either you see people as
individuals or you don't. My God, you can't even say, 'All
of last year's string beans were lousy,' so how can you do it
with *people*?

"Then another cat tells me, 'I've got ten Negroes and six
white men working for me.' Here's a man who's counting
people by color, but he makes a trip across the room to brag
to me that he's a liberal. Do you realize that the only
cliché I escaped is: 'Oh? I didn't even notice you were
colored.' "

"Small world. Somebody said that to *me*."

"George, you're rotten to the core."

He frowned, pleased. "I know."

"Now, Act Two: I'm reaching for an hors d'oeuvre and a
man smiles broadly at me: 'I want to shake your hand. You're

a credit to your people.' Here this phony all-too-liberal is telling me colored people are rotten but *I'm* okay and he's waiting for me to say thank you.

"How do you fight someone like this? The worst thing in the world is when you're up against people *who don't know they're prejudiced.*

"They bring me to their homes, put their arms around my shoulder and walk around the room insulting me, patronizing me, hurting me just as much as a hater would, maybe even more, but *they* expect me to say 'Thank you.' They go to bed puffed up with the satisfaction of being humanitarians, patting themselves on the back: 'I'm not prejudiced, I even had one to my home,' and they fall asleep counting colored people coming to their parties."

I stood up and gave a bar stool a little spin with one finger and watched it wobble slightly as it turned. "I'd be the last person in the world to say that anybody *must* be anything but what he wants to be. And even if he decides he wants to wear the badge of liberal I'm not asking him to turn over his income to the NAACP, or to go ride Freedom Buses— but he's got to know there's more to it than not throwing rocks."

George was looking into his glass, turning it slowly, troubled, seeing something he'd seen around him all his life but which had to look different from the inside.

The doorbell rang. He looked up, and as surely as if he were putting on a different coat I could see him getting ready to hide again behind the façade of sophistication. He grinned. "Your fried chicken is here."

4

FROM

Notes of a Native Son

by James Baldwin
(1924–   )

The frustration due to constant humiliation builds up, and finally some people can contain themselves no longer. In the early 1940s, when the organized civil-rights movement was still a thing of the future, Baldwin lashed out in individual protest. Frightened at his own reaction, Baldwin admits, "The most difficult (and most rewarding) thing in my life has been the fact that I was born a Negro and was forced, therefore, to effect some kind of truce with this reality." Notes of a Native Son is evidence of Baldwin's search for identity as a writer, an American, and a Negro.

James Baldwin was born in Harlem in 1924. His mother delighted in his early literary achievements, but his preacher father was noncommittal at best, hoping James would follow in his ministerial footsteps.

In his late teens Baldwin began writing in earnest. Several years and two books later (both unpublished), he left for France. There he wrote Go Tell It on the Mountain, Giovanni's Room, *and* Another Country. *These books, in addition to* The Fire Next Time, *established his reputation on both continents not only as a writer of merit but as a perceptive social critic as well.*

ON the 29th of July, in 1943, my father died. On the same day, a few hours later, his last child was born. Over a month before this, while all our energies were concentrated in waiting for these events, there had been, in Detroit, one of the bloodiest race riots of the century. A few hours after my father's funeral, while he lay in state in the undertaker's chapel, a race riot broke out in Harlem. On the morning of the 3rd of August, we drove my father to the graveyard through a wilderness of smashed plate glass.

The day of my father's funeral had also been my nineteenth birthday. As we drove him to the graveyard, the spoils of injustice, anarchy, discontent, and hatred were all around us. It seemed to me that God himself had devised, to mark my father's end, the most sustained and brutally dissonant of codas. And it seemed to me, too, that the violence which rose all about us as my father left the world had been devised as a corrective in that apocalypse which had been central to my father's vision; very well, life seemed to be saying, here is something that will certainly pass for an apocalypse until the real thing comes along. I had inclined to be contemptuous of my father for the conditions of his life, for the conditions of our lives. When his life had ended I began to wonder about that life and also, in a new way, to be apprehensive about my own.

I had not known my father very well. We had got on badly, partly because we shared, in our different fashions, the vice of stubborn pride. When he was dead I realized that I had hardly ever spoken to him. When he had been dead a long time I began to wish I had. It seems to be typical of life in America, where opportunities, real and fancied, are thicker than anywhere else on the globe, that the second generation has no time to talk to the first. No one, including my father, seems to have known exactly how old he was. but his mother had been born during slavery. He was of the first generation of free men. He, along with thousands of other Negroes, came North after 1919 and I was part of that generation of what Negroes sometimes call the Old Country.

He had been born in New Orleans and had been a quite young man there during the time that Louis Armstrong, a boy, was running errands for the dives and honky-tonks of what was always presented to me as one of the most wicked of cities—to this day, whenever I think of New Orleans, I also helplessly think of Sodom and Gomorrah. My father never mentioned Louis Armstrong except to forbid us to play his records; but there was a picture of him on our wall for a long time. One of my father's strong-willed female relatives had placed it there and forbade my father to take it down. He never did, but he eventually maneuvered her out of the house and when, some years later, she was in trouble and near death, he refused to do anything to help her.

He was, I think, very handsome. I gather this from photographs and from my own memories of him, dressed in his Sunday best and on his way to preach a sermon somewhere, when I was little. Handsome, proud, and ingrown, "like a toe-nail," somebody said. But he looked to me, as I grew older, like pictures I had seen of African tribal chieftains: he really should have been naked, with war-paint on and barbaric mementos, standing among spears. He could be chilling in the pulpit and indescribably cruel in his personal life and he was certainly the most bitter man I have ever met; yet it must be said that there was something else in him, buried in him, which lent him his tremendous

power and, even, a rather crushing charm. It had something to do with his blackness, I think—he was very black—
with his blackness and his beauty, and with the fact that
he knew that he was black but did not know that he was
beautiful. He claimed to be proud of his blackness but it
had also been the cause of much humiliation and it had
fixed bleak boundaries to his life. He was not a young man
when we were growing up and he had already suffered
many kinds of ruin; in his outrageously demanding and
protective way he loved his children, who were black like
him and menaced, like him; and all these things sometimes
showed in his face when he tried, never to my knowledge
with any success, to establish contact with any of us. When
he took one of his children on his knee to play, the child
always became fretful and began to cry; when he tried to
help one of us with our homework the absolutely unabating
tension which emanated from him caused our minds and
our tongues to become paralyzed, so that he, scarcely knowing why, flew into a rage and the child, not knowing
why, was punished. If it ever entered his head to bring a
surprise home for his children, it was, almost unfailingly,
the wrong surprise and even the big watermelons he often
brought home on his back in the summertime led to the
most appalling scenes. I do not remember, in all those
years, that one of his children was ever glad to see him
come home. From what I was able to gather of his early
life, it seemed that this inability to establish contact with
other people had always marked him and had been one of
the things which had driven him out of New Orleans.
There was something in him, therefore, groping and tenta-
tive, which was never expressed and which was buried
with him. One saw it most clearly when he was facing
new people and hoping to impress them. But he never did,
not for long. We went from church to smaller and more im-

probable church, he found himself in less demand as a minister, and by the time he died none of his friends had come to see him for a long time. He had lived and died in an intolerable bitterness of spirit and it frightened me, as we drove him to the graveyard through those unquiet, ruined streets, to see how powerful and overflowing this bitterness could be and to realize that this bitterness now was mine.

When he died I had been away from home for a little over a year. In that year I had had time to become aware of the meaning of all my father's bitter warnings, had discovered the secret of his proudly pursed lips and rigid carriage: I had discovered the weight of white people in the world. I saw that this had been for my ancestors and now would be for me an awful thing to live with and that the bitterness which had helped to kill my father could also kill me.

He had been ill a long time—in the mind, as we now realized, reliving instances of his fantastic intransigence in the new light of his affliction and endeavoring to feel a sorrow for him which never, quite, came true. We had not known that he was being eaten up by paranoia and the discovery that his cruelty, to our bodies and our minds, had been one of the symptoms of his illness was not, then, enough to enable us to forgive him. The younger children felt, quite simply, relief that he would not be coming home anymore. My mother's observation that it was he, after all, who had kept them alive all these years meant nothing because the problems of keeping children alive are not real for children. The older children felt, with my father gone, that they could invite their friends to the house without fear that their friends would be insulted or, as had sometimes happened with me, being told that their friends were in league with the devil and intended to rob our family of everything we owned. (I didn't fail to wonder, and it made me hate him, what on earth we owned that anybody else would want.)

His illness was beyond all hope of healing before anyone realized that he was ill. He had always been so strange and had lived, like a prophet, in such unimaginably close communion with the Lord that his long silences which were punctuated by moans and hallelujahs and snatches of old songs while he sat at the living-room window never seemed odd to us. It was not until he refused to eat because, he said, his family was trying to poison him that my mother was forced to accept as a fact what had, until then, been only an unwilling suspicion. When he was committed, it was discovered that he had tuberculosis and, as it turned out, the disease of his mind allowed the disease of his body to destroy him. For the doctors could not force him to eat, either, and, though he was fed intravenously, it was clear from the beginning that there was no hope for him.

In my mind's eye I could see him, sitting at the window, locked up in his terrors; hating and fearing every living soul including his children who had betrayed him, too, by reaching towards the world which had despised him. There were nine of us. I began to wonder what it could have felt like for such a man to have had nine children whom he could barely feed. He used to make little jokes about our poverty, which never, of course, seemed very funny to us; they could not have seemed very funny to him, either, or else our feeble response to them would never have caused such rages. He spent great energy and achieved, to our chagrin, no small amount of success in keeping us away from the people who surrounded us, people who had all-night rent parties to which we listened when we should have been sleeping, people who cursed and drank and flashed razor blades on Lenox Avenue. He could not understand why, if they had so much energy to spare, they could not use it to make their lives better. He treated almost everybody on our block with a most uncharitable asperity and neither they, nor, of course, their children were slow to reciprocate.

The only white people who came to our house were welfare workers and bill collectors. It was almost always my
mother who dealt with them, for my father's temper, which
was at the mercy of his pride, was never to be trusted. It
was clear that he felt their very presence in his home to be a
violation: this was conveyed by his carriage, almost ludi-
crously stiff, and by his voice, harsh and vindictively polite.
When I was around nine or ten I wrote a play which was
directed by a young, white schoolteacher, a woman, who
then took an interest in me, and gave me books to read and,
in order to corroborate my theatrical bent, decided to take
me to see what she somewhat tactlessly referred to as "real"
plays. Theater-going was forbidden in our house, but, with
the really cruel intuitiveness of a child, I suspected that the
color of this woman's skin would carry the day for me.
When, at school, she suggested taking me to the theater,
I did not, as I might have done if she had been a Negro, find
a way of discouraging her, but agreed that she should pick
me up at my house one evening. I then, very cleverly, left
all the rest to my mother, who suggested to my father, as I
knew she would, that it would not be very nice to let such
a kind woman make the trip for nothing. Also, since it was
a schoolteacher, I imagine that my mother countered the idea
of sin with the idea of "education," which word, even
with my father, carried a kind of bitter weight.

Before the teacher came my father took me aside to ask
why she was coming, what *interest* she could possibly have
in our house, in a boy like me. I said I didn't know but I, too,
suggested that it had something to do with education. And
I understood that my father was waiting for me to say something—I didn't quite know what; perhaps that I wanted his
protection against this teacher and her "education." I said
none of these things and the teacher came and we went out.

It was clear, during the brief interview in our living room, that my father was agreeing very much against his will and that he would have refused permission if he had dared. The fact that he did not dare caused me to despise him: I had no way of knowing that he was facing in that living room a wholly unprecedented and frightening situation.

Later, when my father had been laid off from his job, this woman became very important to us. She was really a very sweet and generous woman and went to a great deal of trouble to be of help to us, particularly during one awful winter. My mother called her by the highest name she knew: she said she was a "christian." My father could scarcely disagree but during the four or five years of our relatively close association he never trusted her and was always trying to surprise in her open, Midwestern face the genuine, cunningly hidden, and hideous motivation. In later years, particularly when it began to be clear that this "education" of mine was going to lead me to perdition, he became more explicit and warned me that my white friends in high school were not really my friends and that I would see, when I was older, how white people would do anything to keep a Negro down. Some of them could be nice, he admitted, but none of them were to be trusted and most of them were not even nice. The best thing was to have as little to do with them as possible. I did not feel this way and I was certain, in my innocence, that I never would.

But the year which preceded my father's death had made a great change in my life. I had been living in New Jersey, working in defense plants, working and living among southerners, white and black. I knew about the south, of course, and about how southerners treated Negroes and how they expected them to behave, but it never entered my mind that anyone would look at me and expect *me* to behave that way. I learned in New Jersey that to be a Negro meant, precisely, that one was never looked at but was simply at the mercy of the reflexes the color of one's skin caused in other people. I acted in New Jersey as I had always acted, that is as though I thought a great deal of myself—I had to *act* that way—with results that were, simply, unbelievable. I had scarcely arrived before I had earned the enmity, which was extraordinarily ingenious, of all my superiors and nearly all my co-workers. In the beginning, to make matters worse, I simply did not know what was happening. I did not know what I had done, and I shortly began to wonder what *any-one* could possibly do, to bring about such unanimous, active, and unbearably vocal hostility. I knew about jim-crow but I had never experienced it. I went to the same self-service restaurant three times and stood with all the Princeton boys before the counter, waiting for a hamburger and coffee; it was always an extraordinarily long time before anything was set before me; but it was not until the fourth visit that I learned that, in fact, nothing had ever been set before me: I had simply picked something up. Negroes were not served there, I was told, and they had been waiting for me to realize that I was always the only Negro present. Once I was told this, I determined to go there all the time. But now they were ready for me and, though some dread-ful scenes were subsequently enacted in the restaurant, I never ate there again.

It was the same story all over New Jersey, in bars, bowling alleys, diners, places to live. I was always being forced to leave, silently, or with mutual imprecations. I very shortly became notorious and children giggled behind me when I passed and their elders whispered or shouted—they really believed that I was mad. And it did begin to work on my mind, of course; I began to be afraid to go anywhere and to compensate for this I went places to which I really should not have gone and where, God knows, I had no desire to be.

My reputation in town naturally enhanced my reputation at work and my working day became one long series of acrobatics designed to keep me out of trouble. I cannot say that these acrobatics succeeded. It began to seem that the machinery of the organization I worked for was turning over, day and night, with but one aim: to eject me. I was fired once, and contrived, with the aid of a friend from New York, to get back on the payroll; was fired again, and bounced back again. It took a while to fire me for the third time, but the third time took. There were no loopholes anywhere. There was not even any way of getting back inside the gates.

That year in New Jersey lives in my mind as though it were the year during which, having an unsuspected predilection for it, I first contracted some dread, chronic disease, the unfailing symptom of which is a kind of blind fever, a pounding in the skull and fire in the bowels. Once this disease is contracted, one can never be really carefree again, for the fever, without an instant's warning, can recur at any moment. It can wreck more important things than race relations. There is not a Negro alive who does not have this rage in his blood—one has the choice, merely, of living with it consciously or surrendering to it. As for me, this fever has recurred in me, and does, and will until the day I die.

My last night in New Jersey, a white friend from New York took me to the nearest big town, Trenton, to go to the movies and have a few drinks. As it turned out, he also saved me from, at the very least, a violent whipping. Almost every detail of that night stands out very clearly in my memory. I even remember the name of the movie we saw because its title impressed me as being so patly ironical. It was a movie about the German occupation of France, starring Maureen O'Hara and Charles Laughton and called *This*

Land Is Mine. I remember the name of the diner we walked
into when the movie ended: it was the "American Diner."
When we walked in the counterman asked what we wanted
and I remember answering with the casual sharpness which
had become my habit: "We want a hamburger and a cup of
coffee, what do you think we want?" I do not know why,
after a year of such rebuffs, I so completely failed to antici-
pate his answer, which was, of course, "We don't serve
Negroes here." This reply failed to discompose me, at least
for the moment. I made some sardonic comment about the
name of the diner and we walked out into the streets.

This was the time of what was called the "brown-out,"
when the lights in all American cities were very dim. When
we reentered the streets something happened to me which
had the force of an optical illusion, or a nightmare. The
streets were very crowded and I was facing north. People
were moving in every direction but it seemed to me, in that
instant, that all of the people I could see, and many more
than that, were moving towards me, against me, and that
everyone was white. I remember how their faces gleamed.
And I felt, like a physical sensation, a *click* at the nape of
my neck as though some interior string connecting my head
to my body had been cut. I began to walk. I heard my friend
call after me, but I ignored him. Heaven only knows what
was going on in his mind, but he had the good sense not to
touch me—I don't know what would have happened if he
had—and to keep me in sight. I don't know what was going
on in my mind, either; I certainly had no conscious plan.
I wanted to do something to crush these white faces, which
were crushing me. I walked for perhaps a block or two until
I came to an enormous, glittering, and fashionable restaurant in which I knew not even the intercession of the Virgin
would cause me to be served. I pushed through the doors
and took the first vacant seat I saw, at a table for two, and
waited.

I do not know how long I waited and I rather wonder, until today, what I could possibly have looked like. Whatever I looked like, I frightened the waitress who shortly appeared, and the moment she appeared all my fury flowed towards her. I hated her for her white face, and for her great, astounded, frightened eyes. I felt that if she found a black man so frightening I would make her fright worth while.

She did not ask me what I wanted, but repeated, as though she had learned it somewhere, "We don't serve Negroes here." She did not say it with the blunt, derisive hostility to which I had grown so accustomed, but, rather, with a note of apology in her voice, and fear. This made me colder and more murderous than ever. I felt I had to do something with my hands. I wanted her to come close enough for me to get her neck between my hands. So I pretended not to have understood her, hoping to draw her closer. And she did step a very short step closer, with her pencil poised incongruously over her pad, and repeated the formula: ". . . don't serve Negroes here."

Somehow, with the repetition of that phrase, which was already ringing in my head like a thousand bells of a nightmare, I realized that she would never come any closer and that I would have to strike from a distance. There was nothing on the table but an ordinary water mug half full of water, and I picked this up and hurled it with all my strength at her. She ducked and it missed her and shattered against the mirror behind the bar. And, with that sound, my frozen blood abruptly thawed, I returned from wherever I had been, I *saw*, for the first time, the restaurant, the people with their mouths open, already, as it seemed to me, rising as one man, and I realized what I had done, and where I was, and I was frightened. I rose and began running for the door. A round, potbellied man grabbed me by the nape of the neck just as I reached the doors and began to

beat me about the face. I kicked him and got loose and ran
into the streets. My friend whispered, *"Run!"* and I ran.

My friend stayed outside the restaurant long enough to
misdirect my pursuers and the police, who arrived, he told
me, at once. I do not know what I said to him when he came
to my room that night. I could not have said much. I felt,
in the oddest, most awful way, that I had somehow betrayed
him. I lived it over and over and over again, the way one
relives an automobile accident after it has happened and
one finds oneself alone and safe. I could not get over two
facts, both equally difficult for the imagination to grasp,
and one was that I could have been murdered. But the other
was that I had been ready to commit murder. I saw nothing
very clearly but I did see this: that my life, my *real* life, was
in danger, and not from anything other people might do
but from the hatred I carried in my own heart.

II

I had returned home around the second week in June—in
great haste because it seemed that my father's death and my
mother's confinement were both but a matter of hours. In the
case of my mother, it soon became clear that she had simply
made a miscalculation. This had always been her tendency
and I don't believe that a single one of us arrived in the
world, or has since arrived anywhere else, on time. But none
of us dawdled so intolerably about the business of being
born as did my baby sister. We sometimes amused ourselves,
during those endless, stifling weeks, by picturing the baby
sitting within the safe, warm dark, bitterly regretting the
necessity of becoming a part of our chaos and stubbornly
putting it off as long as possible. I understood her perfectly
and congratulated her on showing such good sense so soon.
Death, however, sat as purposefully at my father's bedside

as life stirred within my mother's womb and it was harder to understand why he so lingered in that long shadow. It seemed that he had bent, and for a long time, too, all of his energies towards dying. Now death was ready for him but my father held back.

All of Harlem, indeed, seemed to be infected by waiting. I had never before known it to be so violently still. Racial tensions throughout this country were exacerbated during the early years of the war, partly because the labor market brought together hundreds of thousands of ill-prepared people and partly because Negro soldiers, regardless of where they were born, received their military training in the south. What happened in defense plants and army camps had repercussions, naturally, in every Negro ghetto. The situation in Harlem had grown bad enough for clergymen, policemen, educators, politicians, and social workers to assert in one breath that there was no "crime wave" and to offer, in the very next breath, suggestions as to how to combat it. These suggestions always seemed to involve playgrounds, despite the fact that racial skirmishes were occurring in the playgrounds, too. Playground or not, crime wave or not, the Harlem police force had been augmented in March, and the unrest grew—perhaps, in fact, partly as a result of the ghetto's instinctive hatred of policemen. Perhaps the most revealing news item, out of the steady parade of reports of muggings, stabbings, shootings, assaults, gang wars, and accusations of police brutality, is the item concerning six Negro girls who set upon a white girl in the subway because, as they all too accurately put it, she was stepping on their toes. Indeed she was, all over the nation.

I had never before been so aware of policemen, on foot, on horseback, on corners, everywhere, always two by two. Nor had I ever been so aware of small knots of people. They were on stoops and on corners and in doorways, and what

was striking about them, I think, was that they did not
seem to be talking. Never, when I passed these groups, did
the usual sound of a curse or a laugh ring out and neither
did there seem to be any hum of gossip. There was certainly,
on the other hand, occurring between them communication
extraordinarily intense. Another thing that was striking was
the unexpected diversity of the people who made up these
groups. Usually, for example, one would see a group of
sharpies standing on the street corner, jiving the passing
chicks; or a group of older men, usually, for some reason,
in the vicinity of a barber shop, discussing baseball scores,
or the numbers, or making rather chilling observations
about women they had known. Women, in a general way,
tended to be seen less often together—unless they were
church women, or very young girls, or prostitutes met together for an unprofessional instant. But that summer I
saw the strangest combinations: large, respectable, churchly
matrons standing on the stoops or the corners with their
hair tied up, together with a girl in sleazy satin whose face
bore the marks of gin and the razor, or heavy-set, abrupt,
no-nonsense older men, in company with the most disrepu-
table and fanatical "race" men, or these same "race" men
with the sharpies, or these sharpies with the churchly
women. Seventh Day Adventists and Methodists and Spirit-
ualists seemed to be hobnobbing with Holyrollers and they
were all, alike, entangled with the most flagrant disbeliev-
ers; something heavy in their stance seemed to indicate that
they had all, incredibly, seen a common vision, and on each
face there seemed to be the same strange, bitter shadow.

The churchly women and the matter-of-fact, no-nonsense
men had children in the Army. The sleazy girls they talked
to had lovers there, the sharpies and the "race" men had
friends and brothers there. It would have demanded an un-
questioning patriotism, happily as uncommon in this

country as it is undesirable, for these people not to have been disturbed by the bitter letters they received, by the newspaper stories they read, not to have been enraged by the posters, then to be found all over New York, which described the Japanese as "yellow-bellied Japs." It was only the "race" men, to be sure, who spoke ceaselessly of being revenged—how this vengeance was to be exacted was not clear—for the indignities and dangers suffered by Negro boys in uniform; but everybody felt a directionless, hopeless bitterness, as well as that panic which can scarcely be suppressed when one knows that a human being one loves is beyond one's reach, and in danger. This helplessness and this gnawing uneasiness does something, at length, to even the toughest mind. Perhaps the best way to sum all this up is to say that the people I knew felt, mainly, a peculiar kind of relief when they knew that their boys were being shipped out of the south, to do battle overseas. It was, perhaps, like feeling that the most dangerous part of a dangerous journey had been passed and that now, even if death should come, it would come with honor and without the complicity of their countrymen. Such a death would be, in short, a fact with which one could hope to live.

It was on the 28th of July, which I believe was a Wednesday, that I visited my father for the first time during his illness and for the last time in his life. The moment I saw him I knew why I had put off this visit for so long. I had told my mother that I did not want to see him because I hated him. But this was not true. It was only that I *had* hated him and I wanted to hold on to this hatred. I did not want to look on him as a ruin: it was not a ruin I had hated. I imagine that one of the reasons people cling to their hates so stubbornly is because they sense, once hate is gone, that they will be forced to deal with pain.

We traveled out to him, his older sister and myself, to

what seemed to be the very end of a very Long Island. It was hot and dusty and we wrangled, my aunt and I, all the way out, over the fact that I had recently begun to smoke and, as she said, to give myself airs. But I knew that she wrangled with me because she could not bear to face the fact of her brother's dying. Neither could I endure the reality of her despair, her unstated bafflement as to what had happened to her brother's life, and her own. So we wrangled and I smoked and from time to time she fell into a heavy reverie. Covertly, I watched her face, which was the face of an old woman; it had fallen in, the eyes were sunken and lightless; soon she would be dying, too.

In my childhood—it had not been so long ago—I had thought her beautiful. She had been quick-witted and quick-moving and very generous with all the children and each of her visits had been an event. At one time one of my brothers and myself had thought of running away to live with her. Now she could no longer produce out of her handbag some unexpected and yet familiar delight. She made me feel pity and revulsion and fear. It was awful to realize that she no longer caused me to feel affection. The closer we came to the hospital the more querulous she became and at the same time, naturally, grew more dependent on me. Between pity and guilt and fear I began to feel that there was another me trapped in my skull like a jack-in-the-box who might escape my control at any moment and fill the air with screaming.

She began to cry the moment we entered the room and she saw him lying there, all shriveled and still, like a little black monkey. The great, gleaming apparatus which fed him and would have compelled him to be still even if he had been able to move brought to mind, not beneficence, but torture; the tubes entering his arm made me think of pictures I had seen when a child, of Gulliver, tied down by the pygmies on that island. My aunt wept and wept, there was a whistling sound in my father's throat; nothing was said; he could not speak. I wanted to take his hand, to say something. But I do not know what I could have said, even if he could have heard me. He was not really in that room with us, he had at last really embarked on his journey; and though my aunt told me that he said he was going to meet Jesus, I did not hear anything except that whistling in his throat. The doctor came back and we left, into that unbearable train again, and home. In the morning came the telegram saying that he was dead. Then the house was suddenly full of relatives, friends, hysteria, and confusion and I quickly left my mother and the children to the care of those impressive women, who, in Negro communities at least, automatically appear at times of bereavement armed with lotions, proverbs, and patience, and an ability to cook. I went downtown. By the time I returned, later the same day, my mother had been carried to the hospital and the baby had been born.

III

For my father's funeral I had nothing black to wear and this posed a nagging problem all day long. It was one of those problems, simple, or impossible of solution, to which the mind insanely clings in order to avoid the mind's real trouble. I spent most of that day at the downtown apartment of a girl I knew, celebrating my birthday with whiskey and wondering what to wear that night. When planning a birthday celebration one naturally does not expect that it will be up against competition from a funeral and this girl had anticipated taking me out that night, for a big dinner and a night club afterwards. Sometime during the course of that long day we decided that we would go out anyway, when

my father's funeral service was over. I imagine *I* decided it,
since, as the funeral hour approached, it became clearer
and clearer to me that I would not know what to do with
myself when it was over. The girl, stifling her very lively
concern as to the possible effects of the whiskey on one
of my father's chief mourners, concentrated on being con-
ciliatory and practically helpful. She found a black shirt
for me somewhere and ironed it and, dressed in the darkest
pants and jacket I owned, and slightly drunk, I made my
way to my father's funeral.

The chapel was full, but not packed, and very quiet.
There were, mainly, my father's relatives, and his children,
and here and there I saw faces I had not seen since childhood, the faces of my father's one-time friends. They were
very dark and solemn now, seeming somehow to suggest
that they had known all along that something like this
would happen. Chief among the mourners was my aunt,
who had quarreled with my father all his life; by which I
do not mean to suggest that her mourning was insincere
or that she had not loved him. I suppose that she was one
of the few people in the world who had, and their inces-
sant quarreling proved precisely the strength of the tie that
bound them. The only other person in the world, as far as
I knew, whose relationship to my father rivaled my aunt's
in depth was my mother, who was not there.

It seemed to me, of course, that it was a very long funeral.
But it was, if anything, a rather shorter funeral than most,
nor, since there were no overwhelming, uncontrollable
expressions of grief, could it be called—if I dare to use the
word—successful. The minister who preached my father's
funeral sermon was one of the few my father had still been
seeing as he neared his end. He presented to us in his sermon a man whom none of us had ever seen—a man
thoughtful, patient, and forbearing, a Christian inspiration

to all who knew him, and a model for his children. And
no doubt the children, in their disturbed and guilty state,
were almost ready to believe this; he had been remote enough
to be anything and, anyway, the shock of the incontrover-
tible, that it was really our father lying up there in that
casket, prepared the mind for anything. His sister moaned
and this grief-stricken moaning was taken as corroboration.
The other faces held a dark, non-committal thoughtfulness.
This was not the man they had known, but they had
scarcely expected to be confronted with *him*; this was, in
a sense deeper than questions of fact, the man they had not
known, and the man they had not known may have been
the real one. The real man, whoever he had been, had suffered and now he was dead; this was all that was sure and
all that mattered now. Every man in the chapel hoped that
when his hour came he, too, would be eulogized, which is
to say forgiven, and that all of his lapses, greeds, errors,
and strayings from the truth would be invested with co-
herence and looked upon with charity. This was perhaps
the last thing human beings could give each other and it
was what they demanded, after all, of the Lord. Only the
Lord saw the midnight tears, only He was present when one
of His children, moaning and wringing hands, paced up
and down the room. When one slapped one's child in anger
the recoil in the heart reverberated through heaven and became part of the pain of the universe. And when the children
were hungry and sullen and distrustful and one watched
them, daily, growing wilder, and further away, and running
headlong into danger, it was the Lord who knew what the
charged heart endured as the strap was laid to the backside;
the Lord alone who knew what one *would* have said if one
had had, like the Lord, the gift of the living word. It was
the Lord who knew of the impossibility every parent in
that room faced: how to prepare the child for the day when

the child would be despised and how to *create* in the child—
by what means?—a stronger antidote to this poison than
one had found for oneself. The avenues, side streets, bars,
billiard halls, hospitals, police stations, and even the playgrounds of Harlem—not to mention the houses of correc-
tion, the jails, and the morgue—testified to the potency of
the poison while remaining silent as to the efficacy of
whatever antidote, irresistibly raising the question of
whether or not such an antidote existed; raising, which
was worse, the question of whether or not an antidote was
desirable; perhaps poison should be fought with poison.
With these several schisms in the mind and with more terrors in the heart than could be named, it was better not to
judge the man who had gone down under an impossible
burden. It was better to remember: *Thou knowest this man's*
fall; but thou knowest not his wrassling.

While the preacher talked and I watched the children—
years of changing their diapers, scrubbing them, slapping
them, taking them to school, and scolding them had had
the perhaps inevitable result of making me love them,
though I am not sure I knew this then—my mind was
busily breaking out with a rash of disconnected impressions.
Snatches of popular songs, indecent jokes, bits of books I
had read, movie sequences, faces, voices, political issues—
I thought I was going mad; all these impressions suspended,
as it were, in the solution of the faint nausea produced
in me by the heat and liquor. For a moment I had the impression that my alcoholic breath, inefficiently disguised
with chewing gum, filled the entire chapel. Then someone
began singing one of my father's favorite songs and,
abruptly, I was with him, sitting on his knee, in the hot,
enormous, crowded church which was the first church we
attended. It was the Abyssinian Baptist Church on 138th
Street. We had not gone there long. With this image, a

host of others came. I had forgotten, in the rage of my growing up, how proud my father had been of me when I was little. Apparently, I had had a voice and my father had liked to show me off before the members of the church. I had forgotten what he had looked like when he was pleased but now I remembered that he had always been grinning with pleasure when my solos ended. I even remembered certain expressions on his face when he teased my mother— had he loved her? I would never know. And when had it all begun to change? For now it seemed that he had not always been cruel. I remembered being taken for a haircut and scraping my knee on the footrest of the barber's chair and I remembered my father's face as he soothed my crying and applied the stinging iodine. Then I remembered our fights, fights which had been of the worst possible kind because my technique had been silence.

I remembered the one time in all our life together when we had really spoken to each other.

It was on a Sunday and it must have been shortly before I left home. We were walking, just the two of us, in our usual silence, to or from church. I was in high school and had been doing a lot of writing and I was, at about this time, the editor of the high school magazine. But I had also been a Young Minister and had been preaching from the pulpit. Lately, I had been taking fewer engagements and preached as rarely as possible. It was said in the church, quite truthfully, that I was "cooling off."

My father asked me abruptly, "You'd rather write than preach, wouldn't you?"

I was astonished at his question—because it was a real question. I answered, "Yes."

That was all we said. It was awful to remember that that was all we had *ever* said.

The casket now was opened and the mourners were

being led up the aisle to look for the last time on the de-
ceased. The assumption was that the family was too overcome with grief to be allowed to make this journey alone and
I watched while my aunt was led to the casket and, muffled
in black, and shaking, led back to her seat. I disapproved
of forcing the children to look on their dead father, considering that the shock of his death, or, more truthfully,
the shock of death as a reality, was already a little more
than a child could bear, but my judgment in this matter had
been overruled and there they were, bewildered and frightened and very small, being led, one by one, to the casket.
But there is also something very gallant about children at
such moments. It has something to do with their silence and
gravity and with the fact that one cannot help them. Their
legs, somehow, seem *exposed*, so that it is at once incredible
and terribly clear that their legs are all they have to hold
them up.

I had not wanted to go to the casket myself and I certainly had not wished to be led there, but there was no way
of avoiding either of these forms. One of the deacons led
me up and I looked on my father's face. I cannot say that it
looked like him at all. His blackness had been equivocated
by powder and there was no suggestion in that casket of
what his power had or could have been. He was simply an
old man dead, and it was hard to believe that he had ever
given anyone either joy or pain. Yet, his life filled that
room. Farther up the avenue his wife was holding his new-
born child. Life and death so close together, and love and
hatred, and right and wrong, said something to me which
I did not want to hear concerning man, concerning the life
of man.

After the funeral, while I was downtown desperately
celebrating my birthday, a Negro soldier, in the lobby of
the Hotel Braddock, got into a fight with a white police-

man over a Negro girl. Negro girls, white policeman, in or out of uniform, and Negro males—in or out of uniform—were part of the furniture of the lobby of the Hotel Braddock and this was certainly not the first time such an incident had occurred. It was destined, however, to receive an unprecedented publicity, for the fight between the policeman and the soldier ended with the shooting of the soldier. Rumor, flowing immediately to the streets outside, stated that the soldier had been shot in the back, an instantaneous and revealing invention, and that the soldier had died protecting a Negro woman. The facts were somewhat different—for example, the soldier had not been shot in the back, and was not dead, and the girl seems to have been as dubious a symbol of womanhood as her white counterpart in Georgia usually is, but no one was interested in the facts. They preferred the invention because this invention expressed and corroborated their hates and fears so perfectly. It is just as well to remember that people are always doing this. Perhaps many of those legends, including Christianity, to which the world clings began their conquest of the world with just some such concerted surrender to distortion. The effect, in Harlem, of this particular legend was like the effect of a lit match in a tin of gasoline. The mob gathered before the doors of the Hotel Braddock simply began to swell and to spread in every direction, and Harlem exploded.

The mob did not cross the ghetto lines. It would have been easy, for example, to have gone over Morningside Park on the west side or to have crossed the Grand Central railroad tracks at 125th Street on the east side, to wreak havoc in white neighborhoods. The mob seems to have been mainly interested in something more potent and real than the white face, that is, in white power, and the principal damage done during the riot of the summer of 1943 was to white business establishments in Harlem. It might

have been a far bloodier story, of course, if, at the hour
the riot began, these establishments had still been open.
From the Hotel Braddock the mob fanned out, east and
west along 125th Street, and for the entire length of Lenox,
Seventh, and Eighth avenues. Along each of these avenues,
and along each major side street—116th, 125th, 135th, and
so on—bars, stores, pawnshops, restaurants, even little
luncheonettes had been smashed open and entered and
looted—looted, it might be added, with more haste than
efficiency. The shelves really looked as though a bomb had
struck them. Cans of beans and soup and dog food, along
with toilet paper, corn flakes, sardines and milk tumbled
every which way, and abandoned cash registers and cases
of beer leaned crazily out of the splintered windows and
were strewn along the avenues. Sheets, blankets, and cloth-
ing of every description formed a kind of path, as though
people had dropped them while running. I truly had not
realized that Harlem *had* so many stores until I saw them
all smashed open; the first time the word *wealth* ever entered
my mind in relation to Harlem was when I saw it scattered
in the streets. But one's first, incongruous impression of
plenty was countered immediately by an impression of
waste. None of this was doing anybody any good. It would
have been better to have left the plate glass as it had been
and the goods lying in the stores.

It would have been better, but it would also have been
intolerable, for Harlem had needed something to smash.
To smash something is the ghetto's chronic need. Most of
the time it is the members of the ghetto who smash each
other, and themselves. But as long as the ghetto walls are
standing there will always come a moment when these outlets do not work. That summer, for example, it was not
enough to get into a fight on Lenox Avenue, or curse out

one's cronies in the barber shops. If ever, indeed, the violence which fills Harlem's churches, pool halls, and bars erupts outward in a more direct fashion, Harlem and its citizens are likely to vanish in an apocalyptic flood. That this is not likely to happen is due to a great many reasons, most hidden and powerful among them the Negro's real relation to the white American. This relation prohibits, simply, anything as uncomplicated and satisfactory as pure hatred. In order really to hate white people, one has to blot so much out of the mind—and the heart—that this hatred itself becomes an exhausting and self-destructive pose. But this does not mean, on the other hand, that love comes easily: the white world is too powerful, too complacent, too ready with gratuitous humiliation, and, above all, too ignorant and too innocent for that. One is absolutely forced to make perpetual qualifications and one's own reactions are always canceling each other out. It is this, really, which has driven so many people mad, both white and black. One is always in the position of having to decide between amputation and gangrene. Amputation is swift but time may prove that the amputation was not necessary—or one may delay the amputation too long. Gangrene is slow, but it is impossible to be sure that one is reading one's symptoms right. The idea of going through life as a cripple is more than one can bear, and equally unbearable is the risk of swelling up slowly, in agony, with poison. And the trouble, finally, is that the risks are real even if the choices do not exist.

"But as for me and my house," my father had said, "we will serve the Lord." I wondered, as we drove him to his resting place, what this line had meant for him. I had heard him preach it many times. I had preached it once myself, proudly giving it an interpretation different from my father's. Now the whole thing came back to me, as though my father and I were on our way to Sunday school and I were memorizing the golden text: *And if it seem evil unto you to serve the Lord, choose you this day whom you will serve; whether the gods which your fathers served that were on the other side of the flood, or the gods of the Amorites, in whose land ye dwell; but as for me and my house, we will serve the Lord.* I suspected in these familiar lines a meaning which had never been there for me before. All of my father's texts and songs, which I had decided were meaningless, were arranged before me at his death like empty bottles, waiting to hold the meaning which life would give them for me. This was his legacy: nothing is ever escaped. That bleakly memorable morning I hated the unbelievable streets and the Negroes and whites who had, equally, made them that way. But I knew that it was folly, as my father would have said, this bitterness was folly. It was necessary to hold on to the things that mattered. The dead man mattered, the new life mattered; blackness and whiteness did not matter; to believe that they did was to acquiesce in one's own destruction. Hatred, which could destroy so much, never failed to destroy the man who hated and this was an immutable law.

It began to seem that one would have to hold in the mind forever two ideas which seemed to be in opposition. The first idea was acceptance, the acceptance, totally without rancor, of life as it is, and men as they are: in the light of this idea, it goes without saying that injustice is a commonplace. But this did not mean that one could be complacent, for the second idea was of equal power: that one must never, in one's own life, accept these injustices as commonplace but must fight them with all one's strength. This fight begins, however, in the heart and it now had been laid to my charge to keep my own heart free of hatred and despair. This intimation made my heart heavy and, now that my father was irrecoverable, I wished that he had been beside me so that I could have searched his face for the answers which only the future would give me now.

II

THE SEEDS OF
BITTERNESS

IF the previous selections illustrate the psychological effects of racism, the following pieces offer an extensive picture of two centuries of deliberate discrimination and subjugation. As far back as the Founding Fathers, democracy and equality were ideals limited to the white population of America. They were not meant to be shared with nonwhites. England was a limited monarchy, and England's child was born a limited democracy. The struggle during the past century has been between the American heritage and the American conscience. That is to say, white Americans were left revolutionary ideals and the problem of deciding whether they would be limited to whites or whether they would include people of color as well.

The bitterness of the slavery controversy grew as the number of slaves leaped to two million during the lifetime of

Charles Ball (1787?–1850?), whose narrative takes us back to the days when black people were held in bondage and slaveholder Thomas Jefferson wrestled with the concept that all men are entitled to life and liberty.

In 1790 there were about 700,000 slaves in the United States, and before the slave trade from overseas was *legally* closed in 1808 an additional 100,000 were hurried across the Atlantic Ocean. The Constitutional provision was unenforceable, however, and it was not until the slave trade was punished in the same manner as piracy some twelve years later that the traffic actually slowed down. Even so, it is estimated that between 1808 and 1865 some 250,000 to 300,000 slaves were smuggled into the United States. By comparison, there were 60,000 free blacks in the United States in 1790, and this number grew to half a million by the outbreak of the Civil War.

Newly freed slaves did what they could to help their more unfortunate brethren by raising money, as in Elizabeth Keckley's case, or by attempting to teach as many blacks as possible to read and write. Educational opportunities increased after emancipation, but at no time did they approach the quality of the facilities available to white children. However, the desire for learning was great. In 1870 at least 81 percent of all Negroes over ten years old were illiterate. Sixty years later only 16 percent of American blacks could not read or write. The second-rate schools which Negro children were forced to attend under the separate but equal doctrine did much to perpetuate the belief in white racial supremacy. They also laid the foundations for the Little Rock protest in which Daisy Bates took so prominent a role.

After the Civil War, job opportunities were extremely limited for nonskilled blacks. Sharecropping, as in Jesse Owens' case, became a way of life for those Negroes who had nowhere to go and for whites who had no knowledge of farming. Under this arrangement, blacks would farm part of a white man's property in return for pay either in food and lodging or money. Illiterate, uneducated in financial matters, the free black sharecroppers soon fell hopelessly in debt to their unscrupulous white landlords. This situation combined with rumors of fantastic opportunities in other parts of the country stimulated an exodus of Negroes from the rural South as early as 1879. Kansas was the direction toward which most of the emigrants turned, and Nat Love was one of the earliest Negroes who heeded the call to go West.

The great migration, however, did not take place until World War I. A severe labor depression in the South, crop failures due to the boll weevil, floods, southern injustice, and seeming opportunities in northern industry all conspired to lead the Negro to urban areas. For the decade ending in 1920 the North and West showed a net gain of 330,000 blacks.

The promised land turned out to be a mirage. Herded into ghettos, openly discriminated against, America's urban Negroes became increasingly frustrated. For every white person on the relief rolls during the Depression, three to four blacks suffered the same fate. Ellen Tarry's determination to find a job under these cruel circumstances is a bitter saga.

The anger resulting from three centuries of pyramiding injustices is finding new outlets in the militant protest of the 1970s. With a swelling awareness of their contribution to American civilization, the black people of this country are demanding a share of its benefits and a voice in its government.

1

FROM

The Life of Olaudah Equiano, or Gustavus Vassa, the African

Written by Himself
(1745–c. 1800)

*It is carefully recorded that a Dutch ship unloaded "20
Negars" off Jamestown in 1619, the first blacks brought to
the New World. From that time until the slave trade was declared piracy in 1820, it brought profit to a great many
whites in both the North and South, and untold misery to
countless blacks.*

*Slavery, however, was not alien to Gustavus Vassa, for he
himself came from a slave-holding family in Nigeria where
he was born. Kidnapped by Africans from his home in 1757
at the age of twelve, Vassa was turned over to white slave
traders for a handsome price. Within the year Vassa made
an unbearable journey across the ocean, and landed in
America, where he spent many years in bondage in Virginia.
Turned over to a Pennsylvania master (slavery was not
abolished in Pennsylvania until after the Revolution), Gustavus was put to work on small trading vessels in the West
Indies as well as on Caribbean plantations. He eventually
purchased his freedom and devoted his later years to anti-
slavery work in England. First published in 1789, Vassa's*

narrative is a shocking indictment of the slave trade and
slavery. Upon reading his description of the voyage from
Africa to the American continent, one may ask: How did so
many blacks survive?

THE first object which saluted my eyes when I arrived on
the coast, was the sea, and a slave ship, which was then riding at anchor, and waiting for its cargo. These filled me
with astonishment, which was soon converted into terror,
when I was carried on board. I was immediately handled,
and tossed up to see if I were sound, by some of the crew;
and I was now persuaded that I had gotten into a world of
bad spirits, and that they were going to kill me. Their complexions, too, differing so much from ours, their long hair,
and the language they spoke (which was very different from
any I had ever heard), united to confirm me in this belief.
Indeed, such were the horrors of my views and fears at the
moment, that, if ten thousand worlds had been my own, I
would have freely parted with them all to have exchanged
my condition with that of the meanest slave in my own
country. When I looked round the ship too, and saw a large
furnace of copper boiling, and a multitude of black people
of every description chained together, every one of their
countenances expressing dejection and sorrow, I no longer
doubted of my fate; and, quite overpowered with horror and
anguish, I fell motionless on the deck and fainted. When I
recovered a little, I found some black people about me, who
I believed were some of those who had brought me on board,
and had been receiving their pay; they talked to me in order
to cheer me, but all in vain. I asked them if we were not to
be eaten by those white men with horrible looks, red faces,
and long hair. They told me I was not, and one of the crew
brought me a small portion of spirituous liquor in a wine
glass; but, being afraid of him, I would not take it out of his

hand. One of the blacks, therefore, took it from him and gave
it to me, and I took a little down my palate, which, instead
of reviving me, as they thought it would, threw me into the
greatest consternation at the strange feeling it produced,
having never tasted any such liquor before. Soon after this,
the blacks who brought me on board went off, and left me
abandoned to despair.

I now saw myself deprived of all chance of returning to
my native country, or even the least glimpse of hope of
gaining the shore, which I now considered as friendly; and
I even wished for my former slavery in preference to my
present situation, which was filled with horrors of every
kind, still heightened by my ignorance of what I was to
undergo. I was not long suffered to indulge my grief; I was
soon put down under the decks, and there I received such a
salutation in my nostrils as I had never experienced in my
life: so that, with the loathsomeness of the stench, and crying together, I became so sick and low that I was not able
to eat, nor had I the least desire to taste anything. I now
wished for the last friend, death, to relieve me; but soon, to
my grief, two of the white men offered me eatables; and, on
my refusing to eat, one of them held me fast by the hands
and laid me across, I think, the windlass, and tied my feet,
while the other flogged me severely. I had never experienced
anything of this kind before, and, although not being used
to the water, I naturally feared that element the first time I
saw it, yet, nevertheless, could I have got over the nettings,
I would have jumped over the side, but I could not; and
besides, the crew used to watch us very closely who were not
chained down to the decks, lest we should leap into the
water; and I have seen some of these poor African prisoners
most severely cut, for attempting to do so, and hourly whipped for not eating. This indeed was often the case with myself. In a little time after, amongst the poor chained men, I

found some of my own nation, which in a small degree gave
ease to my mind. I inquired of these what was to be done
with us. They gave me to understand, we were to be carried
to these white people's country to work for them. I then was
a little revived, and thought, if it were no worse than working, my situation was not so desperate; but still I feared I
should be put to death, the white people looked and acted,
as I thought, in so savage a manner; for I had never seen
among any people such instances of brutal cruelty; and this
not only shown towards us blacks, but also to some of the
whites themselves. One white man in particular I saw, when
we were permitted to be on deck, flogged so unmercifully
with a large rope near the foremast, that he died in conse-
quence of it; and they tossed him over the side as they would
have done a brute. This made me fear these people the more;
and I expected nothing less than to be treated in the same
manner. I could not help expressing my fears and apprehensions to some of my countrymen; I asked them if these
people had no country, but lived in this hollow place (the
ship)? They told me they did not but came from a distant
one. "Then," said I, "how comes it in all our country we
never heard of them?" They told me because they lived so
very far off. I then asked where were their women? had
they any like themselves? I was told they had. "And why,"
said I, "do we not see them?" They answered, because they
were left behind. I asked how the vessel could go. They told
me they could not tell; but that there was cloth put upon
the masts by the help of the ropes I saw, and then the vessel
went on; and the white men had some spell or magic they
put in the water when they liked, in order to stop the vessel.
I was exceedingly amazed at this account, and really thought
they were spirits. I therefore wished much to be from
amongst them, for I expected they would sacrifice me; but
my wishes were vain—for we were so quartered that it was

impossible for any of us to make our escape.

While we stayed on the coast I was mostly on deck; and one day, to my great astonishment, I saw one of these vessels coming in with the sails up. As soon as the whites saw it, they gave a great shout, at which we were amazed; and the more so, as the vessel appeared larger by approaching nearer. At last, she came to anchor in my sight, and when the anchor was let go, I and my countrymen who saw it, were lost in astonishment to observe the vessel stop—and were now convinced it was done by magic. Soon after this the other ship got her boats out, and they came on board of us, and the people of both ships seemed very glad to see each other. Several of the strangers also shook hands with us black people, and made motions with their hands, signifying I suppose, we were to go to their country, but we did not understand them.

At last, when the ship we were in had got in all her cargo, they made ready with many fearful noises, and we were all put under deck, so that we could not see how they managed the vessel. But this disappointment was the least of my sorrow. The stench of the hold while we were on the coast was so intolerably loathsome, that it was dangerous to remain there for any time, and some of us had been permitted to stay on the deck for the fresh air; but now that the whole ship's cargo were confined together, it became absolutely pestilential. The closeness of the place, and the heat of the climate, added to the number in the ship, which was so crowded that each had scarcely room to turn himself, almost suffocated us. This produced copious perspirations, so that the air soon became unfit for respiration, from a variety of loathsome smells, and brought on a sickness among the slaves, of which many died—thus falling victims to the improvident avarice, as I may call it, of their purchasers. This wretched situation was again aggravated by the galling of the chains, now become insupportable, and the filth of the necessary tubs, into which the children often fell, and were almost suffocated. The shrieks of the women, and the groans of the dying, rendered the whole a scene of horror almost inconceivable. Happily perhaps, for myself, I was soon reduced so low here that it was thought necessary to keep me almost always on deck; and from my extreme youth I was not put in fetters. In this situation I expected every hour to share the fate of my companions, some of whom were almost daily brought upon deck at the point of death, which I began to hope would soon put an end to my miseries. Often did I think many of the inhabitants of the deep much more happy than myself. I envied them the freedom they enjoyed, and as often wished I could change my condition for theirs. Every circumstance I met with, served only to render my state more painful, and heightened my apprehensions, and my opinion of the cruelty of the whites.

One day they had taken a number of fishes; and when they had killed and satisfied themselves with as many as they thought fit, to our astonishment who were on deck, rather than give any of them to us to eat, as we expected, they tossed the remaining fish into the sea again, although we begged and prayed for some as well as we could, but in vain; and some of my countrymen, being pressed by hunger, took an opportunity, when they thought no one saw them, of trying to get a little privately; but they were discovered, and the attempt procured them some very severe floggings. One day, when we had a smooth sea and moderate wind, two of my wearied countrymen who were chained together (I was near them at the time), preferring death to such a life of misery, somehow made through the nettings and jumped into the sea; immediately, another quite dejected fellow, who, on account of his illness, was suffered to be out of irons, also followed their example; and I believe many more would very soon have done the same if they had not been prevented by the ship's crew, who were instantly alarmed. Those of us that were the most active were in a moment put down under the deck; and there was such a noise and confusion amongst the people of the ship as I never heard before, to stop her, and get the boat out to go after the slaves. However, two of the wretches were drowned, but they got the other, and afterwards flogged him unmercifully, for thus attempting to prefer death to slavery. In this manner we continued to undergo more hardships than I can now relate, hardships which are inseparable from this accursed trade. Many a time we were near suffocation from the want of fresh air, which we were often without for whole days together. This, and the stench of the necessary tubs, carried off many.

During our passage, I first saw flying fishes, which surprised me very much; they used frequently to fly across the ship, and many of them fell on the deck. I also now first saw the use of the quadrant; I had often with astonishment seen the mariners make observations with it, and I could not think what it meant. They at last took notice of my surprise; and one of them, willing to increase it, as well as to gratify my curiosity, made me one day look through it. The clouds appeared to me to be land, which disappeared as they passed along. This heightened my wonder; and I was now more persuaded than ever that I was in another world, and that every thing about me was magic. At last, we came in sight of the island of Barbadoes, at which the whites on board gave a great shout, and made many signs of joy to us. We did not know what to think of this; but as the vessel drew nearer, we plainly saw the harbor, and other ships of different kinds and sizes, and we soon anchored amongst them, off Bridgetown. Many merchants and planters now came on board, though it was in the evening. They put us in separate parcels, and examined us attentively. They also made us jump, and pointed to the land, signifying we were to go there. We thought by this, we should be eaten by these ugly men, as they appeared to us; and, when soon after we were all put down under the deck again, there was much dread and trembling among us, and nothing but bitter cries to be heard all the night from these apprehensions, insomuch, that at last the white people got some old slaves from the land to pacify us. They told us we were not to be eaten, but to work, and were soon to go on land, where we should see many of our country people. This report eased us much. And sure enough, soon after we were landed, there came to us Africans of all languages.

We were conducted immediately to the merchant's yard, where we were all pent up together, like so many sheep in a fold, without regard to sex or age. As every object was new to me, everything I saw filled me with surprise. What struck me first, was, that the houses were built with bricks and stories, and in every other respect different from those I had seen in Africa; but I was still more astonished on seeing people on horseback. I did not know what this could mean; and, indeed, I thought these people were full of nothing but magical arts. While I was in this astonishment, one of my fellow prisoners spoke to a countryman of his about the horses, who said they were the same kind they had in their country. I understood them, though they were from a distant part of Africa; and I thought it odd I had not seen any horses there; but afterwards, when I came to converse with different Africans, I found they had many horses amongst them, and much larger than those I then saw.

We were not many days in the merchant's custody, before we were sold after their usual manner, which is this: On a signal given (as the beat of a drum), the buyers rush at once into the yard where the slaves are confined, and make choice of that parcel they like best. The noise and clamor with which this is attended, and the eagerness visible in the countenances of the buyers, serve not a little to increase the apprehension of terrified Africans, who may well be supposed to consider them as the ministers of that destruction to which they think themselves devoted. In this manner, without scruple, are relations and friends separated, most of them never to see each other again. I remember, in the vessel in which I was brought over, in the men's apartment, there were several brothers, who, in the sale, were sold in different lots; and it was very moving on this occasion, to see and hear their cries at parting. O, ye nominal Christians! might not an African ask you—Learned you this from your God, who says unto you, Do unto all men as you would men should do unto you? Is it not enough that we are torn from our country and friends, to toil for your luxury and lust of gain? Must every tender feeling be likewise sacrificed to your avarice? Are the dearest friends and relations, now rendered more dear by their separation from their kindred, still to be parted from each other, and thus prevented from cheering the gloom of slavery, with the small comfort of being together, and mingling their sufferings and sorrows? Why are parents to lose their children, brothers their sisters, or husbands their wives? Surely, this is a new refinement in cruelty, which, while it has no advantage to atone for it, thus aggravates distress, and adds fresh horrors even to the wretchedness of slavery.

2

FROM

Fifty Years in Chains or The Life of an American Slave

by Charles Ball
(1781?–1850)

Charles Ball is not the real name of the author of the next selection, and we do not know exactly when he was born. An escaped slave, he was still a slave by the laws of this country when his verbal narrative was taken down and published in 1837.

Charles—it is necessary to call him that for lack of any other information—and his mother were sold separately at a slave auction when he was about four, and he never saw her again. This was one of the greatest tragedies of slavery: the inhuman practice of separating husbands and wives and children on the slave block. Ball himself was forced to leave his own wife and youngsters in Maryland and accompany a new master to Georgia. His anguish and the events of the trip are described fully in the following pages.

The chances of escaping to a free state were remote, but after many years Ball decided to risk it. He chose harvest time so that he would not lack food en route. After five months of traveling only at night, he made his way to his

wife's cabin in Maryland. In the morning when he threw
himself on the mercy of his old master and mistress, he was
advised to conceal himself for a while and then work for
wages.

By 1800, out of approximately 140,000 blacks living in
Maryland, over 8,000 had achieved freedom by escape, pur-
chase, or as a result of white conscience. Of course by living
in a slave state they always ran the risk of being kidnapped
and sold illegally into slavery. Nevertheless, after eight years
Ball saved $400 and with it bought livestock and twelve
acres of land near Baltimore. He and his family were content
for ten years until he was seized by the family he had escaped
from. Ball was returned to Georgia and made a field slave
once more. He escaped, this time to Philadelphia, where he
spent the rest of his life as a fugitive. He never saw his family
again.

MY MASTER kept a store at a small village on the bank of
the Patuxent river, called B—, although he resided at some
distance on a farm. One morning he rose early, and ordered me to take a yoke of oxen and go to the village, to
bring home a cart which was there, saying he would follow
me. He arrived at the village soon after I did, and took his
breakfast with his storekeeper. He then told me to come into
the house and get my breakfast. Whilst I was eating in the
kitchen, I observed him talking earnestly, but low, to a
stranger near the kitchen door. I soon after went out, and
hitched my oxen to the cart, and was about to drive off,
when several men came round about me, and amongst them
the stranger whom I had seen speaking with my master.
This man came up to me, and, seizing me by the collar,

shook me violently, saying I was his property, and must go with him to Georgia. At the sound of these words, the thoughts of my wife and children rushed across my mind, and my heart beat away within me. I saw and knew that my case was hopeless, and that resistance was vain, as there were near twenty persons present, all of whom were ready to assist the man by whom I was kidnapped. I felt incapable of weeping or speaking, and in my despair I laughed loudly. My purchaser ordered me to cross my hands behind, which were quickly bound with a strong cord; and he then told me that we must set out that very day for the South. I asked if I could not be allowed to go to see my wife and children, or if this could not be permitted, if they might not have leave to come to see me; but was told that I would be able to get another wife in Georgia.

My new master, whose name I did not hear, took me that same day across the Patuxent, where I joined fifty-one other slaves, whom he had bought in Maryland. Thirty-two of these were men and nineteen were women. The women were merely tied together with a rope, about the size of a bed-cord, which was tied like a halter round the neck of each; but the men, of whom I was the stoutest and strongest, were differently caparisoned. A strong iron collar was closely fitted by means of a padlock round each of our necks. A chain of iron, about a hundred feet in length, was passed through the hasp of each padlock, except at the two ends, where the hasps of the padlock passed through a link of the chain. In addition to this, we were handcuffed in pairs, with iron staples and bolts, with a short chain, about a foot long, uniting the handcuffs and their wearers in pairs. In this manner we were chained alternately by the right and left hand; and the poor man to whom I was thus ironed, wept like an infant when the blacksmith, with his heavy hammer, fastened the ends of the bolts that kept the stamples from slipping from our arms. For my own part, I felt indifferent to my fate. It appeared to me that the worst had come that could come, and that no change of fortune could harm me.

After we were all chained and handcuffed together, we sat down upon the ground; and here reflecting upon the sad reverse of fortune that had so suddenly overtaken me, I became weary of life, and bitterly execrated the day I was born. It seemed that I was destined by fate to drink the cup of sorrow to the very dregs, and that I should find no respite from misery but in the grave. I longed to die, and escape from the hands of my tormentors; but even the wretched privilege of destroying myself was denied me, for I could not shake off my chains, nor move a yard without the consent of my master. Reflecting in silence upon my forlorn condition, I at length concluded that as things could not become worse—and as the life of man is but a continued round of changes, they must, of necessity, take a turn in my favor at some future day. I found relief in this vague and indefinite hope, and when we received orders to go on board the scow, which was to transport us over the Patuxent, I marched down to the water with a firmness of purpose of which I did not believe myself capable, a few minutes before.

We were soon on the south side of the river, and taking up our line of march, we traveled about five miles that evening, and stopped for the night at one of those miserable public houses, so frequent in the lower parts of Maryland and Virginia, called "ordinaries."

Our master ordered a pot of mush to be made for our supper; after despatching which we all lay down on the naked floor to sleep in our handcuffs and chains. The women, my fellow-slaves, lay on one side of the room; and the men who were chained with me, occupied the other. I slept but little this night, which I passed in thinking of my wife and little children, whom I could not hope ever to see again.

Day at length came, and with the dawn, we resumed our journey towards the Potomac. As we passed along the road, I saw the slaves at work in the corn and tobacco fields. I knew they toiled hard and lacked food; but they were not, like me, dragged in chains from their wives, children and friends. Compared with me, they were the happiest of mortals. . . . Hitherto our master had not offered to sell any of us, and had even refused to stop to talk to any one on the subject of our sale, although he had several times been addressed on this point, before we reached Lancaster; but soon after we departed from this village, we were overtaken on the road by a man on horseback, who accosted our driver by asking him if his *niggers* were for sale. The latter replied, that he believed he would not sell any yet, as he was on his way to Georgia, and cotton being now much in demand, he expected to obtain high prices for us from persons who were going to settle in the new purchase. He, however, contrary to his custom, ordered us to stop, and told the stranger he might look at us, and that he would find us as fine a lot of hands as were ever imported into the country—that we were all prime property, and he had no doubt would command his own prices in Georgia.

The stranger, who was a thin, weather-beaten, sunburned figure, then said, he wanted a couple of breeding wenches, and would give as much for them as they would bring in Georgia—that he had lately heard from Augusta, and that *niggers* were not higher there than in Columbia, and, as he had been in Columbia the week before, he knew what *niggers* were worth. He then walked along our line, as we stood chained together, and looked at the whole of us— then turning to the women, asked the prices of the two pregnant ones. Our master replied, that these were two of the best-breeding wenches in all Maryland—that one was twenty-two, and the other only nineteen—that the first was already the mother of seven children, and the other of four—that he had himself seen the children at the time he bought their mothers—and that such wenches would be cheap at a thousand dollars each; but as they were not able to keep up with the gang, he would take twelve hundred dollars for the two. The purchaser said this was too much, but that he would give nine hundred dollars for the pair. This price was promptly refused; but our master, after some considera-tion, said he was willing to sell a bargain in these wenches, and would take eleven hundred dollars for them, which was objected to on the other side; and many faults and failings were pointed out in the merchandise. After much bargaining, and many gross jests on the part of the stranger, he offered a thousand dollars for the two, and said he would give no more. He then mounted his horse, and moved off; but after he had gone about one hundred yards, he was called back; and our master said, if he would go with him to the next blacksmith's shop on the road to Columbia, and pay for taking the irons off the rest of us, he might have the two women.

This proposal was agreed to, and as it was now about nine o'clock, we were ordered to hasten on to the next house, where, we were told, we must stop for breakfast. At this place we were informed that it was ten miles to the next smith's shop, and our new acquaintance was obliged by the terms of his contract, to accompany us thither. We re-ceived for breakfast, about a pint of boiled rice to each person, and after this was despatched, we again took to the road, eager to reach the blacksmith's shop, at which we expected to be relieved of the iron rings and chains, which had so long galled and worried us. About two o'clock we arrived at the longed-for residence of the smith; but, on in-quiry, our master was informed that he was not at home, and would not return before evening. Here a controversy arose, whether we should all remain here until the smith returned, or the stranger should go on with us to the next smithery, which was said to be only five miles distant. This was a point not easily settled between two such spirits as our master and the stranger; both of whom had been overseers in their time, and both of whom had risen to the rank of proprietors of slaves. The dispute between the two masters was still raging, when, unexpectedly, the black-smith rode up to his house, on a thin, bony-looking horse, and dismounting, asked his wife what these gentlemen were making such a *frolick* about. I did not hear her answer, but both the disputants turned and addressed themselves to the smith—the one to know what price he would demand to take the irons off all these *niggers*, and the other to know how long it would take him to perform the work. The smith at length agreed to take the irons from the whole of us for two dollars and fifty cents, and immediately set about it, with the air of indifference that he would have manifested in tearing a pair of old shoes from the hoofs of a wagon-horse. After we were released from our chains, our master sold the whole lot of irons, which we had borne from Mary-land, to the blacksmith, for seven dollars.

The smith then procured a bottle of rum, and treated his two new acquaintances to a part of its contents—wishing them both good luck with their *niggers*. After these civili-ties were over, the two women were ordered to follow their new master, who shaped his course across the country, by a road leading west. At parting from us, they both wept aloud, and wrung their hands in despair. We all went to them, and bade them a last farewell. Their road led into a wood, which they soon entered, and I never saw them nor heard of them again.

It was now late in the afternoon; but, as we had made lit-

tle progress to-day, and were now divested of the burden of
our chains, as well as freed from the two women, who had
hitherto much retarded our march, our master ordered us to
hasten on our way, as we had ten miles to go that evening. I
had been so long oppressed by the weight of my chains, and
the iron collar about my neck, that for some time after I
commenced walking at my natural liberty, I felt a kind of
giddiness, or lightness of the head. Most of my companions
complained of the same sensation, and we did not recover
our proper feelings until after we had slept one night. It was
after dark when we arrived at our lodging-place, which
proved to be the house of a small cotton-planter, who, it
appeared, kept a sort of a house of entertainment for travelers,
contrary to what I afterwards discovered to be the usual custom of cotton-planters. This man and my master had known
each other before, and seemed to be well acquainted. He
was the first person that we had met since leaving Maryland,
who was known to my master, and as they kept up a very
free conversation, through the course of the evening, and
the house in which they were, was only separated from the
kitchen, in which we were lodged, by a space of a few feet,
I had an opportunity of hearing much that was highly
interesting to me. I slept but little this night, feeling a rest-
lessness when no longer in chains; and pondering over the
future lot of my life, which appeared fraught only with evil
and misfortune. Day at length dawned and with its first
light we were ordered to betake ourselves to the road, which,
we were told, would lead us to Columbia, the place of intended sale of some, if not all of us. For several days past, I
had observed that in the country through which we traveled,
little attention was paid to the cultivation of anything but
cotton. Now this plant was almost the sole possessor of the
fields. It covered the plantations adjacent to the road, as
far as I could see, both before and behind me, and looked

not unlike buckwheat before it blossoms. I saw some small fields of corn, and lots of sweet potatoes, amongst which the young vines of the watermelon were frequently visible. The improvements on the plantations were not good. There were no barns, but only stables and sheds, to put the cotton under, as it was brought from the field. Hay seemed to be unknown in the country, for I saw neither hay-stacks nor meadows; and the few fields that were lying fallow, had but small numbers of cattle in them, and these were thin and meagre. We had met with no flocks of sheep of late, and the hogs that we saw on the road-side were in bad condition. The horses and mules that I saw in the cotton-fields, were poor and badly harnessed, and the half-naked condition of the negroes, who drove them, or followed with the hoe, together with their wan complexions, proved to me that they had too much work, or not enough food. We passed a cotton-gin this morning, the first that I ever saw; but they were not at work with it. We also met a party of ladies and gentlemen on a journey of pleasure, riding in two very handsome carriages, drawn by sleek and spirited horses, very different in appearance from the moving skeletons that I had noticed drawing the ploughs in the fields. The black drivers of the coaches were neatly clad in gay-colored clothes, and contrasted well with their half-naked brethren, a gang of whom were hoeing cotton by the roadside, near them, attended by an overseer in white-linen shirt and pantaloons, with one of the long negro whips in his hand.

I observed that these poor people did not raise their heads, to look at either the fine coaches and horses then passing, or at us; but kept their faces steadily bent towards the cotton-plants, from among which they were removing the weeds. I almost shuddered at the sight, knowing that I myself was doomed to a state of servitude equally cruel and debasing, unless, by some unforeseen occurrence, I might fall into the hands of a master of less inhumanity of temper than the one who had possession of the miserable creatures before me.

The cruel and frequent punishments meted out to slaves often defy belief. While Ball was working as a field hand, he met another slave who was wearing a piece of fine linen tied in front under a ragged shirt. Ball asked the man why he was wearing a piece of "gentleman's linen" and this was his reply:

"I have always been a hard working man, and have suffered a great deal from hunger in my time. It is not possible for a man to work hard every day for several months, and get nothing but a peck of corn a week to eat, and not feel hungry. When a man is hungry, you know, (if you have ever been hungry,) he must eat whatever he can get. I have not tasted meat since last Christmas, and we have had to work uncommonly hard this summer. Master has a flock of sheep, that run in the woods, and they come every night to sleep in the lane near the house. Two weeks ago last Saturday, when we quit work at night, I was very hungry, and as we went to the house we passed along the lane where the sheep lay. There were nearly fifty of them, and some were very fat. The temptation was more than I could bear. I caught one of them, cut its head off with the hoe that I carried on my shoulder, and threw it under the fence. About midnight when all was still about the house, I went out with a knife, took the sheep into the woods, and dressed it by the light of the moon. The carcass I took home, and after cutting it up, placed it in the great kettle over a good fire, intending to boil it and divide it, when cooked between my fellow-slaves (whom I knew to be as hungry as I was) and myself. Unfortunately for me, master Tom, who had been out amongst his friends that day, had not returned at bedtime; and about one o'clock in the morning, at the time when I had a blazing fire under the kettle, I heard the sound of the feet of a horse coming along the lane. The kitchen walls were open so that the light of my fire could not be concealed, and in a moment I heard the horse blowing at the front of the house. Conscious of my danger, I stripped my shirt from my back, and pushed it into the boiling kettle, so as wholly to conceal the flesh of the sheep. I had scarcely completed this act of precaution, when master Tom burst into the kitchen, and with a terrible oath, asked me what I was doing so late at night, with a great fire in the kitchen. I replied, 'I am going to wash my shirt, master, and am boiling it to get it clean.' 'Washing your shirt at this time of night!' said he, 'I will let you know that you are not to sit up all night and be lazy and good for nothing all day. There shall be no boiling of shirts here on Sunday morning,' and thrusting his cane into the kettle, he raised my shirt out and threw it on the kitchen floor.

"He did not at first observe the mutton, which rose to the surface of the water as soon as the shirt was removed; but, after giving the shirt a kick towards the door, he again turned his face to the fire, and seeing a leg standing several inches out of the pot, he demanded of me what I had in there and where I had got this meat! Finding that I was detected, and that the whole matter must be discovered, I said,—'Master, I am hungry, and am cooking my supper.' 'What is it you have in here?' 'A sheep,' said I, and as the words were uttered, he knocked me down with his cane, and after beating me severely, ordered me to cross my hands until he bound me fast with a rope that hung in the kitchen, and answered the double purpose of a clothes line and a cord to tie us with when we were to be whipped. He put

out the fire under the kettle, drew me into the yard, tied
me fast to the mill-post, and leaving me there for the night,
went and called one of the negro boys to put his horse in
the stable, and went to his bed. The cord was bound so
tightly round my wrists, that before morning the blood had
burst out under my finger nails; but I suppose my master
slept soundly for all that. I was afraid to call any one to
come and release me from my torment, lest a still more terrible punishment might overtake me.

"I was permitted to remain in this situation until long
after sunrise the next morning, which being Sunday, was
quiet and still; my fellow-slaves being permitted to take
their rest after the severe toil of the past week, and my old
master and two young ones having no occasion to rise to
call the hands to the field, did not think of interrupting
their morning slumbers, to release me from my painful confinement. However, when the sun was risen about an hour,
I heard the noise of persons moving in the great house,
and soon after a loud and boisterous conversation, which I
well knew portended no good to me. At length they all
three came into the yard where I lay lashed to the post,
and approaching me, my old master asked me if I had any
accomplices in stealing the sheep. I told them none—that it
was entirely my own act—and that none of my fellow-slaves
had any hand in it. This was the truth; but if any of my
companions had been concerned with me, I should not
have betrayed them; for such an act of treachery could not
have alleviated the dreadful punishment which I knew
awaited me, and would only have involved them in the same
misery.

"They called me a thief, loaded me with oaths and imprecations, and each one proposed the punishment which
he deemed the most appropriate to the enormity of the crime
that I had committed. Master Tom was of opinion, that I

should be lashed to the post at the foot of which I lay, and that each of my fellow-slaves should be compelled to give me a dozen lashes in turn, with a roasted and greased hickory *gad*, until I had received, in the whole, two hundred and fifty lashes on my bare back, and that he would stand by, with the whip in his hand, and *compel* them not to spare me; but after a short debate this was given up, as it would probably render me unable to work in the field again for several weeks. My master Ned was in favor of giving me a dozen lashes every morning for a month, with the whip; but my old master said, this would be attended with too much trouble, and besides, it would keep me from my work, at least half an hour every morning, and proposed, in his turn, that I should not be whipped at all, but that the carcass of the sheep should be taken from the kettle in its half-boiled condition, and hung up in the kitchen loft without salt; and that I should be compelled to subsist on this putrid mutton without any other food, until it should be consumed. This suggestion met the approbation of my young masters, and would have been adopted, had not mistress at this moment come into the yard, and hearing the intended punishment, loudly objected to it, because the mutton would, in a day or two, create such an offensive stench, that she and my young mistresses would not be able to remain in the house. My mistress swore dreadfully, and cursed me for an ungrateful sheep thief, who, after all her kindness in giving me soup and warm bread when I was sick last winter, was always stealing everything I could get hold of. She then said to my master, that such villainy ought not to be passed over in a slight manner, and that as crimes, such as this, concerned the whole country, my punishment ought to be public for the purpose of example; and advised him to have me whipped that same afternoon, at five o'clock; first giving notice to the neighborhood to come and see the spectacle, and to bring with them their slaves, that they might be witnesses to the consequences of stealing sheep.

"They then returned to the house to breakfast; but as
the pain in my hands and arms produced by the ligatures
of the cord with which I was bound, was greater than I
could bear, I now felt exceedingly sick, and lost all knowledge of my situation. They told me I fainted; and when I
recovered my faculties, I found myself lying in the shade
of the house, with my hands free, and all the white persons
in my master's family standing around me. As soon as I was
able to stand, the rope was tied round my neck, and the
other end again fastened to the mill post. My mistress said
I had only pretended to faint; and master Tom said, I
would have something worth fainting for before night. He
was faithful to his promise; but for the present, I was suffered to sit on the grass in the shade of the house.

"As soon as breakfast was over, my two young masters
had their horses saddled, and set out to give notice to their
friends of what had happened, and to invite them to come
and see me punished for the crime I had committed. My
mistress gave me no breakfast and when I begged one of the
black boys whom I saw looking at me through the pales, to
bring me some water in a gourd to drink, she ordered him
to bring it from a puddle in the lane. My mistress has always been very cruel to all her black people.

"I remained in this situation until about eleven o'clock,
when one of my young mistresses came to me and gave me
a piece of jonny-cake about the size of my hand, perhaps
larger than my hand, telling me at the same time, that my
fellow-slaves had been permitted to re-boil the mutton that
I had left in the kettle, and make their breakfast of it, but
that her mother would not allow her to give me any part of
it. It was well for them that I had parboiled it with my
shirt, and so defiled it that it was unfit for the table of my

master, otherwise, no portion of it would have fallen to the black people—as it was, they had as much meat as they could consume in two days, for which I had to suffer.

"About twelve o'clock, one of my young masters returned, and soon afterwards the other came home. I heard them tell my old master that they had been round to give notice of my offence to the neighboring planters, and that several of them would attend to see me flogged, and would bring with them some of their slaves, who might be able to report to their companions what had been done to me for stealing.

"It was late in the afternoon before any of the gentlemen came; but, before five o'clock, there were more than twenty white people, and at least fifty black ones present, the latter of whom had been compelled, by their masters, to come and see me punished. Amongst others, an overseer from a neighboring estate attended; and to him was awarded the office of executioner. I was stripped of my shirt, and the waistband of my trousers was drawn closely round me, below my hips, so as to expose the whole of my back, in its entire length.

"It seems that it had been determined to beat me with thongs of raw cow-hide, for the overseer had two of these in his hands, each about four feet long; but one of the gentlemen present said this might bruise my back so badly, that I could not work for some time; perhaps not for a week or two; and as I could not be spared from the field without disadvantage to my master's crop, he suggested a different plan, by which, in his opinion, the greatest degree of pain could be inflicted upon me, with the least danger of rendering me unable to work. As he was a large planter, and had more than fifty slaves, all were disposed to be guided by his counsels, and my master said he would submit the matter entirely to him as a man of judgment and experience in such cases. He then desired my master to have a dozen pods of red pepper boiled in half a gallon of water, and desired the overseer to lay aside his thongs of raw-hide, and put a new cracker of silk, to the lash of his negro whip. Whilst these preparations were being made, each of my thumbs were lashed closely to the end of a stick about three feet long, and a chair being placed beside the mill post, I was compelled to raise my hands and place the stick, to which my thumbs were bound, over the top of the post, which is about eighteen inches square; the chair was then taken from under me, and I was left hanging by the thumbs, with my face towards the post, and my feet about a foot from the ground. My two great toes were then tied together, and drawn down the post as far as my joints could be stretched; the cord was passed round the post two or three times and securely fastened. In this posture I had no power of motion except in my neck, and could only move that at the expense of beating my face against the side of the post.

"The pepper tea was now brought, and poured into a basin to cool, and the overseer was desired to give me a dozen lashes just above the waist-band; and not to cover a space of more than four inches on my back, from the waist-band upwards. He obeyed the injunction faithfully, but slowly, and each crack of the whip was followed by a sensation as painful as if a red hot iron had been drawn across my back. When the twelve strokes had been given, the operation was suspended, and a black man, one of the slaves present, was compelled to wash the gashes in my skin, with the scalding pepper tea, which was yet so hot that he could not hold his hand in it. This doubly-burning liquid was thrown into my raw and bleeding wounds, and produced a tormenting smart, beyond the description of language. After a delay of ten minutes, by the watch, I received another dozen lashes, on the part of my back which was immediately above the bleeding and burning gashes of the former whipping; and again the biting, stinging, pepper tea was applied to my lacerated and trembling muscles. This operation was continued at regular intervals, until I had received ninety-six lashes, and my back was cut and scalded from end to end. Every stroke of the whip had drawn blood; many of the gashes were three inches long; my back burned as if it had been covered by a coat of hot embers, mixed with living coals; and I felt my flesh quiver like that of animals that have been slaughtered by the butcher and are flayed whilst yet half alive. My face was bruised, and my nose bled profusely, for in the madness of my agony, I had not been able to refrain from beating my head violently against the post.

"Vainly did I beg and implore for mercy. I was kept bound to the post with my whole weight hanging upon my thumbs, an hour and a half, but it appeared to me that I had entered upon eternity, and that my sufferings would never end. At length, however, my feet were unbound, and afterwards my hands; but when released from the cords, I was so far exhausted as not to be able to stand, and my thumbs were stiff and motionless. I was carried into the kitchen, and laid on a blanket, where my mistress came to see me; and after looking at my lacerated back, and telling me that my wounds were only skin deep, said I had come off well after what I had done, and that I ought to be thankful that it was not worse with me. She then bade me not to groan so loud, nor make so much noise, and left me to myself. I lay in this condition until it was quite dark, by which time the burning of my back had much abated, and was succeeded by an aching soreness, which rendered me unable to turn over, or bend my spine in the slightest manner. My mistress again visited me, and brought with her about half a pound of fat bacon, which she made one of the black women roast before the fire on a fork, until the oil ran freely from it, and then rub it warm over my back. This was repeated until I was greased from the neck to the hips, effectually. An old blanket was then thrown over me, and I was left to pass the night alone. Such was the terror stricken into my fellow-slaves, by the example made of me, that although they loved and pitied me, not one of them dared to approach me during the night.

"My strength was gone, and I at length fell asleep, from which I did not awake until the horn was blown the next morning, to call the people to the corn crib, to receive their weekly allowance of a peck of corn. I did not rise, nor attempt to join the other people, and shortly afterwards my master entered the kitchen, and in a soft and gentle tone of voice, asked me if I was dead. I answered him that I was not dead, and making some effort, found I was able to get upon my feet. My master had become frightened when he missed me at the corn crib, and being suddenly seized with an apprehension that I was dead, his heart had become softened, not with compassion for my sufferings, but with the fear of losing his best field hand; but when he saw me stand before him erect, and upright, the recollection of the lost sheep revived in his mind, and with it, all his feelings of revenge against the author of its death.

" 'So you are not dead yet, you thieving rascal,' said he, and cursing me with many bitter oaths, ordered me to go along to the crib and get my corn, and go to work with the rest of the hands. I was forced to obey, and taking my basket of corn from the door of the crib, placed it in the kitchen loft, and went to the field with the other people.

"Weak and exhausted as I was, I was compelled to do the work of an able hand, but was not permitted to taste the mutton, which was all given to the others, who were carefully guarded whilst they were eating, lest they should give me some of it."

This man's back was not yet well. Many of the gashes made by the lash were yet sore, and those that were healed had left long white stripes across his body. He had no notion of leaving the service of his tyrannical master, and his spirit was so broken and subdued that he was ready to suffer and to bear all his hardships: not, indeed, without complaining, but without attempting to resist his oppressors or to escape from their power. I saw him often whilst I remained at this place, and ventured to tell him once, that if I had a master who would abuse me as he had abused him, I would run away.

3

FROM

Behind the Scenes

by Elizabeth Keckley
(1824–1907)

Elizabeth Keckley was born into slavery in America's oldest colony, Virginia. With the help of friends and with a great deal of thrift on her own part, she managed to amass $1200 to buy freedom for herself and her son (who was fathered by a white slaveholder). Armed with her free papers, she went to Washington, D.C., in 1860 in the hope of finding work as a seamstress. At that time there were about half a million free blacks in the United States.

In the capital she was employed by the wife of the Senator from Mississippi—Mrs. Jefferson Davis. In time, Mrs. Davis asked Mrs. Keckley to go South with her family, saying that war was soon to come and that the South would surely win because "the North will yield when it sees the South is in earnest rather than engage in a long and bloody war."

Mrs. Keckley chose to remain in Washington and was referred to Mrs. Abraham Lincoln by a client, shortly after Lincoln's first inauguration. She became not only Mrs. Lincoln's seamstress but a close and trusted friend. Her intimacy with President and Mrs. Lincoln during the war years provides a remarkable memoir.

IN the summer of 1862, freedmen began to flock into Washington from Maryland and Virginia. They came with a great hope in their hearts, and with all their worldly goods on their backs. Fresh from the bonds of slavery, fresh from the benighted regions of the plantation, they came to the Capital looking for liberty, and many of them not knowing it when they found it. Many good friends reached forth kind hands, but the North is not warm and impulsive. For one kind word spoken, two harsh ones were uttered; there was something repelling in the atmosphere, and the bright joyous dreams of freedom to the slave faded—were sadly altered, in the presence of that stern, practical mother, reality. Instead of flowery paths, days of perpetual sunshine, and bowers hanging with golden fruit, the road was rugged and full of thorns, the sunshine was eclipsed by shadows, and the mute appeals for help too often were answered by cold neglect. Poor dusky children of slavery, men and women of my own race—the transition from slavery to freedom was too sudden for you! The bright dreams were too rudely dispelled; you were not prepared for the new life that opened before you, and the great masses of the North learned to look upon your helplessness with indifference— learned to speak of you as an idle, dependent race. Reason should have prompted kinder thoughts. Charity is ever kind.

One fair summer evening I was walking the streets of Washington, accompanied by a friend, when a band of music was heard in the distance. We wondered what it could mean, and curiosity prompted us to find out its meaning. We quickened our steps, and discovered that it came from the house of Mrs. Farnham. The yard was brilliantly lighted, ladies and gentlemen were moving about, and the band was playing some of its sweetest airs. We approached the sentinel on duty at the gate, and asked what was going on. He told us that it was a festival given for the benefit of the sick and wounded soldiers in the city. This suggested an idea to me. If the white people can give festivals to raise funds for the relief of suffering soldiers, why should not the well-to-do colored people go to work to do something for the benefit of the suffering blacks? I could not rest. The thought was ever present with me, and the next Sunday I made a suggestion in the colored church, that a society of colored people be formed to labor for the benefit of the unfortunate freedmen. The idea proved popular, and in two weeks "the Contraband Relief Association" was organized, with forty working members.

In September of 1862, Mrs. Lincoln left Washington for New York, and requested me to follow her at the Metropolitan Hotel. I was glad of the opportunity to do so, for I thought that in New York I would be able to do something in the interests of our society. Armed with credentials, I took the train for New York, and went to the Metropolitan, where Mrs. Lincoln had secured accommodations for me. The next morning I told Mrs. Lincoln of my project; and she immediately headed my list with a subscription of $200. I circulated among the colored people, and got them thoroughly interested in the subject, when I was called to Boston by Mrs. Lincoln, who wished to visit her son Robert, attending college in that city. I met Mr. Wendell Phillips, and other Boston philanthropists, who gave me all the assistance in their power. We held a mass meeting at the Colored Baptist Church. Rev. Mr. Grimes, in Boston, raised a sum of money, and organized there a branch society. The society was organized by Mrs. Grimes, wife of the pastor, assisted by Mrs. Martin, wife of Rev. Stella Martin. This branch of the main society, during the war, was able to send us over eighty large boxes of goods, contributed exclusively by the colored people of Boston. Returning to New York, we held a successful meeting at the Shiloh Church, Rev. Henry Highland Garnet, pastor. The Metropolitan Hotel, at that time as now, employed colored help. I suggested the object of my mission to Robert Thompson, Steward of the Hotel, who immediately raised quite a sum of money among the dining-room waiters. Mr. Frederick Douglass contributed $200, besides lecturing for us. Other prominent colored men sent in liberal contributions. From England a large quantity of stores was received. Mrs. Lincoln made frequent contributions, as also did the President. In 1863 I was re-elected President of the Association, which office I continue to hold. . . .

Mrs. Keckley goes on to describe life in the White House during the war years.

For two years after Willie's death the White House was the scene of no fashionable display. The memory of the dead boy was duly respected. In some things Mrs. Lincoln was an altered woman. Sometimes, when in her room, with no one present but myself, the mere mention of Willie's name would excite her emotion, and any trifling memento that recalled him would move her to tears. She could not bear to look upon his picture; and after his death she never crossed the threshold of the Guest's Room in which he died, or the Green Room in which he was embalmed. There was something supernatural in her dread of these things, and something that she could not explain. Tad's nature was the opposite of Willie's, and he was always regarded as his father's favorite child. His black eyes fairly sparkled with mischief.

The war progressed, fair fields had been stained with blood, thousands of brave men had fallen, and thousands of eyes were weeping for the fallen at home. There were desolate hearthstones in the South as well as in the North, and as the people of my race watched the sanguinary struggle, the ebb and flow of the tide of battle, they lifted their faces Zionward, as if they hoped to catch a glimpse of the Promised Land beyond the sulphureous clouds of smoke which shifted now and then but to reveal ghastly rows of new-made graves. Sometimes the very life of the nation seemed to tremble with the fierce shock of arms. In 1863 the Confederates were flushed with victory, and sometimes it looked as if the proud flag of the Union, the glorious old Stars and Stripes, must yield half of its nationality to the tri-barred flag that floated grandly over long columns of gray. These were sad, anxious days to Mr. Lincoln, and those who saw the man in privacy only could tell how much he suffered. One day he came into the room where I was fitting a dress on Mrs. Lincoln. His step was slow and heavy, and his face sad. Like a tired child he threw himself upon a sofa, and shaded his eyes with his hands. He was a complete picture of dejection. Mrs. Lincoln, observing his troubled look, asked:

"Where have you been, father?"

"To the War Department," was the brief, almost sullen answer.

"Any news?"

"Yes, plenty of news, but no good news. It is dark, dark everywhere."

He reached forth one of his long arms, and took a small Bible from a stand near the head of the sofa, opened the pages of the holy book, and soon was absorbed in reading them. A quarter of an hour passed, and on glancing at the sofa the face of the President seemed more cheerful. The dejected look was gone, and the countenance was lighted up with new resolution and hope. The change was so marked that I could not but wonder at it, and wonder led to the desire to know what book of the Bible afforded so much comfort to the reader. Making the search for a missing article an excuse, I walked gently around the sofa, and looking into the open book, I discovered that Mr. Lincoln las reading that divine comforter, Job. He read with Christian eagerness, and the courage and hope that he derived from the inspired pages made him a new man. I almost imagined that I could hear the Lord speaking to him from out the whirlwind of battle: "Gird up thy loins now like a man: I will demand of thee, and declare thou unto me." What a sublime picture was this! A ruler of a mighty nation going to the pages of the Bible with simple Christian earnestness for comfort and courage, and finding both in the darkest hours of a nation's calamity. Ponder it, O ye scoffers at God's Holy Word, and then hang your heads for very shame!

Frequent letters were received warning Mr. Lincoln of assassination, but he never gave a second thought to the mysterious warnings. The letters, however, sorely troubled his wife. She seemed to read impending danger in every rustling leaf, in every whisper of the wind.

"Where are you going now, father?" she would say to him, as she observed him putting on his overshoes and shawl.

"I am going over to the War Department, mother, to try and learn some news."

"But, father, you should not go out alone. You know you are surrounded with danger."

"All imagination. What does any one want to harm me

for? Don't worry about me, mother, as if I were a little child, for no one is going to molest me"; and with a confident, unsuspecting air he would close the door behind him, descend the stairs, and pass out to his lonely walk.

For weeks, when trouble was anticipated, friends of the President would sleep in the White House to guard him from danger. . . .

Mrs. Lincoln's love for her husband sometimes prompted her to act very strangely. She was extremely jealous of him, and if a lady desired to court her displeasure, she could select no surer way to do it than to pay marked attention to the President. These little jealous freaks often were a source of perplexity to Mr. Lincoln. If it was a reception for which they were dressing, he would come into her room to conduct her downstairs, and while pulling on his gloves ask, with a merry twinkle in his eyes:

"Well, mother, who must I talk with to-night—shall it be Mrs. D.?"

"That deceitful woman! No, you shall not listen to her flattery."

"Well, then, what do you say to Miss C.? She is too young and handsome to practice deceit."

"Young and handsome, you call her! You should not judge beauty for me. No, she is in league with Mrs. D., and you shall not talk with her."

"Well, mother, I must talk with some one. Is there any one that you do not object to?" trying to button his glove, with a mock expression of gravity.

"I don't know as it is necessary that you should talk to anybody in particular. You know well enough, Mr. Lincoln, that I do not approve of your flirtations with silly women, just as if you were a beardless boy, fresh from school."

"But, mother, I insist that I must talk with somebody. I can't stand around like a simpleton, and say nothing. If you will not tell me who I may talk with, please tell me who I may *not* talk with."

"There is Mrs. D. and Miss C. in particular. I detest them both. Mrs. B. also will come around you, but you need not listen to her flattery. These are the ones in particular."

"Very well, mother; now that we have settled the question to your satisfaction, we will go down-stairs"; and always with stately dignity, he proffered his arm and led the way.

The days passed without any incident of particular note disturbing the current of life. On Friday morning, April 14th—alas! what American does not remember the day—I saw Mrs. Lincoln but for a moment. She told me that she was to attend the theatre that night with the President, but I was not summoned to assist her in making her toilette. Sherman had swept from the northern border of Georgia through the heart of the Confederacy down to the sea, striking the death-blow to the rebellion. Grant had pursued General Lee beyond Richmond, and the army of Virginia, that had made such stubborn resistance, was crumbling to pieces. Fort Sumter had fallen;—the stronghold first wrenched from the Union, and which had braved the fury of Federal guns for so many years, was restored to the Union; the end of the war was near at hand, and the great pulse of the loyal North thrilled with joy. The dark war-cloud was fading, and a white-robed angel seemed to hover in the sky, whispering "Peace—peace on earth, good-will toward men!" Sons, brothers, fathers, friends, sweethearts were coming home. Soon the white tents would be folded, the volunteer army be disbanded, and tranquillity again reign. Happy, happy day!—happy at least to those who fought under the banner of the Union. There was great rejoicing throughout the North. From the Atlantic to the Pacific, flags were gayly thrown to the breeze, and at night every city blazed with its tens of thousand lights. But scarcely had the fireworks ceased to play, and the lights been taken down from the windows, when the lightning flashed the most appalling news over the magnetic wires. "The President has been murdered!" spoke the swift-winged messenger, and the loud huzza died upon the lips. A nation suddenly paused in the midst of festivity, and stood paralyzed with horror—transfixed with awe.

Oh, memorable day! Oh, memorable night! Never before was joy so violently contrasted with sorrow.

At 11 o'clock at night I was awakened by an old friend and neighbor, Miss M. Brown, with the startling intelligence that the entire Cabinet had been assassinated, and Mr. Lincoln shot, but not mortally wounded. When I heard the words I felt as if the blood had been frozen in my veins, and that my lungs must collapse for the want of air. Mr. Lincoln shot! the Cabinet assassinated! What could it mean? The streets were alive with wondering awe-stricken people. Rumors flew thick and fast, and the wildest reports came with every new arrival. The words were repeated with blanched cheeks and quivering lips. I waked Mr. and Mrs. Lewis, and told them that the President was shot, and that I must go to the White House. I could not remain in a state of uncertainty. I felt that the house would not hold me. They tried to quiet me, but gentle words could not calm the wild tempest. They quickly dressed themselves, and we sallied out into the street to drift with the excited throng. We walked rapidly toward the White House, and on our way passed the residence of Secretary Seward, which was surrounded by armed soldiers, keeping back all intruders with the point of the bayonet. We hurried on, and as we approached the White House, saw that it too was surrounded with soldiers. Every entrance was strongly guarded, and no one was permitted to pass. The guard at the gate told us that Mr. Lincoln had not been brought home, but refused to give any other information. More excited than ever, we wandered down the street. Grief and anxiety were making me weak, and as we joined the outskirts of a large crowd, I began to feel as meek and humble as a penitent child. A gray-haired old man was passing. I caught a glimpse of his face, and it seemed so full of kindness and sorrow that I gently touched his arm, and imploringly asked:

"Will you please, sir, to tell me whether Mr. Lincoln is dead or not?"

"Not dead," he replied, "but dying. God help us!" and with a heavy step he passed on.

"Not dead, but dying! then indeed God help us!"

We learned that the President was mortally wounded— that he had been shot down in his box at the theatre, and that he was not expected to live till morning; when we returned home with heavy hearts. I could not sleep. I wanted to go to Mrs. Lincoln, as I pictured her wild with grief; but then I did not know where to find her, and I must wait till morning. Never did the hours drag so slowly. Every moment seemed an age, and I could do nothing but walk about and hold my arms in mental agony.

Morning came at last, and a sad morning was it. The flags that floated so gayly yesterday now were draped in black, and hung in silent folds at half-mast. The President was dead, and a nation was mourning for him. Every house was draped in black, and every face wore a solemn look. People spoke in subdued tones, and glided whisperingly, wonderingly, silently about the streets.

About eleven o'clock on Saturday morning a carriage drove up to the door, and a messenger asked for "Elizabeth Keckley."

"Who wants her?" I asked.

"I come from Mrs. Lincoln. If you are Mrs. Keckley, come with me immediately to the White House."

I hastily put on my shawl and bonnet, and was driven at a rapid rate to the White House. Everything about the building was sad and solemn. I was quickly shown to Mrs. Lincoln's room, and on entering, saw Mrs. L. tossing uneasily about upon a bed. The room was darkened, and the only person in it besides the widow of the President was Mrs. Secretary Welles, who had spent the night with her. Bowing to Mrs. Welles, I went to the bedside.

"Why did you not come to me last night, Elizabeth—I sent for you?" Mrs. Lincoln asked in a low whisper.

"I did try to come to you, but I could not find you," I answered, as I laid my hand upon her hot brow.

I afterwards learned, that when she had partially recovered from the first shock of the terrible tragedy in the theatre, Mrs. Welles asked:

"Is there no one, Mrs. Lincoln, that you desire to have with you in this terrible affliction?"

"Yes, send for Elizabeth Keckley. I want her just as soon as she can be brought here."

Three messengers, it appears, were successively despatched for me, but all of them mistook the number and failed to find me.

Shortly after entering the room on Saturday morning, Mrs. Welles excused herself, as she said she must go to her own family, and I was left alone with Mrs. Lincoln.

She was nearly exhausted with grief, and when she became a little quiet, I asked and received permission to go into the Guest's Room, where the body of the President lay in state. When I crossed the threshold of the room, I could not help recalling the day on which I had seen little Willie lying in his coffin where the body of his father now lay. I remembered how the President had wept over the pale beautiful face of his gifted boy, and now the President himself was dead. The last time I saw him he spoke kindly to me, but alas! the lips would never move again. The light had faded from his eyes, and when the light went out the soul went with it. What a noble soul was his—noble in all the noble attributes of God! Never did I enter the solemn chamber of death with such palpitating heart and trembling footsteps as I entered it that day. No common mortal had died. The Moses of my people had fallen in the hour of his triumph. Fame had woven her choicest chaplet for his brow. Though the brow was cold and pale in death, the chaplet should not fade, for God had studded it with the glory of the eternal stars.

When I entered the room, the members of the Cabinet and many distinguished officers of the army were grouped around the body of their fallen chief. They made room for me, and, approaching the body, I lifted the white cloth from the white face of the man that I had worshipped as an idol— looked upon as a demi-god. Notwithstanding the violence of the death of the President, there was something beautiful as well as grandly solemn in the expression of the placid face. There lurked the sweetness and gentleness of child- hood, and the stately grandeur of godlike intellect. I gazed long at the face, and turned away with tears in my eyes and a choking sensation in my throat. Ah! never was man so widely mourned before. The whole world bowed their heads in grief when Abraham Lincoln died.

4

FROM

The Life and Adventures of Nat Love

by Nat Love
(1854–   ?)

The American Negro, in addition to suffering blatant discrimination in this country, has also suffered the humiliation of being ignored. He has been written out of the history books. It is hard to remember, for instance, ever seeing a black cowboy in the hundreds of westerns that have appeared on movie screens. Yet after the Civil War there were perhaps 5,000 Negro cowboys on the range. This was the one place where a black man might be considered for himself and his ability. The frontier was a relatively unstructured society, where the ultimate consideration was survival.

Nat Love was born into slavery in Tennessee less than a

decade before the Civil War. In 1869 he went to Dodge City, Kansas, joined a group of ranch hands, and was promptly nicknamed Red River Dick. Love doesn't mention any of the prejudice which undoubtedly existed in the West, but rather boasts of his adventures and harrowing experiences as a cowboy (some of which is considered apocryphal). Nevertheless, on July 4, 1876, he won a roping and shooting contest at Deadwood City in Dakota Territory and earned a new name—Deadwood Dick.

The railroad eventually made long cattle drives unnecessary, and in 1890 Nat left the range and took a job as a Pullman porter, one of the new positions open to Negroes at that time.

IT was on the tenth day of February, 1869, that I left the old home, near Nashville, Tennessee. I was at that time about fifteen years old, and though while young in years the hard work and farm life had made me strong and hearty, much beyond my years, and I had full confidence in myself as being able to take care of myself and making my way.

I at once struck out for Kansas of which I had heard something. And believing it was a good place in which to seek employment. It was in the west, and it was the great west I wanted to see, and so by walking and occasional lifts from farmers going my way and taking advantage of every thing that promised to assist me on my way, I eventually brought up at Dodge City, Kansas, which at that time was a typical frontier city, with a great many saloons, dance halls, and gambling houses, and very little of anything else. When I arrived the town was full of cow boys from the surrounding ranches, and from Texas and other parts of the west. As Kansas was a great cattle center and market, the wild cow boy, prancing horses of which I was

very fond, and the wild life generally, all had their attrac-
tions for me, and I decided to try for a place with them.
Although it seemed to me I had met with a bad outfit, at
least some of them, going around among them I watched
my chances to get to speak with them, as I wanted to find
some one whom I thought would give me a civil answer to
the questions I wanted to ask, but they all seemed too wild
around town, so the next day I went out where they were in
camp.

Approaching a party who were eating their breakfast, I
got to speak with them. They asked me to have some breakfast with them, which invitation I gladly accepted. During
the meal I got a chance to ask them many questions. They
proved to be a Texas outfit, who had just come up with a
herd of cattle and having delivered them they were pre-
paring to return. There were several colored cow boys
among them, and good ones too. After breakfast I asked
the camp boss for a job as cow boy. He asked me if I could
ride a wild horse. I said "yes sir." He said if you can I will
give you a job. So he spoke to one of the colored cow boys
called Bronko Jim, and told him to go out and rope old
Good Eye, saddle him and put me on his back. Bronko
Jim gave me a few pointers and told me to look out for
the horse was especially bad on pitching. I told Jim I was a
good rider and not afraid of him. I thought I had rode
pitching horses before, but from the time I mounted old
Good Eye I knew I had not learned what pitching was.
This proved the worst horse to ride I had ever mounted in
my life, but I stayed with him and the cow boys were the
most surprised outfit you ever saw, as they had taken me
for a tenderfoot, pure and simple. After the horse got tired
and I dismounted the boss said he would give me a job and
pay me $30.00 per month and more later on. He asked
what my name was and I answered Nat Love, he said to the

boys we will call him Red River Dick. I went by this name for a long time.

The boss took me to the city and got my outfit, which consisted of a new saddle, bridle and spurs, chaps, a pair of blankets and a fine 45 Colt revolver. Now that the business which brought them to Dodge City was concluded, preparations were made to start out for the Pan Handle country in Texas to the home ranch. The outfit of which I was now a member was called the Duval outfit, and their brand was known as the Pig Pen brand. I worked with this outfit for over three years. On this trip there were only about fifteen of us riders, all excepting myself were hardy, experienced men, always ready for anything that might turn up, but they were as jolly a set of fellows as one could find in a long journey. There now being nothing to keep us longer in Dodge City, we prepared for the return journey, and left the next day over the old Dodge and Sun City lonesome trail, on a journey which was to prove the most eventful of my life up to now.

A few miles out we encountered some of the hardest hail storms I ever saw, causing discomfort to man and beast, but I had no notion of getting discouraged but I resolved to be always ready for any call that might be made on me, of whatever nature it might be, and those with whom I have lived and worked will tell you I have kept that resolve. Not far from Dodge City on our way home we encountered a band of the old Victoria tribe of Indians and had a sharp fight.

These Indians were nearly always harassing travelers and traders and the stock men of that part of the country, and were very troublesome. In this band we encountered there were about a hundred painted bucks all well mounted. When we saw the Indians they were coming after us yelling like demons. As we were not expecting Indians at this particular time, we were taken somewhat by surprise.

We only had fifteen men in our outfit, but nothing daunted we stood our ground and fought the Indians to a stand. One of the boys was shot off his horse and killed near me. The Indians got his horse, bridle and saddle. During this fight we lost all but six of our horses, our entire packing outfit and our extra saddle horses, which the Indians stampeded, then rounded them up after the fight and drove them off. And as we only had six horses left us, we were unable to follow them, although we had the satisfaction of knowing we had made several good Indians out of bad ones.

This was my first Indian fight and likewise the first Indians I had ever seen. When I saw them coming after us and heard their blood curdling yell, I lost all courage and thought my time had come to die. I was too badly scared to run, some of the boys told me to use my gun and shoot for all I was worth. Now I had just got my outfit and had never shot off a gun in my life, but their words brought me back to earth and seeing they were all using their guns in a way that showed they were used to it, I unlimbered my artillery and after the first shot I lost all fear and fought like a veteran.

We soon routed the Indians and they left, taking with them nearly all we had, and we were powerless to pursue them. We were compelled to finish our journey home almost on foot, as there were only six horses left to fourteen of us. Our friend and companion who was shot in the fight, we buried on the plains, wrapped in his blanket with stones piled over his grave. After this engagement with the Indians I seemed to lose all sense as to what fear was and thereafter during my whole life on the range I never experienced the least feeling of fear, no matter how trying the ordeal or how desperate my position.

It was a bright, clear fall day, October 4, 1876, that quite a large number of us boys started out over the range hunting strays which had been lost for some time. We had scattered over the range and I was riding along alone when all at once I heard the well-known Indian war whoop and noticed not far away a large party of Indians making straight for me. They were all well mounted and they were in full war paint, which showed me that they were on the war path, and as I was alone and had no wish to be scalped by them I decided to run for it. So I headed for Yellow Horse Canyon and gave my horse the rein, but as I had considerable objection to being chased by a lot of painted savages without some remonstrance, I turned in my saddle every once in a while and gave them a shot by way of greeting, and I had the satisfaction of seeing a painted brave tumble from his horse and go rolling in the dust every time my rifle spoke, and the Indians were by no means idle all this time, as their bullets were singing around me rather lively, one of them passing through my thigh, but it did not amount to much. Reaching Yellow Horse Canyon, I had about decided to stop and make a stand when one of their bullets caught me in the leg, passing clear through it and then through my horse, killing him. Quickly falling behind him I used his dead body for a breast work and stood the Indians off for a long time, as my aim was so deadly and they had lost so many that they were careful to keep out of range.

But finally my ammunition gave out, and the Indians were quick to find this out, and they at once closed in on me, but I was by no means subdued, wounded as I was and almost out of my head, and I fought with my empty gun until finally overpowered. When I came to my senses I was in the Indians' camp.

My wounds had been dressed with some kind of herbs,

the wound in my breast just over the heart was covered thickly with herbs and bound up. My nose had been nearly cut off, also one of my fingers had been nearly cut off. These wounds I received when I was fighting my captors with my empty gun. What caused them to spare my life I cannot tell, but it was I think partly because I had proved myself a brave man, and all savages admire a brave man and when they captured a man whose fighting powers were out of the ordinary they generally kept him if possible as he was needed in the tribe.

Then again Yellow Dog's tribe was composed largely of half breeds, and there was a large percentage of colored blood in the tribe, and as I was a colored man they wanted to keep me, as they thought I was too good a man to die. Be that as it may, they dressed my wounds and gave me plenty to eat, but the only grub they had was buffalo meat which they cooked over a fire of buffalo chips, but of this I had all I wanted to eat. For the first two days after my capture they kept me tied hand and foot. At the end of that time they untied my feet, but kept my hands tied for a couple of days longer, when I was given my freedom, but was always closely watched by members of the tribe. Three days after my capture my ears were pierced and I was adopted into the tribe. The operation of piercing my ears was quite painful, in the method used, as they had a small bone secured from a deer's leg, a small thin bone, rounded at the end and as sharp as a needle. This they used to make the holes, then strings made from the tendons of a deer were inserted in place of thread, of which the Indians had none. Then horn earrings were placed in my ears and the same kind of salve made from herbs which they placed on my wounds was placed on my ears and they soon healed.

The bullet holes in my leg and breast also healed in a surprisingly short time. That was good salve all right. As soon as I was well enough I took part in the Indian dances. One kind or another was in progress all the time. The war dance and the medicine dance seemed the most popular. When in the war dance the savages danced around me in a circle, making gestures, chanting, with every now and then a blood curdling yell, always keeping time to a sort of music provided by stretching buffalo skins tightly over a hoop.

When I was well enough I joined the dances, and I think I soon made a good dancer. The medicine dance varies from the war dance only that in the medicine dance the Indians danced around a boiling pot, the pot being filled with roots and water and they dance around it while it boils. The medicine dance occurs about daylight.

I very soon learned their ways and to understand them, though our conversation was mostly carried on by means of signs. They soon gave me to understand that I was to marry the chief's daughter, promising me 100 ponies to do so, and she was literally thrown in my arms; as for the lady she seemed perfectly willing if not anxious to become my bride. She was a beautiful woman, or rather girl; in fact all the squaws of this tribe were good looking, out of the ordinary, but I had other notions just then and did not want to get married under such circumstances, but for prudence sake I seemed to enter into their plans, but at the same time keeping a sharp lookout for a chance to escape. I noted where the Indians kept their horses at night, even picking out the handsome and fleet Indian pony which I meant to use should opportunity occur, and I seemed to fall in with the Indians' plans and seemed to them so contented that they gave me more and more freedom and relaxed the strict watch they had kept on me, and finally in about thirty days from the time of my capture my opportunity arrived.

My wounds were now nearly well, and gave me no trouble. It was a dark, cloudy night, and the Indians, grown careless in their fancied security, had relaxed their watchfulness. After they had all thrown themselves on the ground and the quiet of the camp proclaimed them all asleep I got up and crawling on my hands and knees, using the greatest caution for fear of making a noise, I crawled about 250 yards to where the horses were picketed, and going to the Indian pony I had already picked out I slipped the skin thong in his mouth which the Indians use for a bridle, one which I had secured in my shirt for some time for this particular purpose, then springing to his back I made for the open prairie in the direction of the home ranch in Texas, one hundred miles away. All that night I rode as fast as my horse could carry me and the next morning, twelve hours after I had left the Indians' camp I was safe on the home ranch again. And my joy was without bounds, and such a reception as I received from the boys. They said they were just one day late, and if it hadn't been for a fight they had with some of the same tribe, they would have been to my relief. As it was they did not expect to ever see me again alive. But that they knew that if the Indians did not kill me, and gave me only half a chance I would get away from them, but now that I was safe home again, nothing mattered much and nothing was too good for me.

It was a mystery to them how I managed to escape death with such wounds as I had received, the marks of which I will carry to my grave and it is as much a mystery to me as the bullet that struck me in the breast just over the heart passed clear through, coming out my back just below the shoulder. Likewise the bullet in my leg passed clear through, then through my horse, killing him.

Those Indians are certainly wonderful doctors, and then I am naturally tough as I carry the marks of fourteen bullet wounds on different parts of my body, most any one of which would be sufficient to kill an ordinary man, but I am not even crippled. It seems to me that if ever a man bore a charm I am the man, as I have had five horses shot from under me and killed, have fought Indians and Mexicans in all sorts of situations, and have been in more tight places than I can remember. Yet I have always managed to escape with only the mark of a bullet or knife as a reminder. The fight with the Yellow Dog's tribe is probably the closest call I ever had, and as close a call as I ever want.

The fleet Indian pony which carried me to safety on that memorable hundred-mile ride, I kept for about five years. I named him "The Yellow Dog Chief." And he lived on the best the ranch afforded, until his death occurred in 1881, never having anything to do except an occasional race, as he could run like a deer. I thought too much of him to use him on the trail and he was the especial pet of every one on the home ranch, and for miles around.

I heard afterwards that the Indians pursued me that night for quite a distance, but I had too much the start and besides I had the fastest horse the Indians owned. I have never since met any of my captors of that time. As they knew better than to venture in our neighborhood again. My wound healed nicely, thanks to the good attention the Indians gave me. My captors took everything of value I had on me when captured. My rifle which I especially prized for old associations sake, also my forty-fives, saddle and bridle, in fact my whole outfit, leaving me only the few clothes I had on at the time.

My comrades did not propose to let this bother me long, however, because they all chipped in and bought me a new outfit, including the best rifle and revolvers that could be secured, and I had my pick of the ranch horses for another mount. During my short stay with the Indians I learned a great deal about them, their ways of living, sports, dances, and mode of warfare which proved of great benefit to me in after years. The oblong shields they carried were made from tanned buffalo skins and so tough were they made that an arrow would not pierce them although I have seen them shoot an arrow clean through a buffalo. Neither will a bullet pierce them unless the ball hits the shield square on, otherwise it glances off.

All of them were exceedingly expert with the bow and arrow, and they are proud of their skill and are always practicing in an effort to excel each other. This rivalry extends even to the children who are seldom without their bows and arrows.

They named me Buffalo Papoose, and we managed to make our wants known by means of signs. As I was not with them a sufficient length of time to learn their language, I learned from them that I had killed five of their number and wounded three while they were chasing me and in the subsequent fight with my empty gun. The wounded men were hit in many places, but they were brought around all right, the same as I was. After my escape and after I arrived home it was some time before I was again called to active duty, as the boys would not hear of me doing anything resembling work, until I was thoroughly well and rested up. But I soon began to long for my saddle and the range.

And when orders were received at the ranch for 2000 head of cattle, to be delivered at Dodge City, Kansas, I insisted on taking the trail again. It was not with any sense of pride or in bravado that I recount here the fate of the men who have fallen at my hand.

It is a terrible thing to kill a man no matter what the

cause. But as I am writing a true history of my life, I cannot leave these facts out. But every man who died at my hands was either seeking my life or died in open warfare, when it was a case of killing or being killed.

5

FROM

Blackthink

by Jesse Owens
(1913–   )

*Olympic champion Jesse Owens was born on a tenant farm
in northern Alabama in the early years of the twentieth
century. His father was a sharecropper—a kind of life
second only to slavery in its economic and psychological
misery.*

*Nevertheless, Owens, as he will readily admit, is proof
that America can be the land of opportunity. He calls
himself an "immoderate moderate" and thus finds "blackthink" (pro-Negro antiwhite bigotry) as destructive as the
doctrine of white racial supremacy.*

In this chapter from Blackthink, *he recounts his early
days on the farm. It was "only one chapter" of his life. But
for the 4 million slaves freed after the Civil War, and for
their children and grandchildren, sharecropping was
closer to an entire book than a single chapter.*

NO ONE called me a nigger until I was seven.
That was because an Alabama sharecropper's child in the

First World War years almost never saw the white man who owned his every breath.

Owned.

In theory, the Emancipation Proclamation had been a wonderful thing. But in 1915 in Alabama it was only a theory. The Negro had been set free—free to work eighteen hours a day, free to see all his labor add up to a debt at the year's end, free to be chained to the land he tilled but could never own any more than if he were still a slave. The black-thinkers of today, often talking from their integrated high-rises, restaurants and universities, don't know what it is to really be shut out like we were then, shut out so tight you actually wondered sometimes if you really existed.

You won't find Oakville, Alabama, on the map today. Eight miles from Decatur, in the northern strip of the state, it was more an invention of the white landowners than a geographical place. Whatever had the smack of civilization to it was in Decatur.

The grocery store was in Oakville, though. Just across the creek. But that wasn't as nice as it sounds. The white man owned the grocery store and he made sure it was awfully convenient. My parents tried not to end up there any more than they had to. Sometimes my father and my older brother Prentis would get up an hour earlier than their usual 4 A.M. to try and shoot a few rabbits for supper. And my mother would find time somehow to tend a little vegetable garden in the back.

But those few rabbits and vegetables didn't go very far with nine mouths to feed. So you always ended up at the owner's store for food, just as you had to go there for tools. My father never paid any money at the grocery. The owner's man just entered our debt on a sheet of paper with #1 at the top—we were the first of eight families who worked his spread of two hundred and fifty acres—and in December of every year, the white man totaled up what you owed against the worth of your crop to find out how much you were ahead.

Only you never came out ahead. It always happened that those "cheap" tools and supplies you bought cost more than the nearly quarter of a million square feet they helped you to plant, just as the weekly potatoes and beans and corn bread (you only bought meat two times a year, on the holidays) always came to more than the six thousand pounds of cotton you enabled the owner to send North.

Each year that it happened, my father went into an angry fit and swore that he was going to learn to read to make sure they were only writing down on that list what he was actually buying. And Mother vowed that she'd learn numbers to check they weren't charging us too much for it. But there was no one in Oakville to teach those things to them and no time to learn anyway. Besides, my father wouldn't go near a book—he was superstitious about them. That was another holdover from slave days. So one December became the next, and with each one we became a little deeper in debt even though we usually put out more cotton every year than the one before, unless the weevils or some fungus disease had come along.

Our debt was small, though, compared to the other sharecroppers'. We were the "luckiest" family for miles around. My father had been blessed with four sons who had lived. I was the only one who couldn't help, not because I was too young but because I was too sick. Every winter for as long as I could remember, I'd come down with pneumonia. A couple of those years, I was close to never seeing spring.

Yet somehow my mother always pulled me through. Afterward, she'd take my father aside and plead with him to think about leaving the South and sharecropping. He sensed that she was right—every Negro we knew was on a never-ending treadmill of poverty and ignorance—but his fear of the unknown was even greater.

A few Negroes had left and gone North. But Henry Owens was over forty years old, an age not made by half a dozen Negro sharecroppers in Morgan County. It was late to pull up roots. And like most other sharecroppers, he was the son of the son of a slave. His own grandfather had told him the stories of being *legally* shut out, stories of death that came in the night, sometimes at the hands of the white man and sometimes through simple starvation. So, deep down in that invisible place where a man decides what to do, my father felt that we could have it even worse than we did in Oakville. He wasn't going to dare take a chance on that. The whole world would have to jerk out of orbit for him to pack us up and leave.

And that's just what happened. The whole world, Henry Owens' world, went completely out of orbit.

The first jolt was when I got sick again. This time was different. This time blood came up every time I coughed, and for about a week I didn't know where I was. My mother worked her homemade magic once more, but we all knew it would be the last time. My lungs were too weak.

Our neighbor a mile down was dead. That was the second jolt. My father began sharecropping about the same time Joe had. Joe was a few years younger, and my father had always kind of treated him like a little brother, telling what he knew about better ways to work the land, even lending out one of my brothers to him when things were pretty good, though that wasn't often.

Joe had to work his land alone because his wife kept having stillborn babies. Each time she'd get pregnant they didn't pray for a son but just for something alive. A child would have made life bearable. Yet the years passed and all Joe and Betsy shared were new grave markers in back of their house each twelve months or so.

Then Joe got a "sign." Something told him that Betsy would become pregnant again soon and that this time the baby would not only live but would be a son. When her belly began to swell, Joe's skeleton of a body stopped feeling tired. He worked as never before and whistled every day until the baby came. It came, dead as always. Only this time it took Betsy with it.

So Joe Steppart killed himself.

My father changed after that. Not enough to leave, but enough to begin to think out loud about what that white man and his system were doing to all of us. The white man's name was John Clannon, by the way, and his home was on the top of one large hill on the other side of the creek. It was too far, of course, for him to see down into our little house. But at night when all the lights were shining on the hill, I imagined I saw him at his big living room window, a window larger than our whole house, watching us.

John Clannon owned two hundred and fifty acres of land with eight men sharecropping it for him. We had the largest spread, fifty acres, because we had the most sons. All the eight houses of the Negroes were on the one side of the creek. John Clannon had never crossed over to that side since he bought the land and carved it up. None of the Negroes ever went on his side, either, unless they were sent for by one of his men.

On a cool night in February of 1921, he sent for my father. We all waited, busying ourselves but not really able to get anything done. "I wonder what the owner can want with

Papa," someone would mutter every now and then. What we really meant was, "What was the owner going to do to Papa?" And to us.

For even though we didn't realize it then, we lived with constant fear. That is the crucial difference between 1920 and, say, 1960. Negroes of a decade or two ago began in poverty and degradation, but the massive machinery of our society was moving to sweep it away. In 1920 there was no machinery. The man on the hill was everything. He was worse in one way than the "benevolent" white despots on slave plantations, because the Negro then wasn't plagued every day by the agonizing choice of what to do with his freedom, whether or not to leave.

In theory, of course, my folks had a fifty-fifty deal with John Clannon, but fifty percent of nothing amounts to nothing. So we lived in fear of him and of his power, and the fear was justified. That February night proved it. My father trudged back into the house almost an hour later and took aside my mother and my older brothers Prentis and Quincy. In our little cardboard house, though, as soon as his voice got agitated it wasn't hard to overhear what he was telling them.

We'd had a particularly good crop that year. Even with exorbitant grocery bills every week, it had still gotten us out of debt. That threatened John Clannon's hold over us, I guess, and he wanted to do something about it right away. What he proposed to do was to revise his deal with my father. Sixty-forty instead of fifty-fifty. Retroactive.

My father had stood still for everything else, but he couldn't stand still for that. The years of resentment had risen up in him and finally become words. He was an uneducated man, but he was a fair man, and he said that this wasn't fair. He didn't get to say it to Clannon himself, though. An "assistant" talked to "the niggers."

"Fair?" the assistant had replied. "What does fair have to do with *you*?" My father was an example, he said. If he could "get the best" of Clannon, the others might think they could too.

"And what about my family?" my father had shot back, finally beginning to lose forty-two years of control. "We work hard. I want my sons to amount to more than I have!"

"Your sons will never amount to anything—just be grateful if they *survive!*" the man had shouted back.

That last statement had stuck in my father's craw. He struggled to spit it out for the next two days, but it only lodged deeper. That Sunday after church he told us that we were leaving Oakville for Cleveland.

We still owed John Clannon some money, but we had our tools and our house and our animals. That would more than pay what we owed and keep us eating in Cleveland long enough, my father figured, for him to find steady work.

My father never found steady work in Cleveland, and we'd had barely enough money to get us North. Clannon offered us next to nothing for everything we owned, including the five mules from Canada my father had scraped and saved for one by one by one. It wasn't just greed that made Clannon do it. He didn't want to let us go. A healthy Negro with three sons who knew the ropes was hard to find.

But we got the hell out. As I said, for my father Cleveland wasn't much different from Oakville. Yet for me it was like another planet. It gave me a chance. And one chance is all you need, no matter what the blackthinkers say.

As I think back, though, I can see part of it was that the white man's words had stuck in my craw, too. *Your sons will never amount to anything.* I wanted to amount to something. I had to. So did a lot of other Negroes whose names you'll never hear, but who *have* amounted to something. That's why when I hear some black militant telling me and them that we've never made anything of ourselves and that our sons and daughters never will, I wonder if it isn't John Clannon's assistant talking again.

It's no accident that the Rap Browns and Stokely Carmichaels sometimes sound like the Clannons.

Because *blackthink*—pro-Negro, antiwhite bigotry—is what makes the new Negro and white extremists of today tick, and it's not much different from John Clannon's *whitethink*. Irrationality and violence, above all, are at blackthink's gut. It might sound shocking at first, what with all the brainwashing that goes on, but if you think about it you'll see that America's blackthinking extremists may be the new George Wallaces.

Bigotry always begins with a hurt. For the John Clannons it might have been when they got off the boat from Ireland and found signs that said NO IRISH ALLOWED or ran into employer after employer who thought that Irish was another word for *drunk*. Some of those John Clannons couldn't take it. And their way of copping out wasn't going on a binge or sailing back to Ireland. What they did was to work their knuckles to the bone, with bitterness their twenty-four-hour-a-day boss, and when they got power and money they took it out on my father and seven other men and their families. The grandsons of some of *those* families became the Raps and Harrys of today.

And the hurt was soul-shattering sometimes. It was rougher than a cancer because, once you had it, you couldn't cut it out even for a single minute. A couple of years before we left Alabama I recall hearing about the white mob in Georgia that lynched a bunch of Negroes because someone there had murdered the white owner. They never knew if that someone was a colored man or not. They didn't care.

When in doubt about anything, murder a Negro—or a bunch of Negroes—was their creed. Only this time one of the men they hung had a wife who was eight months pregnant and who just couldn't stand to see her husband taken away. She clawed at the shoes of the white men as they dragged him to the tree, she screamed to the next county when they put the rope around his neck.

So they strung her up, too. Only they didn't tighten the knot enough to kill her, just to dangle her above the fire they'd made so she'd slowly burn to death. Before she lost consciousness, her ready-to-be-born baby dropped into the flames.

That wasn't the worst of it. As the baby fell into the fire, the white men ran to their homes to call their wives and their children. To watch it roast.

I feel as sorry for those white children who are alive today as for the dead Negro woman and her child. I shudder to imagine what *their* sons and grandsons have become.

So it isn't that some of today's militants don't have their crosses to bear. And all the atrocities against the Negro didn't happen fifty years ago, either. In World War II a colored soldier could be court-martialed for walking into a white USO, even though the next day he might be shipped overseas to stand in the front line against enemy fire. Of course, not all Negroes were shipped overseas. Two dozen in Alexandria, Louisiana, never got to die for their country. They died for whitethink in 1941 when, for no reason except their blackness, they were lined up and shot in cold blood by some lily-white officers.

The one that somehow sticks in my mind most, though, happened about ten years ago. It was only a squib on the obituary page of the daily paper. A young Negro artist in the South had been, without provocation, castrated by three white men. I think that burned my in-

sides deeper than anything. It seemed to epitomize what
so many white men had really tried to do to the Negro.
They hadn't killed him. Worse. They'd taken away the
black man's manhood before the Negro had ever had the
chance to really use it, leaving an emasculated shell to
go through the motions of life for the next forty or fifty or
sixty years. If there is a more sickening crime against the
human soul than that, I don't know what it is.

But I also know that a crime such as this is now the rare
exception. What's more, they are almost always punished,
and properly, whenever and wherever they happen. There
was a time when horror was a way of life for virtually every
Negro and justice was an impossible dream you didn't dare
torture yourself with. My father only talked about things
once or twice, but that was enough to give me the picture.
Whenever my mother was feeling low, she filled in the bits
and pieces that told you what existence—you couldn't call
it *life*—was like for her parents and grandparents.

Volumes have been written on slave times, from the near-
starvation and the incredible work load that went with it
to the intolerable living conditions and the merciless beat-
ings. We've all heard about the fatherly way the plantation
owners treated some of their slaves, and I'm sure there were
some who did. But my grandparents and great-grandparents
never knew any kindly paternalism. It's said that Alabama
was run by the poor white trash, and that could be part of
the reason. I think the deeper truth, though, is that slave
life was sometimes bearable only for those who, not being
able to live any longer with the never-stopping fright of
not knowing what would happen next, gave in to the
tyranny. Like the blackthinkers of today who throw in the
towel of reason and angrily lash out as a way of life when
they feel they just can't take it anymore, those plantation
Toms became allies of the extremists in their day. And let's

not kid ourselves—the white slavemasters *were* the extremists, even though they happened to be the Establishment, too. The Nazis were the Establishment in 1936 Germany.

The difference is that today's black extremist is born with a platinum spoon in his mouth compared to what his great-grandparents had to go through. You wonder at times how any one of them then survived mentally, let alone physically. Historian Lura Beam put it better than I can: "The slave lived subject to the fear, shock and pressure that unhinge people now and send them to mental hospitals."

The moments of gratuitous "friendship" from the owners mainly served to underline the basic relationship of master to servant, dictator to subject, human being to lower animal. The whitethinking world my great-grandparents were born into made George Orwell's crimethinking *Nineteen Eighty-Four* seem mild. My own father was actually afraid to *touch* a book! He believed that if he laid a finger on one, someone in the family would fall suddenly ill, possibly die. Primitive? Not altogether. His parents and their parents had never been allowed to own a book, to say nothing of learning to read one. Slaves had been beaten to death for having books hidden in their homes. When we moved up to Cleveland, the first thing my mother saved to buy (and it took almost a year) was a silver-lettered little Bible. She kept it on a special board high above the fireplace and each day every one of us except my father had to take it down and read a passage from it out loud as best we could, any passage, before we left the house. It took my father many years before he could even take the book in his hands. And he never learned how to read it.

Yet if Henry Owens never was able to read the words of his religion, at least he didn't have to dig a hole in the ground or put a kitchen pot over his head to pray. That's what many slaves were forced to do. If they were caught

praying openly, they'd be beaten within an inch of their
lives, or maybe have their infants—or parents—sold on the
auction block as punishment. And if they ever went so far
as to try and take their loved ones and run, every white
owner had a passel of "nigger hounds" just for the purpose
of tracking them down and cornering them like the animals
they were felt to be.

So if the white man who owned you "loved" you, it wasn't
even in the way that he loved those hounds of his that were
always ready to corner you. When a dog died, there might
have been a few days of sadness on the plantation. When a
slave died, the usual feeling was anger—anger that less
work might be done that day. It was up to the other slaves
to make up for it, unless *they* wanted to be beaten or starved.
Most Negroes didn't have the strength to work any harder,
and so they died, frequently before they were thirty, almost
always before they were forty. It didn't matter much to the
owners, as long as the Negroes kept breeding so a new generation of slaves was constantly growing up to work the
cotton. Many of them weren't born with dark brown or
black skin, however, because they were the offspring of
slave women and the owners. My great-grandfather's wife
had to go to the owner's bed whenever "benevolently"
beckoned. My own skin isn't light brown by accident or
from love, and neither is the skin of any other Negro.

So if Henry Owens was verbally abused, grossly over-
worked and sadistically treated by the system into which he
was thrown, at least he could pray when he wanted and be
sure his wife was his alone to love. Leaving this for the
North was taking a chance on the unknown, and the unknown could only be worse. That's why it took an earth-
quake to pry Negroes like us loose from the cotton fields.
There was always the possibility of a too terrible past
rising up again to haunt us.

I admire my papa fiercely for the decision he made, but

you couldn't say it was any more than what his father or grandfather did. Just to survive, in body and spirit, was an accomplishment for *them*.

I've tried to make something of my life, but when I put it against what Henry Owens did, it doesn't seem like much, considering the opportunity I had. And when I put what most of today's blackthinkers, with their opportunities, have accomplished against what Henry Owens accomplished, it comes out near zero.

6

FROM

A Colored Woman in a White World

by Mary Church Terrell
(1863–1954)

Preventing Negroes of means from buying homes in the suburbs has resulted in a great financial disparity between the thousands of black families clustered together in the central-city ghetto. A glaring example of this is Washington, D.C., where exclusion of blacks from the suburbs has also resulted in a city school system with an 83 percent black population.

Around the turn of the century Mary Church Terrell and her husband sought to buy a house in one of the many white neighborhoods in Washington. In 1900 the District of Columbia was still a sleepy little town with about 86,000 Negroes out of a total population of 278,000—a little more than 30 percent. (It is interesting to note that today Washington proper is approximately 53 percent black.) It is the frustrating search for a place to live in the capital of the United States which Mrs. Terrell describes in the following selection from her autobiography.

*Born the year of the Emancipation Proclamation, Mary
Terrell spent her life writing, teaching, and lecturing. She
was the first president of the National Association of Colored
Women, founded in 1895, and was active in the civil-rights
movement as early as the 1940s. At the outbreak of World
War I she offered her secretarial services to the government,
only to find that she, as a dark-skinned American, received
lower wages than her white counterparts. It caused her some
despair to find discrimination in the nation's capital and
a great deal of unhappiness to learn it was government
sanctioned.*

FOR several years after our marriage we lived in a two-room
apartment in a desirable section of the National Capital,
and then we decided we would start to buy a home. But deciding to do so was much easier than carrying out our plans.
Washington is like most cities in our country. Colored people have to overcome difficulties when they try to buy homes.
How huge they are I did not know until I tackled them myself. It was easy to find houses where self-respecting people
of any color would not care to live. But finding the kind we
wanted which either the owners themselves or their agents
would sell us was a horse of quite another color.

We looked with longing eyes upon many a dear little
house which was just exactly what we wanted in every respect, but we were frankly told we could not buy it, because
we were colored. Finally I selected one, only one house
removed from Howard Town, which was almost exclusively
inhabited by colored people. It was named for General
Howard, under whose supervision a camp for refugees was
established there during the Civil War. The little house was
an English basement with six rooms, a hall room, and a
bath. It was several blocks from Howard University, one of

the finest institutions for colored youth in the United
States. This institution was also named for General
Howard, who was deeply interested in the education of
colored people and was the leading spirit in founding the
university, over which he presided for four years.

Although the house was near the settlement occupied by
colored people, it was located in Le Droit Park, a section
in which nobody but white people lived excepting one
colored family. It is said that the white people used to build
a fence to separate their bailiwick from Howard Town, so
their colored neighbors could not walk through Le Droit
Park on their way to the city. Every night this fence was
kicked down by colored people, according to the story related to me by Major Fleetwood, a colored man who was
awarded a medal by Congress for distinguished bravery
during the Civil War. And every day it was rebuilt by the
whites, who were determined to keep colored people out.

Be that as it may, when the woman who owned the house
which we had selected learned that colored people wanted
it, she refused to sell it to us. Since it was so near a settlement of colored people, I had no idea there would be the
slightest objection to selling it to us. I had been searching
continuously and diligently for several months, and this
was the only desirable house I had seen which I thought I
would like to buy.

It reached the ears of an old, well-established real estate
firm that we wanted this piece of property. Both father and
son came to see us one evening. After I had given a detailed
account of the prolonged strenuous efforts I had made to
find a house, the elder of the two men said, "Do you want
that house in Le Droit Park?" I assured him that I wanted
it very much. "Well, you shall have it," he declared. "I'll
be damned if you shan't."

He fulfilled his promise to get it for me to the letter. He

induced a wealthy man who had a colored secretary (which was indeed a rare thing in Washington) to buy the house for us, and then he sold it to us immediately.

It was in this house, soon after we lost our second baby at birth, that University Park Temple was organized. For several years afterward the services of this church were held in a little mission near Howard University which had been conducted by the First Congregational Church, of which President and Mrs. Coolidge were members during their residence in the White House. Later this church, founded in our home, merged with the Lincoln Memorial Congregational Church, and the union of the two is now known as Lincoln Congregational Temple.

From the English basement we moved into another house in Le Droit Park, which my father gave me. Here we remained fifteen years. When I started to furnish the first house we bought, I discovered that our exchequer was a bit low and economy must be used. Then I acquired the habit of going to a well-known auction and discovered that I could find furniture there which I could not afford to pay for new, but which I could buy at a resonable price second hand. I took great pride in some of the wonderful bargains I got in this auction room in those early days.

Mother died in the second house into which we moved. After that so many things reminded me of her I decided it was my duty to myself to make a change. She had lived with me continuously for fifteen years. It was the first time I had been with my mother longer than a few months at a time since I was a small child. In reviewing the period she spent with me, after she had passed away, it seemed to me that each of us had tried to make up for lost time by concentrating into those fifteen years all the devotion we could have shown each other during the time we had been separated. She was a great comfort, and in spite of physical affliction she was an unalloyed joy to us all. Mr. Terrell and she always combined against me in an argument. Mr. Terrell used to assure his friends that they did not know what real life was until they lived with their mother-in-law.

When I started in quest of a house for the second time and asked several real estate firms to show me what they had on their list, I discovered they took me to see nothing but residences which had been discarded by discriminating people, because they were old-fashioned and devoid of modern improvements. Then it dawned upon me that, as a colored woman, I would be unable even to SEE the kind of house I desired. I decided to devise some sort of scheme by which I would be able to look at desirable houses with modern improvements without benefit of real estate agents.

I felt then, as I feel now, that people who are discriminated against solely on account of race, color, or creed are justified in resorting to any subterfuge, using any disguise, or playing any trick, provided they do not actually break the law, if it will enable them to secure the advantages and obtain the rights to which they are entitled by outwitting their prejudice-ridden foes.

As I motored through a street one day, I saw a "For Sale" sign on a house which, judging from the exterior, I thought I would like. My daughter Mary and I went to see it next day, and the caretaker who was showing it was eager to have me take it. It was new, and the man told me that the purchaser would be allowed to paper it and select the fixtures to suit his taste. Then I went to a real estate agent who had been highly recommended to me by a friend. "He sold me my house in this fine neighborhood," she said, "and I feel sure he would sell you one. I have had no trouble at all. After my neighbors saw I had neither hoofs nor claws, they almost embarrassed me with their attention."

I went to this agent and threw my cards on the table at

once. I asked him frankly whether he would object to selling a house to me in the neighborhood designated. I would not bother him further, I stated, if he had any scruples whatever on the subject. Referring to the record in the city which my husband and I had made, the real estate agent declared that "anybody would be glad to live next to Judge Terrell and his wife." But, knowing my city as well I did, I took this assertion with several grains of salt.

It was a reflection upon my intelligence and my knowledge of conditions on general principles for the gentleman to deliver himself of any such speech as that and expect me to believe it. If our dear Lord and Saviour should come to this country in the form of a colored man, He would be obliged to say again, "The Son of man hath not where to lay his head," unless He was accommodated by colored people or was willing to take anything He could get. There are exceptions to all general rules, and there is no doubt that there are a goodly number who would give shelter to a colored man or woman, just as Robert G. Ingersoll opened his house to Frederick Douglass in Peoria, Illinois, when he had been refused accommodations at all the hotels.

The agent appeared perfectly willing to negotiate the purchase of the house, and I commissioned him to do it. I gave him the required deposit and urged him to close the deal as soon as he could. He promised to let me hear from him in a short while. I grew apprehensive about getting the house, but my daughter, who had heard the agent give me positive assurance that there would be no trouble about buying it for me, read me delightful little lectures about worrying unnecessarily. "You just like to borrow trouble, Mother," she would say, "and you dearly love to worry. Mr. L. said he would get that house for you, and of course he will keep his word." My dear little girl was filled with the faith of youth, because she had had no experience battling with the Race Problem, as her mother had had.

So much confidence did she repose in the agent's promise that she planned a house party for the Christmas holidays and assigned each of the prospective guests to her respective room. Not only did she complete all her plans for the housewarming, but she wrote her name with the new address upon newspapers, paper bags, and anything else she dared inscribe that she happened to come upon, when she had a lead pencil in her hand.

Several times I 'phoned the agent, urging him to complete the transaction as soon as he could, so that we might move into our new home before the opening of the fall term, which was not far away. He would tell me that I would have to wait a little longer, but that everything was going all right. Finally, I went to his office just before school opened to get a definite reply. He then returned my deposit and frankly admitted that he could not sell me the house, because the owner had discovered that a colored family wanted it and refused to let us have it. It is quite probable that after having promised to negotiate the purchase of the property the agent had had an attack of cold feet and changed his mind.

"It is well for you," said the agent, returning my deposit, "that you did not succeed in getting that house. If you had, you would have been boycotted by everybody upon whom you would have had to depend for supplies. Neither the milkman nor the iceman would have served you. And every time you or the other members of your family appeared on the street, the boys in the neighborhood would have pelted you with bricks and stones."

"Such a fearsome prospect as that would not have frightened me a bit," I replied, "if I could have gained possession of that house. There is always a cure for violence like that due to race prejudice, if one goes about it in the right way."

After that dismal failure I decided that never again would I attempt to buy a house in Washington. To that decision I adhered for a long time, and we lived in a rented house. But the times change and we all change with them. Circumstances seemed to demand that we should get a house of our own after a while, and I started on a wild-goose chase of house-hunting again.

We had no car at that time, so I trudged many weary miles before I finally found a residence which appealed to all our family as desirable. I had decided definitely not to buy a house that had a kitchen in the basement. I had had enough of that arrangement in the second house to last me for the rest of my natural life. No more basements for me, running up and down the steps to answer the doorbell when I was busy in the kitchen and there was no one to help me!

The house which I finally selected had the kitchen on the first floor and was bright with sunshine the greater part of the day. A colored real estate agent had shown us this house and he assured me he could get it for me. There was absolutely no doubt about that, he said, so I gave him the deposit. After he had kept it for several months and had been unable to complete the deal, the deposit was returned. He had failed. But I could not bear to give the house up. It had taken me a long time to find it, and the thought of being obliged to go through another ordeal of house-hunting was nerve-racking.

I 'phoned the real estate agent who had it for sale and urged him to sell it to us. Without mincing matters at all, he told me right off the reel that he would not sell that house to colored people, no matter who they were. "But a colored family already lives next door to the house I want to buy," I said, "and there are several others on the same side of the street." "But they do not own their homes," he replied. "They rent them." This statement did not tally with the facts. I knew that one of the teachers in the colored high school, who lived four or five doors below the coveted house, had bought his home. I was at my wits' end. There seemed nothing more that I could do. Wherever I turned, disappointment stared me in the face.

As a last resort I called up a colored man who was in the District tax office, whom I had known from girlhood, and asked him to ascertain the name of the owner of the house which I wanted so much to buy. I explained the situation fully. He promised he would help me get the house if he possibly could.

A few days afterward a white agent came to see me to inquire whether I would like to purchase the house in question, and to assure me he could make arrangements to get it for me. I called his attention to the fact that there were several colored families living in the block on the same side of the street, and a colored family lived next door to the one I wanted to buy. The agent kept his word. I had to pay several thousand dollars more for the house than the price at which it was originally offered, and I was obliged to make a much larger deposit than the one which was at first required. But I was glad to be relieved of all the worry and trouble incident to hunting another house, and I cheerfully accepted the terms.

And so, after many troubles and trials, we finally obtained possession of the house which we now call home, which, by the way, is on the same street, several blocks away, on which both President Wilson and President Hoover once lived.

It is not because colored people are so obsessed with the desire to live among white people that they try to buy property in a white neighborhood. They do so because the houses there are modern, as a rule, and are better in every way than are those which have been discarded and turned over to their own group. If colored people could find houses on a street restricted to themselves which were as well built and as up to date as are those in white districts, they would make no effort to thrust themselves upon their fair-skinned brothers and sisters who object to having them in close proximity.

When we were obliged to pay several thousand dollars more for our house than the price which was first quoted, we were not being subjected to a hardship from which other colored people are generally exempt. It is well known that from $8 to $10 more rent per month is demanded from colored people than white people have to pay for the same kind of house. As a rule, they also have to pay much more for the property they buy than do others. For instance, the price charged us for the house in which we are now living was at least $2,000 more than a white purchaser would have been obliged to pay.

African blood is truly a luxury in the United States for which those who show it or acknowledge it pay dearly indeed.

7

FROM

Lady Sings the Blues

by Billie Holiday
(1915–1959)

Although there may have been black singing stars, the entertainment business as a whole has been no more receptive to blacks than any other American industry. There are virtually no black producers, union sound men, makeup artists, or any vice-presidents at any TV network or major film studio. More ironic is that, off the stage and on the road, even the superstar is not immune to the humiliation and outrages suffered by every other black person, as this selection by Billie Holiday illustrates.

DON'T tell me about those pioneer chicks hitting the trail in those slip-covered wagons with the hills full of redskins. I'm the girl who went West in 1937 with sixteen white cats, Artie Shaw and his Rolls-Royce—and the hills were full of white crackers.

It all began one night at Clarke Monroe's Uptown House.

Artie came in and got to talking and dreaming about his new band. He thought he needed something sensational to give it a shove.

"Something sensational? That's easy," I told him. "Hire a good Negro singer."

That did it. Artie waited for me all night at the Uptown House and put me right in his car to take me to Boston for the opening. Georgie Auld, Tony Pastor, and Max Kaminsky were with him. Before we left, we drove over to Mom's and she fixed fried chicken for a 6:30 A.M. breakfast for the whole gang. The chicken knocked Artie out. He never ate anything like she fixed it. When the chicken was gone, we piled into his car and were off.

Boston was jumping then. We were booked in Roseland. Glenn Miller was working just around the corner, and a block away there was Chick Webb and his band with Ella Fitzgerald. Chick's group was the best known; but we were still better known than Miller.

The sight of sixteen men on a bandstand with a Negro girl singer had never been seen before—in Boston or anywhere. The question of how the public would take to it had to be faced opening night at Roseland. Naturally Sy Schribman, the owner of Roseland and a guy who did a lot for bands like Dorsey, Miller, and others, was worried.

But Artie was a guy who never thought in terms of white and coloured. "I can take care of the situation," was his answer. "And I know Lady can take care of herself."

"As far as I'm concerned," I told Artie, "I don't care about sitting on the bandstand. When it comes time for me to sing a number, you introduce me, I sing, then I'm gone."

Artie disagreed. "No," he insisted. "I want you on the bandstand like Helen Forrest and Tony Pastor and everyone else." So that's what I did. Everything up in Boston was straight—but the real test was coming up. We were heading for Kentucky.

Kentucky is like Baltimore—it's only on the border of being the South, which means people there take their Dixie stuff more seriously than the crackers farther down.

Right off, we couldn't find a place that would rent me a room. Finally Artie got sore and picked out the biggest hotel in town. He was determined to crack it—or he was going to sue. I tried to stop him. "Man," I said, "are you trying to get me killed?"

Artie had taken the band on the road for a good reason— he wanted to play to as many people as possible before risking a New York opening. The band had enough work to do without looking for lawsuits around every corner and doing a job for the NAACP.

But there was no moving Artie. He's a wild one; he has his own peculiarities but he's amazing and a good cat deep down. He's not one to go back on his word. Whatever he says, Jack, you can believe that's it. Whatever he'd set out to do, he would believe in it. He might find he was wrong, but rather than go back on his word, he'd suffer. That's the way he was and that's why I liked him, and that's why he wouldn't listen to me in Kentucky. He got eight cats out of the band and they escorted me to the registration desk at the biggest hotel in that little old Kentucky town.

I don't think anybody black had ever got a room there before, but the cats in the band acted like it was as natural as breathing. I think the man at the desk figured it couldn't be true what he thought he saw, and I couldn't be a Negro or nobody would act like that. I think they thought I was Spanish or something, so they gave me a nice room and no back talk.

The cats had a little taste of triumph, so they went on from there. All eight of them waltzed into the dining room, carrying me with them like I was the *Queen Mary* and they were a bunch of tugboats. We sat down, ordered food all around and champagne, acting up like we were a sensation. And we were.

After that scene I guess the management thought they were getting off easy in letting me have a room.

It was a one-man town. And the sheriff was the man. He ran things. He was on the scene that night when we opened in a real-life natural rock cave. The sheriff was haunting the place, letting kids in for half price. They were selling kids whisky right under his nose. But he didn't pay any mind to that. He was too busy dogging me.

When it came time to go on, I told Artie I didn't want any trouble and didn't want to sit on the bandstand.

"It just don't make sense," I told him. "This is the damn South." But Artie didn't want to give in. He was unhappy. I was unhappy. Finally we compromised and agreed I would come out on the stand and sit just before my numbers.

I could smell this sheriff a mile off. I told the cats in the band he was looking for trouble.

"He wants to call me nigger so bad he's going to find a way," I told them. And so I bet Tony Pastor, Georgie Auld and Max Kaminsky two bucks apiece he would make it.

He did.

When I came on the sheriff walked up to the raised bandstand; Artie's back was to the dance floor, so he pulled Artie's pants leg and said, "Hey you!" Artie turned around. "Don't touch me," he hollered over the music.

But the sheriff didn't give up so easy. I had money riding on what he would do, so I was watching him real close. So were the cats I had the bet with. They were keeping a free eye on him. He pulled Artie's leg again. "Hey you," he said.

Artie turned around. "You want to get kicked?" he asked him.

Still the old cracker sheriff didn't give up. Back he came again. "Hey you," he said. Then he turned to me and, so loud everybody could hear, he said, "What's Blackie going to sing?"

Artie looked like it was the end of the world—and the tour. I guess he thought I was going to break down and have a collapse or something. But I was laughing like hell. I turned to Georgie, Tony, and Max, put my hand out, and said, "Come on now, give me the money."

We had another big scene like this one time in St. Louis. We were scheduled to play the ballroom in one of the biggest hotels in town. The man who hired us just leased the ballroom from the hotel. But this day, of all days, after two months of one-nighters and a chance to sit still for three whole weeks, we were rehearsing and in wandered this old cracker who owned the hotel, the city block, the works. He was older than God and hadn't been seen around there in ten years. But he picked this day to come scooting around in his wheel chair to look over his property.

Naturally, the first thing he saw was me. And the first thing he said was, "What's that nigger doing there? I don't have niggers to clean up around here."

Artie tried to tell him I was his vocalist, but he wasn't listening. He wasn't saying anything but "nigger."

So I stepped in and said, "Man, can't you say nothing else? I'm tired of being called nigger." Besides, I knew I could whip him.

Tony was so sore and red in the face, I didn't know what he might do, when this old cracker ordered Artie and him and me and all of us out of the hotel. If you've got one of those Italian boys like Tony in your corner, they'll go to hell for you and die for you. If one of those cats loves you, I'm sorry, you've got you a buddy-boy.

So with Tony beside me I walked up to this old cracker and stared him down.

"Listen," I told him. "Artie Shaw has been very nice to me. I know you don't even have niggers clean up your hotel. But I'm a Negro or whatever you want to call me, and I'll make you a bet. You let us open in this damn ballroom, and if I don't go over better than anyone else, you can throw me and Artie and all of us out. You want to take the bet or don't you?"

He didn't know what to say. He didn't want to take it. But he didn't want to scoot off in his wheel chair either. There were quite a few spectators on the scene, and people began saying he was a drag if he didn't take the bet. So he did, and we opened.

I knew that night I had the future of the whole band riding on me, so I really worked. First I did "I Cried for You." Then I followed with "Them There Eyes." And then I finished with a thing called "What You Gonna Do When There Ain't No Swing?" Swing was the thing then.

When I ended the number I held onto the word "ain't," then I held "no." Then I held my breath, thinking the jury was out and wondering what the verdict would be, and I sang the word "swing." I hadn't got the word shaped with my mouth when people stood up whistling and hollering and screaming and clapping. There was no arguing. I was the best, so we stayed there for six weeks instead of three.

It wasn't long before the roughest days with the Basie band began to look like a breeze. It got to the point where I hardly ever ate, slept, or went to the bathroom without having a major NAACP-type production.

Most of the cats in the band were wonderful to me, but I got so tired of scenes in crummy roadside restaurants over getting served, I used to beg Georgie Auld, Tony Pastor, and Chuck Peterson to just let me sit in the bus and rest— and let them bring me out something in a sack. Some places they wouldn't even let me eat in the kitchen. Some places they would. Sometimes it was a choice between me eating and the whole band starving. I got tired of having a federal case over breakfast, lunch, and dinner.

One time we stopped at a dirty little hole in the wall, and the whole band piled in. I was sitting at the counter next to Chuck Peterson. Everybody else gets waited on and this blonde bitch waitress ignores me like I'm not even there. Chuck called her first and then Tony Pastor got real sore. "This is Lady Day." He hollered at her, "Now you feed her."

I pleaded with him not to start anything, but Tony let loose, the cats in the band started throwing things around. When they wouldn't serve me, the whole band pitched in and wrecked the joint. Everybody grabbed their food, and when the bus pulled out, you could hear the old sheriff's police siren coming after us. Even Artie jumped into that fight.

Getting a night's sleep was a continual drag, too. We were playing big towns and little towns, proms and fairs. A six-hundred-mile jump overnight was standard. When we got to put up at a hotel, it was usually four cats to a room. We might finish at Scranton, Pennsylvania, at two in the morning, grab something to eat, and make Cleveland, Ohio, by noon the next day. The boys in the band had worked out a deal for getting two nights' sleep for one night's rent.

We'd drive all night, hit a town in the morning, register and turn in early, and sleep until time to go to work. When the job was through, we'd sleep the rest of the night, clear out in the morning, and hit the road. This would work every other day and save loot. On the $125 a week I made, that was still very important.

This would have been fine except that I had to double up with another vocalist. I don't think she liked Negroes much, and especially not me. She didn't want to sleep in the same room with me. She only did because she had to.

Artie had asked me to help her to phrase her lyrics; this

made her jealous. Then once I made the mistake of telling somebody we got along fine, and to prove it I mentioned how she let me help her phrase. This made her sore. It was true, there were some places where the management wouldn't let me appear, and I'd have to sit in the bus while she did numbers that were arranged for me. She was always happy when she could sing and I couldn't.

I'll never forget the night we were booked at this fancy boys' school in New England. She was real happy because she was sure I was going to have to sit in the bus all night again because I was too black and sexy for those young boys.

But when the time came to open, the head man of the school came out and explained that it wasn't me, they just didn't want any female singers at all. So the two of us had to sit in the bus together all night and listen to the band playing our songs.

Did I razz her! "You see, honey," I said, "you're so fine and grand. You may be white, but you're no better than me. They won't have either of us here because we're both women."

Almost every day there was an "incident."

In a Boston joint they wouldn't let me go in the front door; they wanted me to come in the back way. The cats in the band flipped and said, "If Lady doesn't go in the front door, the band doesn't go in at all." So they caved.

Eating was a mess, sleeping was a problem, but the biggest of all was a simple little thing like finding a place to go to the bathroom.

Sometimes we'd make a six-hundred-mile jump and only stop once. Then it would be a place where I couldn't get served, let alone crash the toilet without causing a scene. At first I used to be so ashamed. Then finally I just said to hell with it. When I had to go I'd just ask the bus driver to stop and let me off at the side of the road. I'd rather go in the bushes than take a chance in the restaurants and towns. . . .

When we got to Detroit, we played on the same stage in the same big theatre where they tried to black me up because I was too light for the boys in the Basie band. The management never asked me to wear pink make-up to sing with a white band, but if they had I wouldn't have been surprised.

Detroit was almost as far north as we ever went, but it was still full of crackers and I was always uneasy. One night Chuck Peterson asked me to go with him to a little backstage bar on the corner and have a drink. I didn't want to go for the same old reason. But he insisted, and so we did.

In a matter of minutes some woman at the bar piped out that she wasn't going to drink in the place if that nigger stood there, making clear she meant me. Chuck wanted to answer back, but I talked him out of it and we went on to finish our drink.

The next thing we knew, a man came over and started after Chuck. "What the hell's going on ?" he said. "A man can't bring his wife in a bar any more without you tramp white men bringing a nigger woman in."

Chuck wouldn't stand for that, but before he knew it this guy and a couple more were on him, beating and kicking him. While everyone else stood around with their mouths open, this guy kept kicking Chuck in the mouth and saying, "I'll fix it so you don't play trumpet tonight."

If my maid hadn't come in just then from backstage to tell me it was show time and helped me get him out of there, they might have beat him to death.

I was sick for the rest of the booking in Detroit. Eventually Chuck's mother, who happens to be a lawyer, sued the management for damages and collected a few thousand dollars.

There's something weird about that town. Ten years later, it didn't seem so much better. When I was headlining at the

Paradise Theatre in Detroit's Negro section in 1949, I
walked in a nearby bar. The bartender greeted me by telling
me he couldn't serve me because I had enough.

I asked him what he meant. "Do you really think I had
enough or don't you serve Negroes?"

"There she goes," he said, "trying to start trouble. She
must be drunk."

The next time there was a riot in Detroit, I heard that this
particular little saloon got taken apart. . . .

After surviving months of being bugged by sheriffs,
waitresses, hotel clerks, and crackers of kinds in the South,
I got the crummiest deal of all when we got back to New
York—New York, my own home town.

We were set to open at the Blue Room of Maria Kramer's
Lincoln on 43rd Street. The Lincoln hadn't been a good
spot for bands, but there was a coast-to-coast radio wire in
the room—and in those days radio was everything. This
was my chance to sing on the radio coast to coast every
night. A few weeks of this and any band or any singer
could be made. This was big time.

I should have known something was shaking when the
hotel management gave me a suite. I didn't need a place to
sleep. I was staying home with Mom. I didn't even need a
place to dress. I could come to the hotel every night dressed,
and Artie always wanted me to sit on the bandstand all night
and look pretty, anyway.

Artie was getting pressure from all over—the hotel, the
booking agency, the networks. But he didn't have the heart
to tell me. The excuse for giving me the suite was that I was
supposed to stay there until it was time for me to sing, and
not mingle with the guests.

The next thing I knew, the management wanted me to
come in the back door of the hotel. When a little joint in
Boston tried this, the whole band had said, "If Lady doesn't

use the door the band doesn't either." But Artie and the cats in the band had taken months of hell for this New York engagement, and nobody was in a position to push a hotel chain, a broadcasting network, and the talent agency around.

So I had to come in the back door. I don't know why I didn't walk out then and there, except Mom got such a kick out of listening to our nightly broadcasts. She was crazy about sitting home and hearing me on the radio.

The next thing I knew, I was singing less and less. Some nights I'd only be on for one song all night—and that would be before or after the band had been on the air.

Finally, when they cut me off the air completely, I said to hell with it. I just fired myself. I told Artie he should have told me when the big wheels cracked down on him. "Down South I can dig this kind of stuff, but I can't take it in New York."

The sheriff in Kentucky was at least honest. A real good cracker says, "I don't like Negroes period." Or "dot," as they say in the South. Some just say, "I don't want to socialize with Negroes." They don't tell you that behind your back, they tell it right to your face, and you know it. A cracker just wants you to clean up his house or take care of his kids and then get the hell out.

Even when they insult you they do it to your face. That's the only way they can let you know they're superior to you. They might die and leave you all their money, but somewhere in fine print in that will they've got to let you know you were a good nigger but you're still a nigger.

This sheriff in Kentucky called me "blackie" to my face. The big-deal hotels, agencies, and networks in New York were giving me a fast shove behind my back.

I had been with Artie a year and a half. We had had some real times. I'll always remember the night I sat on the piano bench in his hotel suite, looking across the Boston Back Bay for twelve hours, pounding out two bass notes while he finished writing his theme song, "Nightmare."

There aren't many people who fought harder than Artie against the vicious people in the music business or the crummy side of second-class citizenship which eats at the guts of so many musicians. He didn't win. But he didn't lose either. It wasn't long after I left that he told them to shove it like I had. And people still talk about him as if he were nuts because there were things more important to him than a million damn bucks a year.

8

FROM

The Big Sea

by Langston Hughes
(1902–1967)

*Negroes were not even free of discrimination in Harlem,
where in the 1920s the black intellectuals met, and where
curious whites came after dark for the entertainment the
various cabarets provided. When white patrons refused to
visit clubs which also accepted black customers, nightclub
owners, anxious for the revenue, shrugged and accepted the
jim crowism.*

*Langston Hughes, who describes Harlem during this
period, was frequently introduced as the poet laureate of
the Negro people or the poet laureate of Harlem. Hughes
used every literary form imaginable to express the plight of
his people. The most prolific of modern black writers,
Hughes began his career in 1921 when* The Crisis *published his poem "The Negro Speaks of Rivers," and over
the next forty-five years poured out fiction (*Not Without
Laughter, *the "Simple" stories), poetry, two autobiographies, drama (*Mulatto), *and numerous essays, anthologies,
and books for young readers.*

Hughes' contemporaries during the era of Harlem's renaissance included Countee Cullen, Claude McKay, and Arna Bontemps.

THE 1920's were the years of Manhattan's black Renaissance. It began with *Shuffle Along, Running Wild*, and the Charleston. Perhaps some people would say even with *The Emperor Jones*, Charles Gilpin, and the tom-toms at the Provincetown. But certainly it was the musical revue, *Shuffle Along*, that gave a scintillating send-off to that Negro vogue in Manhattan, which reached its peak just before the crash of 1929, the crash that sent Negroes, white folks, and all rolling down the hill toward the Works Progress Administration.

Shuffle Along was a honey of a show. Swift, bright, funny, rollicking, and gay, with a dozen danceable, singable tunes. Besides, look who were in it: The now famous choir director, Hall Johnson, and the composer, William Grant Still, were a part of the orchestra. Eubie Blake and Noble Sissle wrote the music and played and acted in the show. Miller and Lyles were the comics. Florence Mills skyrocketed to fame in the second act. Trixie Smith sang "He May Be Your Man But He Comes to See Me Sometimes." And Caterina Jarboro, now a European prima donna, and the internationally celebrated Josephine Baker were merely in the chorus. Everybody was in the audience —including me. People came back to see it innumerable times. It was always packed.

To see *Shuffle Along* was the main reason I wanted to go to Columbia. When I saw it, I was thrilled and delighted. From then on I was in the gallery of the Cort Theatre every time I got a chance. That year, too, I saw Katharine Cornell in *A Bill of Divorcement*, Margaret Wycherly in *The Verge*, Maugham's *The Circle* with Mrs. Leslie Carter, and the

Theatre Guild production of Kaiser's *From Morn Till Midnight*. But I remember *Shuffle Along* best of all. It gave just the proper push—a pre-Charleston kick—to that Negro vogue of the '20's, that spread to books, African sculpture, music, and dancing.

Put down the 1920's for the rise of Roland Hayes, who packed Carnegie Hall, the rise of Paul Robeson in New York and London, of Florence Mills over two continents, of Rose McClendon in Broadway parts that never measured up to her, the booming voice of Bessie Smith and the low moan of Clara on thousands of records, and the rise of that grand comedienne of song, Ethel Waters, singing: "Charlie's elected now! He's in right for sure!" Put down the 1920's for Louis Armstrong and Gladys Bentley and Josephine Baker.

White people began to come to Harlem in droves. For several years they packed the expensive Cotton Club on Lenox Avenue. But I was never there, because the Cotton Club was a Jim Crow club for gangsters and monied whites. They were not cordial to Negro patronage, unless you were a celebrity like Bojangles. So Harlem Negroes did not like the Cotton Club and never appreciated its Jim Crow policy in the very heart of their dark community. Nor did ordinary Negroes like the growing influx of whites toward Harlem after sundown, flooding the little cabarets and bars where formerly only colored people laughed and sang, and where now the strangers were given the best ringside tables to sit and stare at the Negro customers—like amusing animals in a zoo.

The Negroes said: "We can't go downtown and sit and stare at you in your clubs. You won't even let us in your clubs." But they didn't say it out loud—for Negroes are practically never rude to white people. So thousands of whites came to Harlem night after night, thinking the

Negroes loved to have them there, and firmly believing that all Harlemites left their houses at sundown to sing and dance in cabarets, because most of the whites saw nothing but the cabarets, not the houses.

Some of the owners of Harlem clubs, delighted at the flood of white patronage, made the grievous error of barring their own race, after the manner of the famous Cotton Club. But most of these quickly lost business and folded up, because they failed to realize that a large part of the Harlem attraction for downtown New Yorkers lay in simply watching the colored customers amuse themselves. And the smaller clubs, of course, had no big floor shows or a name band like the Cotton Club, where Duke Ellington usually held forth, so, without black patronage, they were not amusing at all.

Some of the small clubs, however, had people like Gladys Bentley, who was something worth discovering in those days, before she got famous, acquired an accompanist, specially written material, and conscious vulgarity. But for two or three amazing years, Miss Bentley sat, and played a big piano all night long, literally all night, without stopping—singing songs like "The St. James Infirmary," from ten in the evening until dawn, with scarcely a break between the notes, sliding from one song to another, with a powerful and continuous underbeat of jungle rhythm. Miss Bentley was an amazing exhibition of musical energy—a large, dark, masculine lady, whose feet pounded the floor while her fingers pounded the keyboard—a perfect piece of African sculpture, animated by her own rhythm.

But when the place where she played became too well known, she began to sing with an accompanist, became a star, moved to a larger place, then downtown, and is now in Hollywood. The old magic of the woman and the piano and the night and the rhythm being one is gone. But every-

thing goes, one way or another. The '20's are gone and lots
of fine things in Harlem night life have disappeared like
snow in the sun—since it became utterly commercial,
planned for the downtown tourist trade, and therefore
dull.

The lindy-hoppers at the Savoy even began to practise
acrobatic routines, and to do absurd things for the entertainment of the whites, that probably never would have
entered their heads to attempt merely for their own effortless
amusement. Some of the lindy-hoppers had cards printed
with their names on them and became dance professors
teaching the tourists. Then Harlem nights became show
nights for the Nordics.

Some critics say that this is what happened to certain
Negro writers, too—ceased to write to amuse themselves and
began to write to amuse and entertain white people, and in
so doing distorted and over-colored their material, and left
out a great many things they thought would offend their
American brothers of a lighter complexion. Maybe—since
Negroes have writer-racketeers, as has any other race. But I
have known almost all of them, and most of the good ones
have tried to be honest, write honestly, and express their
world as they saw it.

All of us know that the gay and sparkling life of the so-
called Negro Renaissance of the '20's was not so gay and
sparkling beneath the surface as it looked. Carl Van Vechten, in the character of Byron in *Nigger Heaven*, captured
some of the bitterness and frustration of literary Harlem that
Wallace Thurman later so effectively poured into his *Infants
of the Spring*—the only novel by a Negro about that fantastic period when Harlem was in vogue.

It was a period when, at almost every Harlem uppercrust
dance or party, one would be introduced to various distinguished white celebrities there as guests. It was a period

when almost any Harlem Negro of any social importance at
all would be likely to say casually: "As I was remarking the
other day to Heywood—," meaning Heywood Broun. Or:
"As I said to George—," referring to George Gershwin. It
was a period when local and visiting royalty were not at
all uncommon in Harlem. And when the parties of A'Lelia
Walker, the Negro heiress, were filled with guests whose
names would turn any Nordic social climber green with
envy. It was a period when Harold Jackman, a handsome
young Harlem school teacher of modest means, calmly
announced one day that he was sailing for the Riviera for a
fortnight, to attend Princess Murat's yachting party. It was
a period when Charleston preachers opened up shouting
churches as sideshows for white tourists. It was a period
when at least one charming colored chorus girl, amber
enough to pass for a Latin American, was living in a pent
house, with all her bills paid by a gentleman whose name
was banker's magic on Wall Street. It was a period when
every season there was at least one hit play on Broadway
acted by a Negro cast. And when books by Negro authors
were being published with much greater frequency and
much more publicity than ever before or since in history. It
was a period when white writers wrote about Negroes more
successfully (commercially speaking) than Negroes did
about themselves. It was the period (God help us!) when
Ethel Barrymore appeared in blackface in *Scarlet Sister
Mary!* It was the period when the Negro was in vogue.

I was there. I had a swell time while it lasted. But I
thought it wouldn't last long. (I remember the vogue for
things Russian, the season the Chauve-Souris first came to
town.) For how could a large and enthusiastic number of
people be crazy about Negroes forever? But some Harlemites
thought the millennium had come. They thought the race
problem had at last been solved through Art plus Gladys

Bentley. They were sure the New Negro would lead a new life from then on in green pastures of tolerance created by Countee Cullen, Ethel Waters, Claude McKay, Duke Ellington, Bojangles, and Alain Locke.

I don't know what made any Negroes think that—except that they were mostly intellectuals doing the thinking. The ordinary Negroes hadn't heard of the Negro Renaissance. And if they had, it hadn't raised their wages any. As for all those white folks in the speakeasies and night clubs of Harlem—well, maybe a colored man could find *some* place to have a drink that the tourists hadn't yet discovered.

9

FROM
The Third Door

by Ellen Tarry
(1909–   )

Ellen Tarry was so fair that she could easily pass for white, and it was because she refused to do so that she was constantly humiliated.

She spent her early years in Birmingham, Alabama, and originally wanted to go to Africa to become a missionary. After teaching for a short time in Alabama, however, she decided there was enough work for her in America. At the age of twenty-three, she boarded a train for New York and the Columbia School of Journalism. Forced to put off her enrollment until she earned enough money for tuition, Miss Tarry bitterly learned that jobs for Negroes in New York were even fewer and farther between than for whites—especially during the Depression when the Negro was no longer in vogue.

THE New York-bound train jerked to a stop at the crossing opposite Sloss-Sheffield's foundry. The only other occupant of the Jim-Crow coach with its musty plush seats and dirty spittoons was a man who had gone into the smoker. I thought of all the times I had stood at the top of the mountain and watched the sky steal an orange glow from the rivers of molten lead which ran in and out of troughs at this foundry. Overhead was a bridge where we usually stopped the car to give visitors a closer view of the thrilling spectacle, and of the men who worked this industrail magic, their goggled eyes and half-naked bodies filling out the picture. This, I knew, was part of my way of life. Shorty was, too. So was the *Truth*, my church, Mama, Nannie, the children, and Cousin Mabel. So was Woodlawn Cemetery, where White Mama and Papa were buried.

"There's still time," I thought as I stood up, "to grab my bags and get off this train. I'll run back to the station and tell my friends that I'm not leaving. I'll not run away. I'm going to stay right here where I belong and fight!"

Someone honked the horn of an automobile. I ran from one window to the other. Long lines of cars were parked on either side of the train. I remembered all the times I had waited—impatient to be on my way—blowing the horn when the driver in front was slow to start after the train pulled away. A few hours earlier I had passed this same spot on my way to pick up a friend who was supposed to accompany me on this trip, only to find her dangerously ill and unable to travel.

I tried to move my suitcase but it was too heavy, and I was alone. Soon I would really be alone, for though the trip was to be broken by a visit at Rock Castle and Belmead, New York was my destination. Then I would be a thousand miles from all these things and all of the people who mattered most to me.

A dining car waiter who lived in Birmingham came through the coach. "You're traveling in style," he said. "Got a whole car to yourself. Anything wrong?"

"No," I lied, "nothing's wrong. I—I was trying to arrange my baggage. Would you push the big one back, please?"

The train started again and I knew, as I sank down on the seat, that there was no turning back.

It was a sultry August afternoon when friends met me at Union Station in Washington, and drove me around the city. Late that afternoon we went to a Marine Band concert given on the steps of the Capitol. When the white-uniformed marines played the familiar "Stars and Stripes Forever," I looked up at the red and blue of the flag. Crashing cymbals cut through the dusk, which was settling around us. Then somebody pushed a button and there was light where there had been near darkness. The band played "The Star Spangled Banner," and I understood for the first time how the old women at Mama's church felt when they shouted. I was happy and I wanted to shout, too. Geographical boundaries were ignored. To me, this was the right side of the Mason-Dixon line.

"I'm free! I'm free!" I kept whispering to my friends, who could not understand my reaction to anything so commonplace as a Marine Band concert on the steps of the Capitol at lamp-lighting time. They all looked relieved when they put me on an excursion train for New York the following night.

August 11 is always a day of sober reflection and quiet celebration for me. It was on that day in 1929 that I finally crossed the Hudson River on a ferry, took a subway train to Lenox Avenue and 145th Street, then rode a trolley over to St. Nicholas Avenue. From the one window in the room which my classmate had found for me, the buildings looked as gray as the sky above. New York had temporarily lost its enchantment.

Glancing backward, I remember that nothing in New York seemed familiar. In Alabama we had already begun to feel the pinch of tight money, which we always expected during a Republican administration. In New York everybody seemed to be enjoying prosperity. Every third woman I talked with had two jobs and two men paying court. It was the latter circumstance that caused me to write Mama and tell her that New York was so wicked I was afraid God *would* destroy the city. The contempt with which so many New Yorkers spoke of Alabama worried me and I became angry when people complimented me on a dress and said, "Don't tell me you got *that* in Alabama. I didn't know they sold dresses like that down there."

I accepted the fact that I had an accent, since everybody talked or laughed about it. But it was more than the accent that got me into trouble at the corner grocery store. The clerks said they did not know I wanted white bread when I asked for "light bread." My requests for sweet milk and white meat required explanations also, but it was only after I asked a red-haired clerk named Pat for five pounds of Irish potatoes that I decided to check my lists with Mother Ysaguirre, with whom I roomed, before I went shopping. After overcoming these petty irritations, the two New York customs I found hardest to accept were the pew rent boxes at the doors of Catholic churches where a coin was dropped before entering and the men who remained seated on public vehicles while women stood. Years later I conceded that both were logical and practical.

I had never looked for a job before in my life and now that I was actually on my own the prospects were bewildering. I spoke to the people with whom I lived and to a classmate who lived upstairs in the same apartment building and they suggested that I look in the help-wanted ads. But most of the ads for young women wanted young white women and the others were for "settled or mature Negro" women to cook, nurse, or keep house. I saw one or two for a "Light colored girl to keep a small bachelor apartment. Work pleasant," but my friends said I would not like that kind of job. Wherever I went people laughed at my accent and I began to wonder why I ever had come to New York. The prospect of going to school was not enough to cancel out my disappointment.

My classmate told me to stop asking people what they did for a living. The musicians I met and the pretty girls I saw on the street late at night who, I was told, were show girls seemed to be the only Negroes I knew who were proud of their jobs.

I went to the stores on 125th Street, the shopping center for Harlem, but all of the salesgirls were white. And I did not see any Negroes working in the department stores downtown.

I rode on the subway and sat wherever I wanted. I ate in restaurants and drank sodas at the lunch counters downtown, too. I did not see any signs saying "colored" or "white" but a few days after I came to New York I learned that these signs were stamped on the minds of many of the men concerned with employment. For the first time in my life I was thrown into contact with "working people" and I began to suspect that most of the professional people I knew would have felt just as lost as I did. My friends did not encourage me to go to any of the Negro papers. They said I would never make any money that way and I knew I had to have money to live and to go to school.

Gladys Hunter, who stood with me when I was baptized, was teaching in one of the Harlem schools conducted by the Sisters of the Blessed Sacrament. During her vacations Gladys worked for one of the large chain restaurants. My money was gone and Gladys suggested that I take a job as a waitress at a Barclay Street store. My rent was due and though I wondered what the people in Birmingham would have said if they had known, I had no alternative. I kept reminding myself that Mama often said, "Honest labor is no disgrace."

It was difficult for me to understand the curt chatter of the customers and more difficult for them to understand my relaxed drawl. I never laughed at them, though many of them made no attempt to conceal their amusement when I spoke. I had never seen so many people rushing around as poured in and out of the store during lunchtime. I moved slowly and it took me a few days to understand that fewer customers meant fewer tips.

My feet became tender and swollen from long hours of standing and I had to go to bed each evening as soon as I got home. Each time I counted my daily tips I was reminded that it would take me a long, long time to save the $1,057 which the information bulletin listed as the minimum estimate of expenses for one year of journalism at Columbia. Two weeks of supporting myself in New York forced me to concede defeat. I knew I would have to wait another year before I registered for the course that had lured me to New York.

My expenses seemed exorbitant, but this was because my earnings were so meager. Lucille had secured a room for me with a family from Honduras, who had only been in New York a few years. The older brother, Bobby Ysaguirre, a musician, was seldom home, and his sister, Florence, ran the household. Mother Ysaguirre was a Carib Indian whose children had been fathered by a Spaniard who spoke "real Castile." Her two grandchildren, Doris and Constance, supplied the homelike atmosphere to which I was accustomed.

It was Mother Ysaguirre who bathed my swollen feet each night and showed me how to stretch the few dollars I brought home. Though her English was broken and mine was Alabama-grown, we had no difficulty understanding each other. She introduced me to tropical foods which were cheap and filling, and initiated me into the art of bargaining with shopkeepers.

Flo, as they called her daughter, was an excellent pianist and life in the six-room apartment revolved around the grand piano which almost filled the living room. I usually sang to Flo's accompaniment. It was not long before we had an audience of young men who came visiting.

I soon learned that courtship in New York was different from courtship in Alabama. With the exception of Bill, who lived nearby, the young men made no attempt to hide their ultimate intentions, which did not include marriage. But I was twenty years old, weighed 118 lbs., and felt equal to the occasion.

I was fascinated by the beautifully dressed women I saw on the streets of New York. The waitresses with whom I worked only averaged a few dollars more than I brought home, but they dressed even more expensively than older teachers I had known in Birmingham, who had unlimited credit. After I paid carfare and room rent, and bought food each week, I despaired of ever having enough money to buy a dress. I was curious about how other self-supporting women managed and instead of asking one of them, I admitted my curiosity to a young man whom I had many reasons to trust. He was also a Southerner and one of the few Catholic men I knew.

"Most of them have help." He laughed in a way I did not understand then. He went on to tell me that most women in New York could dress well because they lived with their families, were married, or had some other source of income.

"There must be other women in New York like me," I persisted.

"That gives me an idea." He looked at me closely. "I may have something good for you."

"A good job?" I jumped at the suggestion. "What is it? What do I have to do?"

"You just wait. I'll have to talk it over with someone, but I'll let you know in a few days," he promised.

I told Mother Ysaguirre and Flo about the "good job" I was expecting and walked around in a state of expectation. It was the next weekend before my friend called. Everything was arranged, he said, so we were to celebrate my good luck by going to dinner and the theater. All the time we were downtown, my friend was vague about the details of my new job. He said he would give me the name of the woman I was to call when we got home. I asked about the nature of my duites but he said she would tell me everything, including how much money I would make. We were standing at the Ysaguirres' door when he told me about the blond, blue-eyed girl he was engaged to and that she had a benefactor who was a wealthy white broker. The broker had a business associate who wanted a girl, too. "Someone like you, you can pass," he said. "And who knows how to keep her mouth shut."

My feet were hurting, anyway, so all I had to do was pull off one shoe and advance on my unsuspecting friend, who had made such a fool of me. He also made good time down the four flights of steps.

Only Negro waitresses were employed in the restaurant where I worked. I was the youngest in the group and they knew all the tricks of getting the best stations and the best customers. The lunch hour, when the surrounding buildings dumped many of their occupants into our store, was the busiest time. Though my "Yes, ma'am," and "No, sir," made most of the customers laugh, my speech was also a mark of distinction. Within a few weeks I had built up a following of the more leisurely customers—all male. Even so, I never felt comfortable when they called me "Honey Chile" or greeted me with "How're yo' all today?"

My cousin, Edward Hutchinson, was finishing his course at Meharry Medical College in Nashville, and had been working in and out of New York that summer. He came to see me and told me that money was "getting tight" everywhere. I did not pay much attention to what he said until September 26, my birthday, when we heard the first serious talk about the Wall Street market. My customers seemed more preoccupied at each meal and my tips suffered. Then came the day in October when the newsboys on the streets shouted: "Extra! Read all about the Wall Street CRASH!"

For the next few days, nobody joked with me when they came in the store. Groups of men bunched around tables and ordered extra coffee. They sat and smoked longer than usual but they left smaller tips. A week or two passed and I was forced to start looking for another job.

Bill worked at the College Station branch post office around the corner from my St. Nicholas Avenue address. During World War I, Bill had lied about his age in order to enlist and when I met him in 1929 he was still saving money to go back to medical school. He and Sam, another cousin, had an apartment on Bradhurst Avenue. A young woman around my age, who was distantly related to Bill and Sam, kept house for them. Just before I met him Bill had been jilted by a girl he loved and from the start our conversation turned to books and our respective ambitions. After I met Bill's family, most of my Sundays were spent at their apartment in an easy chair with the books Bill lent me on a table at my elbow. I would go straight to their house after I left Mass at St. Charles' and breakfast was always waiting.

Bill and his family tried to be helpful when I started looking for another job. Sam read through the help-wanted sections and marked the jobs he thought would be of interest to me. Invariably, these ads stated that only white or Ameri-

can females need apply. Sam and Bill spent long anxious
hours telling me that I was "American" and there was
nothing wrong about my answering an ad for a "young
white woman" because I was young and my skin was white.
They lost patience when I said I did not want to sail under
false colors and I felt hurt because they did not understand.

I continued to write "Negro" in the space on job applica-
tions opposite "nationality." I became accustomed to the
change in expressions when interviewers saw the word
Negro. Smiles froze and receptions which had been cordial
became curt. Then came the stock reply: "We don't have
anything today, but we'll keep your application on file,"
or "We will get in touch with you as soon as there's a vac-
ancy."

Flo, who was an elevator operator in one of New York's
oldest department stores, knew I was broke and she got me
a job where she worked. The elevator girls were much
more congenial than the waitresses and when Bill invited
me to my first formal dance in New York, they shopped all
over the store to make sure I was correctly dressed for the
occasion. Flo did not tell me until the day we found the
blue satin gown I finally selected that this party would be
the first affair Bill had attended since his girl friend married.
I could not afford evening slippers and one of the girls lent
a pair of hers. I wore a triple A and my friend's slippers
were C width, but they had to serve the purpose. Before I
left the store, the girls insisted that I let them see how the
evening dress looked on me and I became alarmed over its
low cut. Mama had warned me not to pull off my knit
undershirt during cold weather. She said she knew too
many people who had "gone into the decline" as a result of
not wearing enough clothes after changing climates.

The night of the affair, Mother Ysaguirre solved this
problem by massaging my arms and shoulders with alcohol,

assuring me that I would not catch cold. I made my New York debut at the old New Star Casino.

Monotony is one of the evils that dog an operator on a bank of slow electric elevators. Most of the customers knew that a clause in the founder's will had stipulated that only Negro men and women should be employed as elevator operators in the store. On slow days when the up and down motion of the elevator was lulling me to sleep, some customer usually pulled me out of my lethargy by asking, "Who was white? Your mother or your father?" In the beginning, I tried to explain my parentage, even when some frustrated bargain hunter said, "Did your father and mother really get married?"

The girls who came to relieve me heard one or two of these quiz sessions and gave me some sound advice. They told me that when the next customer asked "Who was white?" I should say: "My mother." At least that answer made them catch their breath, though many of them could not resist the urge to ask me the name of the shop where I got my permanent wave. I resented that more than the inquiries about my parentage, because all my life I had been trying to brush the waves out of my hair and they had persisted in spite of the hair tonic and water I used to try and get rid of them.

Most of the Rock Castle girls I met in New York had married. After Gladys Hunter added Brauer to her name and moved to Long Island I felt more alone than ever. My friend who lived over the Ysaguirres was a nurse and she was busy most of the time. Though Flo introduced me to her friends they were new and untried. Near me lived, I knew, Beatrice Walker, who had shared that wonderful December

8 in Rock Castle with me, but after I left the elevated train which brought me uptown each night I was so weary I kept postponing the visit I had planned to Bea's home. I had only seen her once on the street; she was so beautiful she reminded me of a brown velvet rose tinged with red. So I promised myself I would stop by her apartment the next Sunday on the way home from Mass.

But I never got to see her. A few nights after I made myself the promise I found a note stuck under my door. Beatrice Walker had been found dead. Another Rock Castle girl wrote that all of the gas jets were on when they found her, but she had set her canary outside the door of her apartment before she lay down.

Death has a way of suggesting an inventory, and I had to face the fact I could expect to be laid off any day. Already there had been cuts and we had heard that only a skeleton staff would be retained. Almost every night, Mother Ysaguirre told us about someone in the building who had lost a job.

People who had never "taken in roomers" began letting it be known that they had a vacant room. As men lost their jobs mothers who had been staying home found part-time work as house maids. I heard a lot of talk about the Negro being "the last to be hired and the first to be fired." Yet I was surprised at first that suicides were much more common among the whites until I realized that my people were used to hard times and that they were experienced in finding ways to dispel the fear, in "laughing to keep from crying." When I mentioned the fact that I had heard of not a single wedding or funeral, other than Bea's, a friend told me that few Negroes had enough money to get married and caskets were too expensive for them to consider dying.

Though the Ysaguirres treated me like a member of the

family, I did not want to impose on their generosity. The school year was coming to a close and it looked as if another year would come and go before I could register. I had no energy for writing, and I was bored with the Saturday night parties my friends gave because I knew I needed a new job and new interests. And I never worried too much until the last dollar was broken.

Jobs for Negroes were few and hard to find during the summer of 1930 and I seemed to have a talent for arriving on the spot just as the "No Help Wanted" sign was hung out. But among the memories of these uncertain days of employment agency lines, hot-dog stands, and apples that I bought from men who stood on corners singing "Brother, Can You Spare a Dime?" are also little acts of human kindness from unexpected sources.

There was a tiny luncheonette on 145th Street at Bradhurst Avenue. After a disappointing day of job hunting I would walk one block west to get my evening meal. When there was only one nickel left I had to decide between a hot dog or a glass of milk. The West Indian girl who served as waitress and short-order cook was lacking in the social graces, but she was an expert at judging human nature. She watched me grow shabbier and hungrier each day as we grew friendlier. Each morning she would save me a paper that someone had left on the counter. She insisted that I eat even when I tried to tell her I did not have money for the morning toast or evening frankfurter and dismissed my protests with a frown so that she could serve a paying customer. Each time she fed me I remembered that if we both were living in Birmingham I would not have been allowed to invite her to my club's formal dance.

One morning she shoved a paper at me. It was folded to the "Help Wanted" page and she had marked an ad for a governess. No racial or religious stipulations were included.

"That one is made to order for you," she laughed, "providing you tell them what they ask and nothing more."

She was right. From the information given in the ad it certainly seemed I had the necessary qualifications for the governess job. I was glad of the Riverside Drive address because I could save a nickel by walking to the interview.

I was greeted by a pleasant, youngish-looking woman with snow-white hair. I could tell she was impressed when I told her about my teaching experience and my newspaper work. Then she told me that her child, a girl of twelve, had received a brain injury at birth. She was unable to take care of any of her body needs and required constant care, which meant the governess had to sleep in the room with her. The child was also given to seizures or fits and whoever cared for her had to know what to do in these emergencies. It was a grim picture, but I was broke, my rent was due, and there was a piece of cardboard over the hole in one of my shoes. When the mother asked if I would take the job, I remembered what the waitress had said and agreed to do so before the woman had a chance to ask about my race. She assured me that her husband would abide by her decision.

I missed the Ysaguirres, and there were many unpleasant aspects to the job, but these were forgotten when payday came. I wrote Mama and told her about my young charge and the sorrow the child's condition had caused the parents. I told her that they had not been the least concerned about my racial background and mentioned how I had felt one day when a black woman sat near us on a park bench and the child started screaming because she said she was afraid the black would rub off on her. I insisted, however, that I was going to grit my teeth and stick it out because any Negro who had a job was lucky and I was so sorry for the mother. I put the letter on a chest of drawers I was using, intending to take it to the corner mailbox as soon as the child was asleep. The mother came in the room while I was busy and offered to mail the letter when she went to get a paper.

Two days later the woman came to me in tears. "My husband's business is so bad," she said. "I will have to let you go at the end of next week. You've been such a help I don't know what I will do without you, but I'll write you a good reference."

When I returned to the Ysaguirres I found a letter from Mama. She was pleased that I had a job where I could be of service, but cautioned me about not properly sealing my letters. I realized then that my employers had opened the letter I wrote my mother.

The next ad I answered was another one for a governess. It was placed by one of the few Wall Street brokers who was not broke by that time. He asked me to come in for an interview in his office. A clerk took my name and address as soon as I entered the expensively furnished suite. I was the first of six or seven applicants. The others were all well-dressed, poised white women who sat around the room smoking and reading magazines as though they were waiting for a showing of the latest Parisian fashions.

"This is just a waste of my time, he'll never take me," I thought and was trying to think up an excuse to leave the room when an inner door opened and a red-faced man of medium height with an unruly shock of auburn hair walked out. The clerk handed him the paper with our names on it and pointed out each applicant. He worked from the bottom of the list and I was the last one to be called to the inner office. He stood when I entered the room and motioned me to a chair.

"I could have let all the others go without talking to them," the man said, "because when I looked out there in that room I knew you were the only one who was young enough to get down on the floor with this rough kid of mine." He pointed to a handsomely framed picture of a robust baby boy.

I was so excited I just shook my head when he offered me a cigarette and lighted a cigar for himself as he told me all about his son and what an exceptionally smart and active child he was at the advanced age of two years. "He's talking already and I want you to start teaching him at once. What do you think?" he asked.

I explained that I had taught fourth and fifth grades and my experience with two-year-olds had been limited. "But I'll do my best," I promised.

Salary, working hours, and conditions were settled, and I was getting happier by the second when my new employer made an admission. "You know," he leaned over and spoke softly as he looked in the direction of the clerk who was visible through the open door, "when you talked with me over the telephone you sounded like a darky."

"A darky?"

"Yes, all of you Southerners do. Particularly the ones from Alabama. Take Tom Heflin, for instance. He sounds just like my darky cook. I knew another man from Alabama once..." He went on and on.

I thought about all that Bill and his family had told me. I tried to keep my mouth shut, as my waitress friend said I should. My eyes never left the face of the man before me, but in my mind I was appraising a weekly pay check, a summer in Long Beach rolling on the sand with the baby whose picture rested on the desk, then a comfortable winter in a Park Avenue apartment with a warm coat, warm gloves, and shoes without cardboard over the holes. I even saw a bank account on which I would write the check which would enable me to go back to school.

When my daydream ended, he was saying, "With all their faults, you have to admit the darkies are loyal, though. Now take our cook . . ."

"I'm afraid you have made a mistake." I spoke quietly. "I *am* a Negro. You did not ask or I would have told you."

"You—you can't be!" he insisted as he left his chair and closed the door. "You just can't be! Look," he pulled back his sleeve baring a portion of his arm. "You are whiter than I am."

"I'm fairer than you, but I am still a Negro. Does it make that much difference?"

"Well, now," he began, "I'll have to take that up with my wife. Don't think I don't like the darkies, er, the Negroes. They are fine people! We treat our cook just like one of the family. It's just that we never thought of having a Negro governess for my son. But you leave it to me. I'll discuss the matter with my wife tonight and call you the first thing in the morning. I'm sure it will be all right. You'll hear from me tomorrow morning!" he called as I walked through the outer door, knowing he would not call.

I took the El to 145th Street, thinking I might sit on one of the benches on Edgecombe Avenue until I felt like facing the Ysaguirres. As I walked the block between Bradhurst and Edgecombe an elderly white woman approached me.

"Isn't it beautiful up there?" She pointed toward upper Edgecombe Avenue and the rows of apartment houses high on the hill overlooking the park. "I used to live there. It was even more beautiful then. But that was before the niggers came. They've ruined everything."

"It may interest you to know"—I advanced on my whipping boy—"that you are talking about me and my mother and my sisters and my father and my grandmother!" I screamed.

The woman ran up the hill toward St. Nicholas Avenue; a crowd of people quickly gathered around me.

"What happened? Did she try to rob you?" asked one of

the men who had eaten with me at the luncheonette down the street.

"Nothing. It was nothing," I answered as the people looked at me in astonishment. "I'm just tired of looking at the promised land and then getting pushed away."

My next venture was better organized. When I went to the office of Editor No. 2, I had typed up a work sheet, which I handed him along with a scrapbook containing clippings from the *Truth* and a sample feature story. After an interview which lasted for hours, he offered me a job as a society editor—without salary. When I explained that I had to live off my earnings he assured me that I could get money from the people I wrote about. He laughed when I insisted that such an arrangement was a violation of journalistic ethics. We left his office at the same time and he offered to drive me home. Instead, he drove up the Speedway to a roadside rendezvous and I came home via bus and trolley car.

The next week when his paper came out with the core of my sample feature woven into an article which carried his by-line, neither Johnny, Ray, nor Ted made the usual charge that I was "all worked up over nothing." When I told them what had happened, Ray was angry, but Ted and Johnny tried to answer the questions that were bothering me.

When I asked why I ran into so many embarrassing situations Ted said he thought my southern manner of open friendliness was misleading. He said I should be more direct and strictly professional.

"Living alone," he added, "is another strike against you."

Johnny, who spared few words, leaned back in a wing chair and blew smoke rings from a big cigar. "Men look at you," he said, "then they listen to you talk. By that time, they've seen the cornshucks that are still in your hair and they decide you're a natural pushover."

The boys had to draw pictures before I understood the important principles of male psychology which they were trying to explain to me, and realized I had to learn how to live in a world dominated by men. I determined to build up a stern exterior as an aid to survival.

While I was perfecting this new approach, the flame which had been ignited the night I saw a white policeman kick Shorty was rekindled. The mailman rang impatiently the morning he brought the airmail-special-delivery letter which supplied the match. I had just had a letter from Mama the day before and I wondered why she had written again. When I tore the letter open, a clipping dropped to the floor. As I stooped to pick it up I read: " . . . Edna Davis . . . a Negro woman . . . fatally wounded by Detective . . . for resisting an officer of the law. . . ."

"Edna Davis," I thought. "This can't be *my* Edna Davis. She's coming to live with me as soon as I can send for her. She can't be dead. She's only eighteen years old."

My feet and legs felt numb, the way they had felt the night Papa was dying and I tried to run back to him. I managed to get to the living room and sank down on a chair. I read the letter. It was, I soon realized, my Edna. Mama had pieced the details together as best she could. She wrote that Edna had gone to a party in a section of the city where we seldom ventured. During the evening, a woman Edna barely knew became intoxicated and when one of the other guests lost a pocketbook the drunken woman was accused. When the woman failed to return the pocketbook she was alleged to have stolen, her accusers attempted to beat her. It was then that Edna got into the fight.

According to the story Mama picked up, Edna knew her drunken friend was innocent because she had seen another guest actually steal the missing purse. Instead of exposing the thief, Edna fought off the attackers. Three inches short of being six feet tall, with a frame which was covered with sound flesh, Edna had always reminded me of Africa at its proudest. When angered, she was powerful and it was not difficult for me to imagine her beating off a crowd of revelers. Then she took the woman to the house where she had gone to live after I left Birmingham. It was said that the angered party crowd called police headquarters and told the officers to go to "913 North Sixteenth Street. And you'd better go armed to kill because there's a bad Negro woman there."

When the policeman walked into Edna's house she was in the act of changing her shoes. We had often laughed about the way Edna insisted upon wearing shoes one or two sizes too small, and her first act upon entering the house was to slip off her shoes and put on house slippers.

That night when the officers said, "Put up your hands!" Edna, leaning over her shoes, looked up to see what was happening. A bullet tore through her forehead, right between the eyes. And Edna Davis, aged eighteen, died before she had ever lived.

"They say she died calling your name," Mama wrote. "I had to get down on my knees and thank God that you were not here, because if you had been in Birmingham that night I know they would have had to kill you, too."

I closed my eyes and relived the day when I had told Edna I was going to New York. We sat looking at each other for awhile; finally, she said: "You go ahead and study. Maybe you'll get to be a real good writer. But be sure to send for me as soon as you get a place. You need me to look after you." This I had remembered all during the hungry, jobless days. Now Edna was dead and I could never send for her.

Now I really knew hate. I hated the white man who had killed Edna. I hated the Negroes who had sent the police to her home and, secretly, I hated myself because I had left her in Birmingham to be killed. Mama used to explain my ability to weep easily by saying that God forgot to close Papa's tear ducts and he had passed the trouble on to me. But my eyes were dry that day when Mabel, who for six years, had been my constant friend and companion, pushed open the door I had left ajar and walked in. I was still sitting on the side of the chair with the clipping in my hand. Without speaking, I handed it to Mabel.

Although Mabel was not a Negro, she shared my indignation. She knew how much Edna had meant to me and her sympathy broke my silence. She closed the windows and let me scream out my hatred for Edna's murderer and the system which allowed him to go free. Mabel got other friends to sit with me when she had to leave. She said later that they had tried to talk to console me, to tell me that I could not carry the problem on my back. But they were mere shadows and the only voice I could hear was Edna's, calling out to me for help, too late.

I thought of all the white friends I had known and loved as a child. How, I asked myself, could they live year after year in a town where men who had been entrusted with the task of upholding the law of the land openly defied God's laws and murdered helpless men and women whenever they chose? How, I asked, could decent people see these things and not cry out?

It was weeks before I could follow a normal routine. I only laughed when Mama wrote that the NAACP was investigating the circumstances surrounding Edna's death, because I knew no white man would be punished in Alabama for killing a Negro woman. I went to the Sacraments but found no peace because the hate in my heart was sinful. I stopped writing Sister Timothy and the other white nuns who had taught me. I went to parties, dances, night clubs, and after-hours spots. Every white man I met became Edna's murderer. I half-prayed, half-hated, half-ate, and slept only when I was too exhausted to do otherwise—until another letter came.

When I read the second clipping I could only say, "God forgive me!" The detective who killed Edna had in turn been killed by an alleged criminal in the act of "resisting an officer of the law."

III

PROTEST

Anger and frustration are hard to contain, and black Americans have struck back at their persecutors since the first slave ships crossed the Atlantic. One of the most bloody shipboard rebellions occurred in 1839 on the *Amistad*, bound for the Caribbean with its African cargo. The mutineers eventually turned themselves over to the authorities in New England where they were tried for murder, convicted, and eventually freed by the United States Supreme Court.

Blacks accepted the risks of a revolt as the price of liberty, but the very rumor of an impending conspiracy struck terror in the hearts of whites and prompted harsh counteraction. In August of 1800 Gabriel Prosser and Jack Bowler led 1,000 slaves to within six miles of Richmond, but a violent storm and two informers helped to end the uprising. Within a short time, scores of slaves were arrested, and thirty-five executed (including Prosser). For the most part they maintained silence, but one insurgent declared: "I have nothing more to offer than what General Washington would have had to offer, had he been taken by British officers and put to trial by them. I have ventured my life in endeavoring to obtain the liberty of my countrymen, and am a willing sacrifice to their cause." The irony was undoubtedly lost on the terrified white population of Virginia.

In the decade before the war with England, plots against the slave masters were reported and discovered up and down the eastern seaboard. In 1810 a conspiracy was uncovered in Lexington, Kentucky, and the following year more than four hundred rebellious slaves in Louisiana were restrained by federal and state troops. The most elaborate attempt at insurgence was the Denmark Vesey insurrection. Over a period of several years Vesey, a free black, rounded up weapons and followers, and by July, 1822, felt strong enough to attack. Any attempt at so large a rebellion could hardly go by unnoticed, and the white population began to round up suspects. At least 139 Negroes were arrested, forty-seven of whom were condemned. The estimates of the number of slaves involved ran as high as 9,000. Down to and throughout the Civil War, blacks such as Nat Turner expressed their violent abhorrence for the "peculiar institution" by rising up against it.

Significantly more effective as a protest against slavery was the highly organized Underground Railroad. A striking example of black and white cooperation, the Railroad was in use before 1800, its network spreading wider and wider but always north. The most courageous conductor of the Railroad was Harriet Tubman. It is said that she personally spirited more than three hundred slaves out of the South. Between 1810 and 1850, the slaveholding states probably lost 100,000 runaway blacks valued at more than thirty million dollars. To minimize risk, the Underground Railroad almost always operated at night. The runaways would take supplies from their masters and disguise themselves as best they could. The conductors provided covered wagons, closed carriages, and farm wagons with secret compartments for their human cargo. "Stations," where those fleeing could rest, eat and take shelter, were ten to twenty miles apart. During the day the runaways were hidden in barns, attics, caves, and other places. Meanwhile, the word was "telegraphed" by messengers to succeeding stations that the fugitives were on their way.

Far from playing the passive role in the Civil War that many historians have attributed to them, Negroes were active participants from the beginning. Barred from actual military duty until 1862, most of the free blacks and escaped slaves worked as laborers in the war effort. Eventually 200,000 Negroes fought in the Union army and navy. Historian James McPherson feels that "without their help, the North could not have won the war as soon as it did, and perhaps it could not have won at all."

Confident that equality was not far off, Negroes began the post-Civil War years optimistically. They soon learned it would take more than an Emancipation Proclamation to bring them into the mainstream of American life. Continued belief in white supremacy, jim-crow legislation, constitutional disenfranchisement, lynchings, frequent race riots soon convinced even the most sanguine black men that they were not welcome participants in the American community.

In this climate the NAACP was formed in 1910. Within the first year of its existence, it launched a program to widen industrial opportunities for Negroes, to seek greater police protection for blacks in the South, and to carry on a crusade against lynching and racial lawlessness. Within fifteen years the legal committee had won three important civil rights decisions before the United States Supreme Court. *Guinn* v. *United States* was the most significant because it declared the Oklahoma and Maryland "grandfather clauses" repugnant to the Fifteenth Amendment of the U. S. Constitution. Over the years resistance by militant whites continued and intensified. Determined to stifle any real effects of the 1954 school-desegregation decision, members of white citizens' councils called on their members to use economic reprisals against those Negroes who were active in the fight to desegregate schools. In retaliation, blacks began to boycott businesses operated by members of the councils. The Montgomery bus boycott, which Dr. Martin Luther King describes in this section, set an example that was followed in other cities.

By this time the black revolution was so widespread that many groups with diverse goals and different ideas about implementing these goals were competing with one another. Elijah Muhammad's Black Muslims, who had preached complete racial separation since 1930, continued to attract followers, and the Congress of Racial Equality (founded in 1942) intensified its efforts to secure equal rights for blacks by sending Freedom Riders into the South to test segregation laws. Spurred on by success, other groups, such as the new Student Nonviolent Coordinating Committee, joined in and sent more than a thousand volunteers on Freedom Rides throughout the South. Voter-registration drives were conducted, and people like Gus Courts could finally cast their ballots without intimidation.

While such successes were welcomed, between 1949 and 1964 the relative participation of Negroes in the total economic life of the country declined. Unemployment was up, blacks were still unable to secure adequate housing or provide a wholesome environment for their families. The bitter frustration that resulted erupted in a race riot far more serious than the Detroit riot of 1943. The reasons were the same but this time the locale was Watts, Los Angeles, and the year 1965. By the time the smoke had cleared from the looting and burning, the toll had reached thirty-four dead, 1,032 injured, and 3,952 arrested. Property damage was estimated at $40 million.

The most revolutionary of the black organizations, the Black Panther Party, was founded a year later. The Panthers, who believe in arming blacks for their own defense, provide an example of a people no longer willing to support a system which denies them the rights and benefits of that system, yet expects them to obey its laws.

1

FROM

Nat Turner's Confession

by Nat Turner
(1800–1831)

*Slave insurrections occurred frequently enough in different
sections of the slave states to cause alarm, but Nat Turner's
revolt spread terror throughout the entire South. On a hot
night during the summer of 1831, in Southampton County,
Virginia, Turner and his band went from house to house
systematically murdering every white person in their path.
Before their bloody spree was over, sixty whites had been
clubbed, stabbed, or shot by Turner's group, and over one
hundred blacks had been killed by those attempting to put
down the revolt.*

*As the initial band led by Turner went to each plantation
or farm, its ranks swelled to sixty or seventy. Of that number
thirteen were eventually hanged, including Turner, and the
rest either jailed or deported. Before his execution, Turner
dictated the following "confession" to his attorney, Thomas*

Gray, whose questions and comments are included in the text.

SIR, you have asked me to give a history of the motives which induced me to undertake the late insurrection, as you call it. To do so I must go back to the days of my infancy, and even before I was born. I was thirty-one years of age the 2nd of October last and born the property of Benj. Turner, of this county. In my childhood a circumstance occurred which made an indelible impression on my mind and laid the groundwork of that enthusiasm which has terminated so fatally to many both white and black, and for which I am about to atone at the gallows. It is here necessary to relate this circumstance, trifling as it may seem; it was the commencement of that belief which has grown with time, and even now, sir, in this dungeon, helpless and forsaken as I am, I cannot divest myself of. Being at play with other children, when three or four years old, I was telling them something, which my mother overhearing, said it had happened before I was born; I stuck to my story, however, and related some things which went in the opinion to confirm it; others being called on were greatly astonished, knowing that these things had happened, and caused them to say in my hearing, I surely would be a prophet, as the Lord had shown me things that had happened before my birth. And my father and mother strengthened me in this my first impression, saying in my presence, I was intended for some great purpose, which they had always thought from certain marks on my head and breast [a parcel of excrescences which I believe are not at all uncommon, particularly among Negroes, as I have seen several with the same. In this case he had either cut them off, or they have nearly disappeared].

My grandmother, who was very religious and to whom I

was much attached, my master, who belonged to the church, and other religious persons who visited the house, and whom I often saw at prayers, noticing the singularity of my manners, I suppose, and my uncommon intelligence for a child, remarked I had too much sense to be raised and if I was, I would never be of any service to anyone as a slave. To a mind like mine, restless, inquisitive and observant of everything that was passing, it was easy to suppose that religion was the subject to which it would be directed, and although this subject principally occupied my thoughts, there was nothing that I saw or heard of to which my attention was not directed. The manner in which I learned to read and write not only had great influence on my own mind—as I acquired it with the most perfect ease; so much so, that I have no recollection whatever of learning the alphabet—but to the astonishment of the family, one day, when a book was shown to me to keep me from crying, I began spelling the names of different objects. This was a source of wonder to all in the neighborhood, particularly the blacks; and this learning was constantly improved at all opportunities. When I got large enough to go to work, while employed, I was reflecting on many things that would present themselves to my imagination, and, whenever an opportunity occurred of looking at a book, when the school children were getting their lessons, I would find many things that the fertility of my own imagination had depicted to me before; all my time not devoted to my master's service was spent either in prayer, or in making experiments in casting different things in molds made of earth, in attempting to make paper, gunpowder, and many other experiments that, although I could not perfect, yet convinced me of its practicability if I had the means.

I was not addicted to stealing in my youth, nor have ever been. Yet such was the confidence of the Negroes in the neighborhood, even at this early period of my life, in my superior judgment, that they would often carry me with them when they were going on any roguery, to plan for them. Growing up among them, with this confidence in my superior judgment, and when this, in their opinions, was perfected by Divine inspiration, from the circumstances already alluded to in my infancy, and which belief was ever afterwards zealously inculcated by the austerity of my life and manners, which became the subject of remark with white and black.

Having soon discovered to be great, I must appear so and, therefore, studiously avoided mixing in society and wrapped myself in mystery, devoting my time to fasting and prayer. By this time, having arrived to man's estate and hearing the Scriptures commented on at meetings, I was struck with that particular passage which says: "Seek ye the kingdom of Heaven and all things shall be added unto you." I reflected much on this passage and prayed daily for light on this subject: As I was praying one day at my plow, the Spirit spoke to me, saying "Seek ye the kingdom of Heaven and all things shall be added unto you."

Question: What do you mean by the Spirit?

Answer: The Spirit that spoke to the prophets in former days.

And I was greatly astonished and for two years prayed continually, whenever my duty would permit. And then again I had the same revelation, which fully confirmed me in the impression that I was ordained for some great purpose in the hands of the Almighty.

Several years rolled round, in which many events occurred to strengthen me in this belief. At this time I reverted in my mind to the remarks made of me in my childhood, and the things that had been shown me, and as it had been said of me in my childhood by those by whom I had been taught to pray, both white and black, and in whom I had the greatest confidence, that I had too much sense to be raised, and if I was I would never be of any use to anyone as a slave. Now finding I had arrived to man's estate and was a slave, and these revelations being made known to me, I began to direct my attention to this great object, to fulfill the purpose for which, by this time, I felt assured I was intended. Knowing the influence I had obtained over the minds of my fellow servants (not by the means of conjuring and such like tricks, for to them I always spoke of such things with contempt), but by the communion of the Spirit whose revelations I often communicated to them, and they believed and said my wisdom came from God. I now began to prepare them for my purpose, by telling them something was about to happen that would terminate in fulfilling the great promise that had been made to me.

About this time I was placed under an overseer, from whom I ran away; and after remaining in the woods thirty days, I returned, to the astonishment of the Negroes on the plantation, who thought I had made my escape to some other part of the country, as my father had done before. But the reason of my return was, that the Spirit appeared to me and said I had my wishes directed to the things of this world, and not to the kingdom of Heaven, and that I should return to the service of my earthly master, "For he who knoweth his Master's will, and doeth it not, shall be beaten with many stripes, and thus have I chastened you." And the Negroes found fault, and murmured against me, saying that if they had my sense they would not serve any master in the world. And about this time I had a vision, and I saw white spirits and black spirits engaged in battle, and the sun was darkened, the thunder rolled in the heavens, and blood flowed in streams, and I heard a voice saying, "Such is your luck, such you are called to see, and let it come rough or smooth, you must surely bear it."

I now withdrew myself as much as my situation would permit from the intercourse of my fellow servants, for the avowed purpose of serving the Spirit more fully, and it appeared to me and reminded me of the things it had already shown me, and that it would then reveal to me the knowledge of the elements, the revolution of the planets; the planets, the operation of tides, and changes of the seasons. After this revelation in the year 1825 and the knowledge of the elements being made known to me, I sought more than ever to obtain true holiness before the great day of judgment should appear, and then I began to receive the true knowledge of faith. And from the first steps of righteousness until the last, was I made perfect; and the Holy Ghost was with me, and said "Behold me as I stand in the Heavens," and I looked and saw the forms of men in different attitudes, and there were lights in the sky to which the children of darkness gave other names than what they really were, for they were the lights of the Savior's hands, stretched forth from east to west, even as they were extended on the cross on Calvary for the redemption of sinners. And I wondered greatly at these miracles, and prayed to be informed of a certainty of the meaning thereof, and shortly afterwards, while laboring in the field, I discovered drops of blood on the corn, as though it were dew from heaven, and I communicated it to many, both white and black in the neighborhood; and I then found on the leaves in the woods hieroglyphic characters and numbers, with the forms of men in different attitudes, portrayed in blood, and representing the figures I had seen before in the heavens. And now the Holy Ghost had revealed itself to me and made plain the miracles it had shown me. For as the blood of Christ had been shed on this earth, and had ascended to heaven for the salvation of sinners, and was now returning to earth again in the form of dew, and as the leaves on the trees bore the impression of the figures I had seen in the heavens, it was plain to me that the Savior was about to lay down the yoke He had borne for the sins of men, and the great day of judgment was at hand.

About this time, I told these things to a white man (Etheldred T. Brantley) on whom it had a wonderful effect, and he ceased from his wickedness and was attacked immediately with a cutaneous eruption, and blood oozed from the pores of his skin, and after praying and fasting nine days, he was healed, and the Spirit appeared to me again and said, as the Savior had been baptized, so should we be also; and when the white people would not let us be baptized by the church, we went down into the water together, in the sight of many who reviled us, and were baptized by the Spirit. After this I rejoiced greatly, and gave thanks to God. And on May 12, 1828, I heard a loud noise in the heavens, and the Spirit instantly appeared to me and said the Serpent was loosened, and Christ had laid down the yoke He had borne for the sins of men, and that I should take it on and fight against the Serpent, for the time was fast approaching, when the first should be last and the last should be first.

Question: Do you not find yourself mistaken now?

Answer: Was not Christ crucified?

And by signs in the heavens that it would make known to me when I should commence the great work, and until the first sign appeared, I should conceal it from the knowledge of men. And on the appearance of the sign (the eclipse of the sun last February), I should arise and prepare myself and slay my enemies with their own weapons. And immediately on the sign appearing in the heavens, the seal was removed from my lips, and I communicated the great work laid out for me to do, to four in whom I had the greatest confidence (Henry, Hark, Nelson, and Sam). It was intended by us to have begun the work of death on the

4th of July last. Many were the plans formed and rejected by us, and it affected my mind to such a degree that I fell sick, and the time passed without our coming to any determination how to commence; still forming new schemes and rejecting them, when the sign appeared again, which determined me not to wait longer.

Since the commencement of 1830, I had been living with Mr. Joseph Travis, who was to me a kind master and placed the greatest confidence in me; in fact, I had no cause to complain of his treatment to me. On Saturday evening, the 20th of August, it was agreed between Henry, Hark and myself, to prepare a dinner the next day for the men we expected, and then to concert a plan, as we had not yet determined on any. Hark on the following morning brought a pig, and Henry Brandy, and being joined by Sam, Nelson, Will, and Jack, they prepared in the woods a dinner, where, about three o'clock, I joined them.

Question: Why were you so backward in joining them?

Answer: The same reason that had caused me not to mix with them for years before.

I saluted them on coming up and asked Will how came he there; he answered, his life was worth no more than others, and his liberty as dear to him. I asked him if he thought to obtain it. He said he would, or lose his life. This was enough to put him in full confidence. Jack, I knew, was only a tool in the hands of Hark, it was quickly agreed we should commence at home (Mr. J. Travis') on that night, and until we had armed and equipped ourselves and gathered sufficient force, neither age nor sex was to be spared (which was invariably adhered to).

We remained at the feast until about two hours in the night, when we went to the house and found Austin; they all went to the cider press and drank, except myself. On returning to the house, Hark went to the door with an axe, for the purpose of breaking it open, as we knew we were strong enough to murder the family, if they were awaked by the noise; but, reflecting that it might create an alarm in the neighborhood, we determined to enter the house secretly and murder them while sleeping. Hark got a ladder and set it against the chimney on which I ascended and, hoisting a window, entered and came down stairs, unbarred the door, and removed the guns from their places. It was then observed that I must spill the first blood. On which, armed with a hatchet and accompanied by Will, I entered my master's chamber. It being dark, I could not give a death blow; the hatchet glanced from his head; he sprang from the bed and called his wife. It was his last word. Will laid him dead with a blow of his axe, and Mrs. Travis shared the same fate, as she lay in bed.

The murder of this family, five in number, was the work of a moment, not one of them awoke; there was a little infant, sleeping in a cradle, that was forgotten until we had left the house and gone some distance, when Henry and Will returned and killed it; we got here four guns that would shoot and several old muskets, with a pound or two of powder. We remained some time at the barn, where we paraded; I formed them in a line as soldiers and, after carrying them through all the maneuvers I was master of, marched them off to Mr. Salathul Francis', about 600 yards distant. Sam and Will went to the door and knocked. Mr. Francis asked who was there; Sam replied it was him and he had a letter for him, on which he got up and came to the door; they immediately seized him, and dragging him out a little from the door, he was dispatched by repeated blows on the head; there was no other white person in the family.

We started from there for Mrs. Reese's, maintaining the most perfect silence on our march, where finding the door unlocked, we entered and murdered Mrs. Reese in her bed, while sleeping; her son awoke, but it was only to sleep the sleep of death. He had only time to say who is that, and he was no more. From Mrs. Reese's we went to Mrs. Turner's, a mile distant, which we reached about sunrise on Monday morning. Henry, Austin, and Sam went to the still, where, finding Mr. Peebles, Austin shot him, and the rest of us went to the house; as we approached, the family discovered us and shut the door. Vain hope! Will, with one stroke of his axe, opened it, and we entered and found Mrs. Turner and Mrs. Newsome in the middle of a room almost frightened to death. Will immediately killed Mrs. Turner with one blow of his axe. I took Mrs. Newsome by the hand, and with the sword I had when I was apprehended, I struck her several blows over the head, but not being able to kill her, as the sword was dull. Will turned around and discovering it, dispatched her also.

A general destruction of property and search for money and ammunition always succeeded the murders. By this time my company amounted to fifteen, and nine men mounted, who started for Mrs. Whitehead's (the other six were to go through a by way to Mr. Bryant's and rejoin us at Mrs. Whitehead's). As we approached the house we discovered Mr. Richard Whitehead standing in the cotton patch, near the lane fence; we called him over into the lane, and Will, the executioner, was near at hand, with his fatal axe, to send him to an untimely grave. As we pushed on to the house, I discovered some one run round the garden, and, thinking it was some of the white family, I pursued them, but finding it was a servant girl belonging to the house, I returned to commence the work of death, but they whom I left had not been idle; all the family were already murdered but Mrs. Whitehead and her daughter Margaret. As I came round to the door I saw Will pulling Mrs. Whitehead out of the house, and at the step he nearly severed her head from her body with his broad axe. Miss Margaret, when I discovered her, had concealed herself in the corner formed by the projection of the cellar cap from the house; on my approach she fled, but was soon overtaken, and after repeated blows with a sword, I killed her by a blow on the head with a fence rail. By this time, the six who had gone by Mr. Bryant's rejoined us and informed me they had done the work of death assigned them.

We again divided, part going to Mr. Richard Porter's, and from thence to Nathaniel Francis', the others to Mr. Howell Harris' and Mr. T. Doyle's. On my reaching Mr. Porter's, he had escaped with his family. I understood there, that the alarm had already spread, and I immediately returned to bring up those sent to Mr. Doyle's and Mr. Howell Harris', having told them I would join them in that neighborhood. I met these sent to Mr. Doyle's and Mr. Harris' returning, having met Mr. Doyle on the road and killed him; and learning from some one who joined them that Mr. Harris was from home, I immediately pursued the course taken by the party gone on before; but knowing they would complete the work of death and pillage at Mr. Francis' before I could get there, I went to Mr. Peter Edwards', expecting to find them there, but they had been here also. I then went to Mr. John T. Barrow's; they had been here and murdered him. I pursued on their track to Capt. Newit Harris', where I found the greater part mounted and ready to start; the men now amounting to about forty, shouted and hurrahed as I rode up; some were in the yard, loading their guns, others drinking. They said Captain Harris and his family had escaped, the property in the house they destroyed, robbing him of money and other valuables. I ordered them to mount and march instantly, this was about nine or ten o'clock Monday morning.

I proceeded to Mr. Levi Waller's, two or three miles distant. I took my station in the rear, and as it was my object to carry terror and devastation wherever we went, I placed fifteen or twenty of the best mounted and most to be relied on in front, who generally approached the houses as fast as their horses could run; this was for two purposes, to prevent their escape and strike terror to the inhabitants; on this account I never got to the houses, after leaving Mrs. White-head's until the murders were committed, except in one case. I sometimes got in sight in time to see the work of death completed, viewed the mangled bodies as they lay, in silent satisfaction, and immediately started in quest of other victims.

Having murdered Mrs. Waller and ten children, we started for Mr. William Williams'; having killed him and two little boys that were there; while engaged in this, Mrs. Williams fled and got some distance from the house, but she was pursued, overtaken, and compelled to get up behind one of the company, who brought her back, and after showing her the mangled body of her lifeless husband, she was told to get down and lay by his side, where she was shot dead. I then started for Mr. Jacob Williams', where the family were murdered. Here we found a young man named Drury, who had come on business with Mr. Williams; he was pursued, overtaken and shot. Mrs. Vaughan's was the next place we visited, and, after murdering the family here, I determined on starting for Jerusalem. Our number amounted now to fifty or sixty, all mounted and armed with guns, axes, swords, and clubs.

On reaching Mr. James W. Parker's gate, immediately on the road leading to Jerusalem and about three miles distant, it was proposed to me to call there, but I objected, as I knew he was gone to Jerusalem, and my object was to reach there as soon as possible; but some of the men having relations at Mr. Parker's, it was agreed that they might call and get his people. I remained at the gate on the road with seven or eight; the others going across the field to the house about half a mile off. After waiting some time for them, I became impatient and started to the house for them, and on our return we were met by a party of white men, who had pursued our bloodstained track, and who had fired on those at the gate and dispersed them, which I knew nothing of, not having been at that time rejoined by any of them.

Immediately on discovering the whites, I ordered my men to halt and form, as they appeared to be alarmed. The white men, eighteen in number, approached us in about one hundred yards, when one of them fired (this was against the positive orders of Captain Alexander P. Peete, who commanded, and who had directed the men to reserve their fire until within thirty paces). And I discovered about half of them retreating. I then ordered my men to fire and rush on them; the few remaining stood their ground until we approached within fifty yards, when they fired and retreated. We pursued and overtook some of them who we thought we left dead (they were not killed); after pursuing them about two hundred yards and rising a little hill, I discovered they were met by another party, and had halted and were reloading their guns. (This was a small party from Jerusalem who knew the Negroes were in the field and had just tied their horses to await their return to the road knowing that Mr. Parker and family were in Jerusalem, but knew nothing of the party that had gone in with Captain Peete. On hearing the firing they immediately rushed to the spot and arrived just in time to arrest the progress of these barbarous villains and save the lives of their friends and fellow citizens.)

Thinking that those who retreated first, and the party who fired on us at fifty or sixty yards distant, had all only fallen back to meet others with ammunition. As I saw them reloading their guns, and more coming up than I saw at first, and several of my bravest men being wounded, the others became panic struck and scattered over the field; the white men pursued and fired on us several times. Hark had his horse shot under him, and I caught another for him as it was running by me; five or six of my men were wounded, but none left on the field; finding myself defeated here I instantly determined to go through a private way and cross the Nottoway River at the Cypress Bridge, three miles below Jerusalem, and attack that place in the rear, as I expected they would look for me on the other road, and I had a great desire to get there to procure arms and ammunition. After going a short distance in this private way, accompanied by about twenty men, I overtook two or three who told me the others were dispersed in every direction. After trying in vain to collect a sufficient force to proceed to Jerusalem, I determined to return, as I was sure they would make back to their old neighborhoods, where they would rejoin me, make new recruits, and come down again. On my way back, I called at Mrs. Thomas', Mrs. Spencer's, and several other places, the white families having fled; we found no more victims to gratify our thirst for blood. We stopped at Maj. Ridley's quarter for the night, and being joined by four of his men, with the recruits made since my defeat, we mustered now about forty strong.

After placing out sentinels, I laid down to sleep, but was quickly roused by a great racket; starting up, I found some mounted and others in great confusion; one of the sentinels having given the alarm that we were about to be attacked. I ordered some to ride around and reconnoiter, and on their return the others being more alarmed, not knowing who they were, fled in different ways, so that I was reduced to about twenty again, with this I determined to attempt to recruit, and proceed on to rally in the neighborhood I had left. Dr. Blunt's was the nearest house, which we reached just before day; on riding up the yard, Hark fired a gun. We expected Dr. Blunt and his family were at Maj. Ridley's, as I knew there was a company of men there; the gun was fired to ascertain if any of the family were at home; we were immediately fired upon and retreated leaving several of my men. I do not know what became of them, as I never saw them afterwards.

Pursuing our course back and coming in sight of Captain Harris', where we had been the day before, we discovered a party of white men at the house, on which all deserted me but two (Jacob and Nat). We concealed ourselves in the woods until near night, when I sent them in search of Henry, Sam, Nelson, and Hark, and directed them to rally all they could at the place we had had our dinner the Sunday before, where they would find me, and I accordingly returned there as soon as it was dark and remained until Wednesday evening, when discovering white men riding around the place as though they were looking for some one, and none of my men joining me, I concluded Jacob and Nat had been taken and compelled to betray me.

On this I gave up all hope for the present; and on Thursday night, after having supplied myself with provisions from Mr. Travis', I scratched a hole under a pile of fence rails in a field, where I concealed myself for six weeks, never leaving my hiding place but for a few minutes in the dead of night to get water, which was very near. Thinking by this time I could venture out, I began to go about in the night and eavesdrop the houses in the neighborhood; pursuing this course for about a fortnight and gathering little or no intelligence, afraid of speaking to any human being, and returning every morning to my cave before the dawn of day. I know not how long I might have led this life, if accident had not betrayed me. A dog in the neighborhood, passing by my hiding place one night while I was out, was attracted by some meat I had in my cave, and crawled in and stole it, and was coming out just as I returned. A few nights after, two Negroes having started to go hunting with the same dog, and passed that way, the dog came again to the place, and having just gone out to walk about, discovered me and barked, on which thinking myself discovered, I spoke to them to beg concealment. On making myself known, they fled from me. Knowing then they would betray me, I immediately left my hiding place and was pursued almost incessantly until I was taken a fortnight afterwards by Mr. Benjamin Phipps, in a little hole I had dug out with my sword, for the purpose of concealment, under the top of a fallen tree. On Mr. Phipps discovering the place of my concealment, he cocked his gun and aimed at me. I requested him not to shoot, and I would give up, upon which he demanded my sword. I delivered it to him, and he brought me to prison. During the time I was pursued, I had many hairbreadth escapes, which your time will not permit you to relate. I am here loaded with chains, and willing to suffer the fate that awaits me.

2

FROM

The Life and Times of Frederick Douglass

by Frederick Douglass
(1817?–1895)

Contrary to belief, whites were not the first abolitionists. Even before the War for Independence, slaves in Massachusetts pressed for their freedom in court. By 1800, many prominent blacks, such as Benjamin Banneker, Prince Hall, and Richard Allen, cried out against the slave trade and urged emancipation. By 1830 there were at least fifty Negro abolitionist organizations located in all the major cities. When the period of militant abolitionism began, black organizations joined forces with abolitionist William Lloyd Garrison and his followers.

Frederick Douglass was the most outstanding black abolitionist. He fled from slavery in 1838 and made his way to New York City. Douglass attended an antislavery convention in Massachusetts in 1841, spoke, and was promptly hired by a number of organizations to lecture on behalf of the

antislavery movement. He was elected president of the New
England Anti-Slavery Society in 1847. No one worked
harder than Frederick Douglass for the Negro people be-
fore, during, and after the Civil War.

ABOUT the time I began my enterprise in Rochester I
chanced to spend a night and a day under the roof of a man
whose character and conversation, and whose objects and
aims in life, made a very deep impression upon my mind
and heart. His name had been mentioned to me by several
prominent Negro men, among whom were the Rev. Henry
Highland Garnet and J. W. Loguen. In speaking of him
their voices would drop to a whisper, and what they said of
him made me very eager to see and to know him.

Fortunately, I was invited to see him in his own house.
At the time to which I now refer this man was a respectable
merchant in a populous and thriving city, and our first
place of meeting was at his store. This was a substantial
brick building on a prominent, busy street. A glance at the
interior, as well as at the massive walls without, gave me
the impression that the owner must be a man of considerable
wealth. My welcome was all that I could have asked. Every
member of the family, young and old, seemed glad to see
me, and I was made much at home in a very little while.

I was, however, a little disappointed with the appearance
of the house and its location. After seeing the fine store I
was prepared to see a fine residence in an eligible locality,
but this conclusion was completely dispelled by actual
observation. In fact, the house was neither commodious nor
elegant, nor its situation desirable. It was a small wooden
building on a back street, in a neighborhood chiefly occupied by laboring men and mechanics; respectable enough, to
be sure, but not quite the place, I thought, where one would

look for the residence of a flourishing and successful merchant.

Plain as was the outside of this man's house, the inside
was plainer. Its furniture would have satisfied a Spartan. It
would take longer to tell what was not in this house than
what was in it. There was an air of plainness about it
which almost suggested destitution. My first meal passed
under the misnomer of tea, though there was nothing about
it resembling the usual significance of that term. It consisted
of beef-soup, cabbage, and potatoes—a meal such as a man
might relish after following the plow all day or performing
a forced march of a dozen miles over a rough road in frosty
weather. Innocent of paint, veneering, varnish, or table-
cloth, the table announced itself unmistakably of pine and
of the plainest workmanship. There was no hired help
visible. The mother, daughters, and sons did the serving,
and did it well. They were evidently used to it, and had no
thought of an impropriety or degradation in being their
own servants. It is said that a house in some measure reflects
the character of its occupants; this one certainly did. In it
there were no disguises, no illusions, no make-believes.
Everything implied stern truth, solid purpose, and rigid
economy.

I was not long in company with the master of this house
before I discovered that he was indeed the master of it, and
was likely to become mine too if I stayed long enough with
him. He fulfilled St. Paul's idea of the head of the family.
His wife believed in him, and his children observed him
with reverence. Whenever he spoke his words commanded
earnest attention. His arguments, which I ventured at some
points to oppose, seemed to convince all; his appeals
touched all, and his will impressed all. Certainly I never felt
myself in the presence of a stronger religious influence than
while in this man's house.

In person he was lean, strong, and sinewy, of the best New England mold, built for times of trouble and fitted to grapple with the flintiest hardships. Clad in plain American woolen, shod in boots of cowhide leather, and wearing a cravat of the same substantial material, under six feet high, less than a hundred and fifty pounds in weight, aged about fifty, he presented a figure straight and symmetrical as a mountain pine. His bearing was singularly impressive. His head was not large, but compact and high. His hair was coarse, strong, slightly gray and closely trimmed, and grew low on his forehead. His face was smoothly shaved, and revealed a strong, square mouth, supported by a broad and prominent chin. His eyes were bluish-gray, and in conversation they were full of light and fire. When on the street, he moved with a long, springing, race-horse step, absorbed by his own reflections, neither seeking nor shunning observation. Such was the man whose name I had heard in whispers; such was the spirit of his house and family; such was the house in which he lived; and such was Captain John Brown, whose name has now passed into history, as that of one of the most marked characters and greatest heroes known to American fame.

After the strong meal already described, Captain Brown cautiously approached the subject which he wished to bring to my attention; for he seemed to apprehend opposition to his view. He denounced slavery in look and language fierce and bitter, thought that slaveholders had forfeited their right to live, that the slaves had the right to gain their liberty in any way they could, did not believe that moral suasion would ever liberate the slave, or that political action would abolish the system. He said that he had long had a plan which could accomplish this end, and he had invited me to his house to lay that plan before me. He said he had been for some time looking for Negro men to whom he could safely reveal his secret, and at times he had almost despaired of finding such men; but that now he was encouraged, for he saw heads of such rising up in all directions. He had observed my course at home and abroad, and he wanted my cooperation.

His plan as it then lay in his mind had much to commend it. It did not, as some suppose, contemplate a general rising among the slaves, and a general slaughter of the slave-masters. An insurrection, he thought, would only defeat the object; but his plan did contemplate the creating of an armed force which should act in the very heart of the South. He was not averse to the shedding of blood, and thought the practice of carrying arms would be a good one for the Negro people to adopt, as it would give them a sense of their manhood. No people, he said, could have self-respect, or be respected, who would not fight for their freedom. He called my attention to a map of the United States, and pointed out to me the far-reaching Alleghenies, which stretch away from the borders of New York into the Southern states.

"These mountains," he said, "are the basis of my plan. God has given the strength of the hills to freedom; they were placed here for the emancipation of the Negro race; they are full of natural forts, where one man for defense will be equal to a hundred for attack; they are full also of good hiding places, where large numbers of brave men could be concealed, and baffle and elude pursuit for a long time. I know these mountains well, and could take a body of men into them and keep them there despite all the efforts of Virginia to dislodge them. The true object to be sought is first of all to destroy the money value of slave property; and that can only be done by rendering such property insecure. My plan, then, is to take at first about twenty-five picked men, and begin on a small scale; supply them with arms and ammuni-

tion and post them in squads of fives on a line of twenty-
five miles. The most persuasive and judicious of these shall
go down to the fields from time to time, as opportunity
offers, and induce the slaves to join them, seeking and se-
lecting the most restless and daring."

He saw that in this part of the work the utmost care
must be used to avoid treachery and disclosure. Only the
most conscientious and skillful should be sent on this
perilous duty. With care and enterprise he thought he could
soon gather a force of one hundred hardy men, men who
would be content to lead the free and adventurous life to
which he proposed to train them; when these were properly
drilled, and each man had found the place for which he was
best suited, they would begin work in earnest; they would
run off the slaves in large numbers, retain the brave and
strong ones in the mountains, and send the weak and timid
to the North by the Underground Railroad. His operations
would be enlarged with increasing numbers and would not
be confined to one locality.

When I asked him how he would support these men, he
said emphatically that he would subsist them upon the
enemy. Slavery was a state of war, and the slave had a right
to anything necessary to his freedom. "But," said I, "suppose you succeed in running off a few slaves, and thus
impress the Virginia slaveholders with a sense of insecurity
in their slaves, the effect will be only to make them sell their
slaves farther South." "That," said he, "will be what I want
first to do; then I would follow them up. If we could drive
slavery out of *one county*, it would be a great gain; it would
weaken the system throughout the State." "But they would
employ bloodhounds to hunt you out of the mountains."
"That they might attempt," said he, "but the chances are,
we should whip them, and when we should have whipped
one squad, they would be careful how they pursued."

"But you might be surrounded and cut off from your provisions or means of subsistence." He thought that this could not be done so they could not cut their way out, but even if the worst came he could but be killed, and he had no better use for his life than to lay it down in the cause of the slave.

When I suggested that we might convert the slaveholders, he became much excited, and said that could never be, "he knew their proud hearts and that they would never be induced to give up their slaves, until they felt a big stick on their heads." He observed that I might have noticed the simple manner in which he lived, adding that he had adopted this method in order to save money to carry out his purpose. This was said in no boastful tone, for he felt that he had delayed already too long, and had no room to boast either his zeal or his self-denial. Had some men made such a display of rigid virtue, I should have rejected it, as affected, false, and hypocritical, but in John Brown, I felt it to be real as iron or granite.

From this night spent with John Brown in Springfield, Mass., 1847, while I continued to write and speak against slavery, I became all the same less hopeful of its peaceful abolition. My utterances became more and more tinged by the color of this man's strong impressions. Speaking at an Anti-Slavery convention in Salem, Ohio, I expressed this apprehension that slavery could only be destroyed by bloodshed, when I was suddenly and sharply interrupted by my good old friend Sojourner Truth with the question, "Frederick, is God dead?" "No," I answered, "and because God is not dead slavery can only end in blood." My quaint old sister was of the Garrison school of non-resistants, and was shocked at my sanguinary doctrine, but she too became an advocate of the sword when the war for the maintenance of the Union was declared. . . .

At the end of two years, when Clay and Calhoun, two of

the ablest leaders the South ever had, were still in the Senate, we had an attempt at a settlement of differences between the North and South which our legislators meant to be final. What those measures were I need not here enumerate, except to say that chief among them was the Fugitive Slave Bill, framed by James M. Mason of Virginia and supported by Daniel Webster of Massachusetts—a bill undoubtedly more designed to involve the North in complicity with slavery and deaden its moral sentiment than to procure the return of fugitives to their so-called owners.

For a time this design did not altogether fail. Letters, speeches, and pamphlets literally rained down upon the people of the North, reminding them of their constitutional duty to hunt down and return to bondage runaway slaves. In this the preachers were not much behind the press and the politicians, especially that class of preachers known as Doctors of Divinity. A long list of these came forward with their Bibles to show that neither Christ nor his holy apostles objected to returning fugitives to slavery. Now that that evil day is past, a sight of those sermons would, I doubt not, bring the red blush of shame to the cheeks of many.

Living, as I then did, in Rochester, on the border of Canada, I was compelled to see the terribly distressing effects of this cruel enactment. Fugitive slaves who had lived for many years safely and securely in western New York and elsewhere, some of whom had by industry and economy saved money and bought little homes for themselves and their children, were suddenly alarmed and compelled to flee to Canada for safety as from an enemy's land—a doomed city —and take up a dismal march to a new abode, empty-handed, among strangers. My old friend Ward, of whom I have just now spoken, found it necessary to give up the contest and flee to Canada, and thousands followed his example.

Bishop Daniel A. Payne of the African Methodist Episco-

pal Church came to me about this time to consult me as to
whether it was best to stand our ground or flee to Canada.
When I told him I could not desert my post until I saw I
could not hold it, adding that I did not wish to leave while
Garnet and Ward remained, "Why," said he, "Ward?
Ward, he is already gone. I saw him crossing from Detroit
to Windsor." I asked him if he were going to stay, and he
answered: "Yes; we are whipped, we are whipped, and we
might as well retreat in order." This was indeed a stunning
blow. This man had power to do more to defeat this
inhuman enactment than any other Negro man in the land,
for no other could bring such brain power to bear against it.
I felt like a besieged city at news that its defenders had fallen
at its gates.

The hardships imposed by this atrocious and shameless
law were cruel and shocking, and yet only a few of all the
fugitives of the Northern States were returned to slavery
under its infamously wicked provisions. As a means of re-
capturing their runaway property in human flesh the law
was an utter failure. Its efficiency was destroyed by its
enormity. Its chief effect was to produce alarm and terror
among the class subject to its operation, and this it did most
effectually and distressingly.

Even Negro people who had been free all their lives felt
themselves very insecure in their freedom, for under this law
the oaths of any two villains were sufficient to consign a
free man to slavery for life. While the law was a terror to
the free, it was a still greater terror to the escaped bondman.
To him there was no peace. Asleep or awake, at work or at
rest, in church or market, he was liable to surprise and capture. By the law the judge got ten dollars a head for all he
could consign to slavery and only five dollars apiece for any
which he might adjudge free.

Although I was now myself free, I was not without appre-

hension. My purchase was of doubtful validity, having been
bought when out of the possession of my owner and when
he must take what was given or take nothing. It was a
question whether my claimant could be estopped by such a
sale from asserting certain or supposable equitable rights in
my body and soul. From rumors that reached me my house
was guarded by my friends several nights, when kidnappers,
had they come, would have got anything but a cool reception, for there would have been "blows to take as well as
blows to give."

Happily this reign of terror did not continue long. Despite
the efforts of Daniel Webster and Millard Fillmore and our
Doctors of Divinity, the law fell rapidly into disrepute.
The rescue of Shadrack resulting in the death of one of the
kidnappers, in Boston, the cases of Simms and Anthony
Burns, in the same place, created the deepest feeling against
the law and its upholders.

But the thing which more than all else destroyed the
Fugitive Slave Law was the resistance made to it by the
fugitives themselves. A decided check was given to the
execution of the law at Christiana, Penn., where three
Negro men, being pursued by Mr. Gorsuch and his son,
slew the father, wounded the son, and drove away the
officers, and made their escape to my house in Rochester.
The work of getting these men safely into Canada was a
delicate one. They were not only fugitives from slavery but
charged with murder, and officers were in pursuit of them.
There was no time for delay. I could not look upon them
as murderers. To me, they were heroic defenders of the rights
of man against manstealers and murderers. So I fed them,
and sheltered them in my house.

Had they been pursued then and there, my home would
have been stained with blood, for these men who had already
tasted blood were well armed and prepared to sell their

lives at any expense to the lives and limbs of their probable assailants. What they had already done at Christiana and the cool determination which showed very plainly especially in Parker (for that was the name of the leader), left no doubt on my mind that their courage was genuine and that their deeds would equal their words.

The situation was critical and dangerous. The telegraph had that day announced their deeds at Christiana, their escape, and that the mountains of Pennsylvania were being searched for the murderers. These men had reached me simultaneously with this news in the New York papers. Immediately after the occurrence at Christiana, they, instead of going into the mountains, were placed on a train which brought them to Rochester. They were thus almost in advance of the lightning, and much in advance of probable pursuit, unless the telegraph had raised agents already here. The hours they spent at my house were therefore hours of anxiety as well as activity. I dispatched my friend Miss Julia Griffiths to the landing three miles away on the Genesee River to ascertain if a steamer would leave that night for any port in Canada, and remained at home myself to guard my tired, dust-covered, and sleeping guests, for they had been harassed and traveling for two days and nights, and needed rest. Happily for us the suspense was not long, for it turned out that that very night a steamer was to leave for Toronto, Canada.

This fact, however, did not end my anxiety. There was danger that between my house and the landing or at the landing itself we might meet with trouble. Indeed the landing was the place where trouble was likely to occur if at all. As patiently as I could, I waited for the shades of night to come on, and then put the men in my "Democrat carriage," and started for the landing on the Genesee. It was an exciting ride, and somewhat speedy withal. We reached the boat at least fifteen minutes before the time of its departure, and that without remark or molestation. But those fifteen minutes seemed much longer than usual. I remained on board till the order to haul in the gang-plank was given; I shook hands with my friends, received from Parker the revolver that fell from the hand of Gorsuch when he died, presented now as a token of gratitude and a memento of the battle for Liberty at Christiana, and I returned to my home with a sense of relief which I cannot stop here to describe.

This affair, at Christiana, and the Jerry rescue at Syracuse, inflicted fatal wounds on the Fugitive Slave Bill. It became thereafter almost a dead letter, for slaveholders found that not only did it fail to put them in possession of their slaves, but that the attempt to enforce it brought odium upon themselves and weakened the slave system.

3

FROM

Stride Toward Freedom

by Martin Luther King, Jr.
(1929–1968)

*It was in Montgomery, Alabama, that Jefferson Davis took
the oath of office as President of the Confederate States of
America. It was here too that the Confederate flag was un-
furled for the first time. But if Montgomery was the cradle
of the Confederacy, it was also the birthplace of the present-
day civil-rights movement.*

*There were many evidences of segregation in Montgomery
in 1955, but perhaps none quite so humiliating as the city-
wide bus system. Negro passengers were verbally abused.
Sometimes they paid their fares at the front door and were
then told to reboard by the back door. Often the bus pulled
off before they had time to reach the rear door. An even more
degrading custom was the practice of reserving the front
seats of the bus for white passengers and prohibiting
blacks from sitting in them whether or not there were any*

whites on the bus. In addition, if all the "white" seats
were filled, and more whites boarded the bus, the Negroes
were forced to stand so that the whites could sit. If they did
not stand, they were subject to arrest.

Such was the situation in Montgomery on December 1,
1955, when Mrs. Rosa Parks refused to obey the driver's or-
der to get up and move to the back of the bus. The result,
predictably, was her arrest. But that was not the only out-
come. It was the last week that the blacks of Montgomery
would ever ride in segregated buses. Led by the Reverend
Dr. Martin Luther King, Jr., old and young alike boycotted
the buses in protest. They walked to and from work—when
other transportation was not available—for over a year. One
elderly lady spoke for all the blacks of Montgomery: "My
feets is tired, but my soul is at rest."

AFTER the "get-tough" policy failed to stop the movement
the diehards became desperate, and we waited to see what
their next move would be. Almost immediately after the protest started we had begun to receive threatening telephone
calls and letters. Sporadic in the beginning, they increased
as time went on. By the middle of January, they had risen
to thirty and forty a day.

Postcards, often signed "KKK," said simply "get out of
town or else." Many misspelled and crudely written letters
presented religious half-truths to prove that "God do not
intend the White People and the Negro to go to gather if he
did we would be the same." Others enclosed mimeographed
and printed materials combining anti-Semitic and anti-
Negro sentiments. One of these contained a handwritten
postscript: "You niggers are getting your self in a bad place.
The Bible is strong for segregation as of the jews concerning other races. It is even for segregation between 12 tribes

of Isreal. We need and will have a Hitler to get our country straightened out." Many of the letters were unprintable catalogues of blasphemy and obscenity.

Meanwhile the telephone rang all day and most of the night. Often Coretta was alone in the house when the calls came, but the insulting voices did not spare her. Many times the person on the other end simply waited until we answered and then hung up. A large percentage of the calls had sexual themes. One woman, whose voice I soon came to recognize, telephoned day after day to hurl sexual accusations at the Negro. Whenever I tried to answer, as I frequently did in an effort to explain our case calmly, the caller would cut me off. Occasionally, we would leave the telephone off the hook, but we could not do this for long because we never knew when an important call would come in.

When these incidents started, I took them in stride, feeling that they were the work of a few hotheads who would soon be discouraged when they discovered that we would not fight back. But as the weeks passed, I began to see that many of the threats were in earnest. Soon I felt myself faltering and growing in fear. One day, a white friend told me that he had heard from reliable sources that plans were being made to take my life. For the first time I realized that something could happen to me.

One night at a mass meeting, I found myself saying: "If one day you find me sprawled out dead, I do not want you to retaliate with a single act of violence. I urge you to continue protesting with the same dignity and discipline you have shown so far." A strange silence came over the audience.

Afterward, to the anxious group that gathered around, I tried to make light of the incident by saying that my words had not grown from any specific cause, but were just a general statement of principle that should guide our actions in the event of any fatality. But Ralph Abernathy was not satisfied. As he drove me home that night, he said:

"Something is wrong. You are disturbed about something."

I tried to evade the issue by repeating what I had just told the group at the church. But he persisted.

"Martin," he said, "you were not talking about some general principle. You had something specific in mind."

Unable to evade any longer, I admitted the truth. For the first time I told him about the threats that were harassing my family. I told him about the conversation with my white friend. I told him about the fears that were creeping up on my soul. Ralph tried to reassure me, but I was still afraid.

The threats continued. Almost every day someone warned me that he had overheard white men making plans to get rid of me. Almost every night I went to bed faced with the uncertainty of the next moment. In the morning I would look at Coretta and "Yoki" and say to myself: "They can be taken away from me at any moment; I can be taken away from them at any moment." For once I did not even share my thoughts with Coretta.

One night toward the end of January I settled into bed late, after a strenuous day. Coretta had already fallen asleep and just as I was about to doze off the telephone rang. An angry voice said, "Listen, nigger, we've taken all we want from you; before next week you'll be sorry you ever came to Montgomery." I hung up, but I couldn't sleep. It seemed that all of my fears had come down on me at once. I had reached the saturation point.

I got out of bed and began to walk the floor. Finally I went to the kitchen and heated a pot of coffee. I was ready to give up. With my cup of coffee sitting untouched before me I tried to think of a way to move out of the picture without appearing a coward. In this state of exhaustion, when

my courage had all but gone, I decided to take my problem
to God. With my head in my hands, I bowed over the kitchen table and prayed aloud. The words I spoke to God
that midnight are still vivid in my memory. "I am here taking a stand for what I believe is right. But now I am afraid.
The people are looking to me for leadership, and if I stand
before them without strength and courage, they too will
falter. I am at the end of my powers. I have nothing left. I've
come to the point where I can't face it alone."

At that moment I experienced the presence of the Divine
as I had never experienced Him before. It seemed as though
I could hear the quiet assurance of an inner voice saying:
"Stand up for righteousness, stand up for truth; and God
will be at your side forever." Almost at once my fears began
to go. My uncertainty disappeared. I was ready to face
anything.

Three nights later, on January 30, I left home a little
before seven to attend our Monday evening mass meeting at
the First Baptist Church. A member of my congregation,
Mrs. Mary Lucy Williams, had come to the parsonage to keep
my wife company in my absence. After putting the baby to
bed, Coretta and Mrs. Williams went to the living room to
look at television. About nine-thirty they heard a noise in
front that sounded as though someone had thrown a brick.
In a matter of seconds an explosion rocked the house. A
bomb had gone off on the porch.

The sound was heard many blocks away, and word of the
bombing reached the mass meeting almost instantly. Toward the close of the meeting, as I stood on the platform
helping to take the collection, I noticed an usher rushing to
give Ralph Abernathy a message. Abernathy turned and ran
downstairs, soon to reappear with a worried look on his
face. Several others rushed in and out of the church. People

looked at me and then away; one or two seemed about to approach me and then changed their minds. An usher called me to the side of the platform, presumably to give me a message, but before I could get there S. S. Seay had sent him away. By now I was convinced that whatever had happened affected me. I called Ralph Abernathy, S. S. Seay, and E. N. French and asked them to tell me what was wrong. Ralph looked at Seay and French and then turned to me and said hesitantly:

"Your house has been bombed."

I asked if my wife and baby were all right.

They said, "We are checking on that now."

Strangely enough, I accepted the word of the bombing calmly. My religious experience a few nights before had given me the strength to face it. I interrupted the collection and asked all present to give me their undivided attention. After telling them why I had to leave, I urged each person to go straight home after the meeting and adhere strictly to our philosophy of nonviolence. I admonished them not to become panicky and lose their heads. "Let us keep moving," I urged them, "with the faith that what we are doing is right, and with the even greater faith that God is with us in the struggle."

I was immediately driven home. As we neared the scene I noticed hundreds of people with angry faces in front of the house. The policemen were trying, in their usual rough manner, to clear the streets, but they were ignored by the crowd. One Negro was saying to a policeman, who was attempting to push him aside: "I ain't gonna move nowhere. That's the trouble now; you white folks is always pushin' us around. Now you got your .38 and I got mine; so let's battle it out." As I walked toward the front porch I realized that many people were armed. Nonviolent resistance was on the verge of being transformed into violence.

I rushed into the house to see if Coretta and "Yoki" were safe. When I walked into the bedroom and saw my wife and daughter uninjured, I drew my first full breath in many minutes. I learned that fortunately when Coretta and Mrs. Williams had heard the sound of something falling on the front porch, they had jumped up and run to the back of the house. If instead they had gone to the porch to investigate, the outcome might have been fatal. Coretta was neither bitter nor panicky. She had accepted the whole thing with unbelievable composure. As I noticed her calmness I became even more calm myself.

Mayor Gayle, Commissioner Sellers, and several white reporters had reached the house before I did and were standing in the dining room. After reassuring myself about my family's safety, I went to speak to them. Both Gayle and Sellers expressed their regret that "this unfortunate incident has taken place in our city." One of the trustees of my church, who is employed in the public school system of Montgomery, was standing beside me when the mayor and the commissioner spoke. Although in a vulnerable position, he turned to the mayor and said: "You may express your regrets, but you must face the fact that your public statements created the atmosphere for this bombing. This is the end result of your 'get-tough' policy." Neither Mayor Gayle nor Commissioner Sellers could reply.

By this time the crowd outside was getting out of hand. The policemen had failed to disperse them, and throngs of additional people were arriving every minute. The white reporters inside the house wanted to leave to get their stories on the wires, but they were afraid to face the angry crowd. The mayor and police commissioner, though they might not have admitted it, were very pale.

In this atmosphere I walked out to the porch and asked the crowd to come to order. In less than a moment there was complete silence. Quietly I told them that I was all right and that my wife and baby were all right. "Now let's not become panicky," I continued. "If you have weapons, take them home; if you do not have them, please do not seek to get them. We cannot solve this problem through retaliatory violence. We must meet violence with nonviolence. Remember the words of Jesus: 'He who lives by the sword will perish by the sword.' " I then urged them to leave peacefully. "We must love our white brothers," I said, "no matter what they do to us. We must make them know that we love them. Jesus still cries out in words that echo across the centuries: 'Love your enemies; bless them that curse you; pray for them that despitefully use you.' This is what we must live by. We must meet hate with love. Remember," I ended, "if I am stopped, this movement will not stop, because God is with the movement. Go home with this glowing faith and this radiant assurance."

As I finished speaking there were shouts of "Amen" and "God bless you." I could hear voices saying: "We are with you all the way, Reverend." I looked out over that vast throng of people and noticed tears on many faces.

After I finished, the police commissioner began to address the crowd. Immediately there were boos. Police officers tried to get the attention of the Negroes by saying, "Be quiet—the commissioner is speaking." To this the crowd responded with even louder boos. I came back to the edge of the porch and raised my hand for silence. "Remember what I just said. Let us hear the commissioner." In the ensuing lull, the commissioner spoke and offered a reward to the person or persons who could report the offenders. Then the crowd began to disperse.

Things remained tense the whole of that night. The Negroes had had enough. They were ready to meet violence with violence. One policeman later told me that if a Negro had fallen over a brick that night a race riot would probably have broken out because the Negro would have been convinced that a white person had pushed him. This could well have been the darkest night in Montgomery's history. But something happened to avert it: The spirit of God was in our hearts; and a night that seemed destined to end in unleashed chaos came to a close in a majestic group demonstration of nonviolence.

After our many friends left the house late that evening, Coretta, "Yoki," and I were driven to the home of one of our church members to spend the night. I could not get to sleep. While I lay in that quiet front bedroom, with a distant street lamp throwing a reassuring glow through the curtained window, I began to think of the viciousness of people who would bomb my home. I could feel the anger rising when I realized that my wife and baby could have been killed. I thought about the city commissioners and all the statements that they had made about me and the Negro generally. I was once more on the verge of corroding hatred. And once more I caught myself and said: "You must not allow yourself to become bitter."

I tried to put myself in the place of the three commissioners. I said to myself these men are not bad men. They are misguided. They have fine reputations in the community. In their dealings with white people they are respectable and gentlemanly. They probably think they are right in their methods of dealing with Negroes. They say the things they say about us and treat us as they do because they have been taught these things. From the cradle to the grave, it is instilled in them that the Negro is inferior. Their parents probably taught them that; the schools they attended taught them that; the books they read, even their churches and ministers, often taught them that; and above all the very concept of segregation teaches them that. The whole cultural tradition under which they have grown—a tradition blighted with more than 250 years of slavery and more than 90 years of segregation—teaches them that Negroes do not deserve certain things. So these men are merely the children of their culture. When they seek to preserve segregation they are seeking to preserve only what their local folkways have taught them was right.

Midnight had long since passed. Coretta and the baby were sound asleep. It was time for me too to get some rest. At about two-thirty I turned over in bed and fell into a dazed slumber. But the night was not yet over. Some time later Coretta and I were awakened by a slow, steady knocking at the front door. We looked at each other wordlessly in the dim light, and listened as the knocking began again. Through the window we could see the dark outline of a fig- ure on the front porch. Our hosts were sound asleep in the back of the house, and we lay in the front, frozen into in- action. Eventually the sounds stopped and we saw a shad- owy figure move across the porch and start down the steps to the street. I pulled myself out of bed, peered through the curtains, and recognized the stocky, reassuring back of Coretta's father.

Obie Scott had heard the news of the bombing over the radio in Marion and had driven to Montgomery to take Coretta and "Yoki" home with him, "until this things cools off." We talked together for some time, but although Coretta listened respectfully to her father's persuasions, she would not leave. "I'm sorry, Dad," she said, "but I belong here with Martin." And so Obie Scott drove back to Marion alone.

Just two nights later, a stick of dynamite was thrown on the lawn of E. D. Nixon. Fortunately, again no one was hurt. Once more a large crowd of Negroes assembled, but they did not lose control. And so nonviolence had won its first and its second tests.

After the bombings, many of the officers of my church

and other trusted friends urged me to hire a bodyguard and armed watchmen for my house. I tried to tell them that I had no fears now, and consequently needed no protection. But they were insistent, so I agreed to consider the question. I also went down to the sheriff's office and applied for a license to carry a gun in the car; but this was refused.

Meanwhile I reconsidered. How could I serve as one of the leaders of a nonviolent movement and at the same time use weapons of violence for my personal protection? Coretta and I talked the matter over for several days and finally agreed that arms were no solution. We decided then to get rid of the one weapon we owned. We tried to satisfy our friends by having floodlights mounted around the house, and hiring unarmed watchmen around the clock. I also promised that I would not travel around the city alone.

This was a comparatively easy promise to keep, thanks to our friend Bob Williams, professor of music at Alabama State College and a former collegemate of mine at More-house. When I came to Montgomery, I had found him here, and from the moment the protest started he was seldom far from my side or Coretta's. He did most of my driving around Montgomery and accompanied me on several out-of-town trips. Whenever Coretta and "Yoki" went to Atlanta or Marion, he was always there to drive them down and to bring them back. Almost imperceptibly he had become my voluntary "bodyguard," though he carried no arms and could never have been as fierce as the name implied.

In this crisis the officers and members of my church were always nearby to lend their encouragement and active support. As I gradually lost my role as husband and father, having to be away from home for hours and sometimes days at a time, the women of the church came into the house to keep Coretta company. Often they volunteered to cook the meals and clean, or help with the baby. Many of the men took turns as watchmen, or drove me around when Bob Williams was not available. Nor did my congregation ever complain when the multiplicity of my new responsibilities caused me to lag in my pastoral duties. For months my day-to-day contact with my parishioners had almost ceased. I had become no more than a Sunday preacher. But my church willingly shared me with the community, and threw their own considerable resources of time and money into the struggle.

Our local white friends, too, came forward with their support. Often they called Coretta to say an encouraging word, and when the house was bombed several of them, known and unknown to us, came by to express their regret. Occasionally the mail would bring a letter from a white Montgomerian saying, "Carry on, we are with you a hundred per cent." Frequently these were simply signed "a white friend."

Interestingly enough, for some time after the bombing the threatening telephone calls slowed up. But this was only a lull; several months later they had begun again in full force.

In order to sleep at night, it finally became necessary to apply for an unlisted number. This number was passed out to all the members of the church, the members of the MIA, and other friends across the country. And although it had sometimes been suggested that our own group was responsible for the threats we never received another hostile call. Of course, the letters still came, but my secretaries were discreet enough to keep as many of them as possible from my attention.

When the opposition discovered that violence could not block the protest, they resorted to mass arrests. As early as January 9, a Montgomery attorney had called the attention of the press to an old state law against boycotts. He referred to Title 14, Section 54, which provides that when two or

more persons enter into a conspiracy to prevent the operation of a lawful business, without just cause or legal excuse,
they shall be guilty of a misdemeanor. On February 13 the
Montgomery County Grand Jury was called to determine
whether Negroes who were boycotting the buses were violating this law. After about a week of deliberations, the jury,
composed of seventeen whites and one Negro, found the boycott illegal and indicted more than one hundred persons.
My name, of course, was on the list.

At the time of the indictments I was at Fisk University
in Nashville, giving a series of lectures. During this period
I was talking to Montgomery on the phone at least three
times a day in order to keep abreast of developments. Thus
I heard of the indictments first in a telephone call from
Ralph Abernathy, late Tuesday night, February 21. He said
that the arrests were scheduled to begin the following morning. Knowing that he would be one of the first to be arrested, I assured him that I would be with him and the others
in my prayers. As usual he was unperturbed. I told him
that I would cut my trip short in Nashville and come to
Montgomery the next day.

I booked an early morning flight. All night long I
thought of the people in Montgomery. Would these mass
arrests so frighten them that they would urge us to call off
the protest? I knew how hard pressed they had been. For
more than thirteen weeks they had walked, and sacrificed,
and worn down their cars. They had been harassed and in-
timidated on every hand. And now they faced arrest on top
of all this. Would they become battle-weary, I wondered.
Would they give up in despair? Would this be the end of our
movement?

I arose early Wednesday morning, and notified the offi-
cials of Fisk that I had to leave ahead of time because of the
situation in Montgomery. I flew to Atlanta to pick up my

wife and daughter, whom I had left at my parents' home
while I was in Nashville. My wife, my mother and father
met me at the airport. I had told them about the indictments
over the phone, and they had gotten additional information
from a radio broadcast. Coretta showed her usual composure; but my parents' faces wore signs of deep perturbation.

My father, so unafraid for himself, had fallen into a constant state of terror for me and my family. Since the protest
began he had beaten a path between Atlanta and Montgomery to be at our side. Many times he had sat in on our
board meetings and never shown any doubt about the justice
of our actions. Yet this stern and courageous man had
reached the point where he could scarcely mention the protest without tears. My mother too had suffered. After the
bombing she had had to take to bed under doctor's orders,
and she was often ill later. Their expressions—even the way
they walked, I realized as they came toward me at the airport—had begun to show the strain.

As we drove to their house, my father said that he thought
it would be unwise for me to return to Montgomery now.
"Although many others have been indicted," he said, "their
main concern is to get you. They might even put you in
jail without a bond." He went on to tell me that the law en-
forcement agencies in Montgomery had been trying to find
something on my record in Atlanta which would make it
possible to deport me from Alabama. They had gone to the
Atlanta police department, and were disappointed when
Chief Jenkins informed them that I did not have even a minor police record. "All of this shows," my father concluded,
"that they are out to get you."

I listened to him attentively, and yet I knew that I could
not follow his suggestion and stay in Atlanta. I was pro-
foundly concerned about my parents. I was worried about
their worry. I knew that if I continued the struggle I would

be plagued by the pain that I was inflicting on them. But if I eased out now I would be plagued by my own conscience, reminding me that I lacked the moral courage to stand by a cause to the end. No one can understand my conflict who has not looked into the eyes of those he loves, knowing that he has no alternative but to take a dangerous stand that leaves them tormented.

My father told me that he had asked several trusted friends to come to the house in the early afternoon to discuss the whole issue. Feeling that this exchange of ideas might help to relieve his worries, I readily agreed to stay over and talk to them. Among those who came were A. T. Walden, a distinguished attorney; C. R. Yates and T. M. Alexander, both prominent businessmen; C. A. Scott, editor of *Atlanta Daily World*; Bishop Sherman L. Green of A.M.E. Church; Benjamin E. Mays, president of Morehouse College; and Rufus E. Clement, president of Atlanta University. Coretta and my mother joined us.

My father explained to the group that because of his respect for their judgment he was calling on them for advice on whether I should return to Montgomery. He gave them a brief history of the attempts that had been made to get me out of Montgomery. He admitted that the fear of what might happen to me had caused him and my mother many restless nights. He concluded by saying that he had talked to a liberal white attorney a few hours earlier, who had confirmed his feeling that I should not go back at this time.

There were murmurs of agreement in the room, and I listened as sympathetically and objectively as I could while two of the men gave their reasons for concurring. These were my elders, leaders among my people. Their words commanded respect. But soon I could not restrain myself any longer. "I must go back to Montgomery," I protested. "My friends and associates are being arrested. It would be the height of cowardice for me to stay away. I would rather be in jail ten years than desert my people now. I have begun the struggle, and I can't turn back. I have reached the point of no return." In the moment of silence that followed I heard my father break into tears. I looked at Dr. Mays, one of the great influences in my life. Perhaps he heard my unspoken plea. At any rate, he was soon defending my position strongly. Then others joined him in supporting me. They assured my father that things were not so bad as they seemed. Mr. Walden put through two calls on the spot to Thurgood Marshall, general counsel of the NAACP, and Arthur Shores, NAACP counsel in Alabama, both of whom assured him that I would have the best legal protection. In the face of all these persuasions, my father began to be reconciled to my return to Montgomery.

After everybody had gone, Coretta and I went upstairs to our room and had a long talk. She, too, I was glad to find, had no doubt that I must go back immediately. With my own feelings reinforced by the opinions of others I trusted, and with my father's misgivings at rest, I felt better and more prepared to face the experience ahead.

Characteristically, my father, having withdrawn his objections to our return to Montgomery, decided to go along with us, unconcerned with any possible danger or unpleasantness to himself. He secured a driver and at six o'clock Thursday morning we were on the highway headed for Montgomery, arriving about nine. Before we could get out of the car, several television cameras were trained on us. The reporters had somehow discovered the time of our arrival. A few minutes later Ralph Abernathy, released on bail after his arrest the previous day, came to the house. With Ralph and my father, I set out for the county jail, several of my church members following after.

At the jail, an almost holiday atmosphere prevailed. On

the way Ralph Abernathy told me how people had rushed down to get arrested the day before. No one, it seems, had been frightened. No one had tried to evade arrest. Many Negroes had gone voluntarily to the sheriff's office to see if their names were on the list, and were even disappointed when they were not. A once fear-ridden people had been transformed. Those who had previously trembled before the law were now proud to be arrested for the cause of freedom. With this feeling of solidarity around me, I walked with firm steps toward the rear of the jail. After I had received a number and had been photographed and finger-printed, one of my church members paid my bond and I left for home.

The trial was set for March 19. Friends from all over the country came to Montgomery to be with us during the proceedings. Ministers from as far north as New York were present. Negro Congressman Charles C. Diggs (D-Mich.) was on hand. Scores of reporters representing publications in the United States, India, France, and England were there to cover the trial. More than five hundred Negroes stood in the halls and the streets surrounding the small courthouse. Several of them wore crosses on their lapels reading, "Father, forgive them."

Judge Eugene Carter brought the court to order, and after the necessary preliminaries the state called me up as the first defendant. For four days I sat in court listening to arguments and waiting for a verdict. William F. Thetford, solicitor for the state, was attempting to prove that I had disobeyed a law by organizing an illegal boycott. The defense attorneys—Arthur Shores, Peter Hall, Ozell Billingsley, Fred Gray, Charles Langford, and Robert Carter—presented arguments to show that the prosecution's evidence was insufficient to prove that I had violated Alabama's anti-boycott law. Even if the state had proved such action, they asserted, no evidence was produced to show that the Negroes did not have just cause or legal excuse.

In all, twenty-eight witnesses were brought to the stand by the defense. I listened with a mixture of sadness and awe as these simple people—most of them unlettered—sat on the witness stand without fear and told their stories. They looked the solicitor and the judge in the eye with a courage and dignity to which there was no answer.

Perhaps the most touching testimony was that of Mrs. Stella Brooks. Her husband had climbed on a bus. After paying his fare he was ordered by the driver to get off and reboard by the back door. He looked through the crowded bus and seeing that there was no room in back he said that he would get off and walk if the driver would return his dime. The driver refused; an argument ensued; and the driver called the police. The policeman arrived, abusing Brooks, who still refused to leave the bus unless his dime was returned. The policeman shot him. It happened so suddenly that everybody was dazed. Brooks died of his wounds.

Mrs. Martha Walker testified about the day when she was leading her blind husband from the bus. She had stepped down and as her husband was following the driver slammed the door and began to drive off. Walker's leg was caught. Although Mrs. Walker called out, the driver failed to stop, and her husband was dragged some distance before he could free himself. She reported the incident, but the bus company did nothing about it.

The stories continued. Mrs. Sadie Brooks testified that she heard a Negro passenger threatened because he did not have the correct change. "The driver whipped out a pistol and drove the man off the bus." Mrs. Della Perkins described being called an "ugly black ape" by a driver.

I will always remember my delight when Mrs. Georgia

Gilmore—an unlettered woman of unusual intelligence—
told how an operator demanded that she get off the bus after paying her fare and board it again by the back door, and
then drove away before she could get there. She turned to
Judge Carter and said: "When they count the money, they do
not know Negro money from white money."

On Thursday afternoon, March 22, both sides rested.
All eyes were turned toward Judge Carter, as with barely a
pause he rendered his verdict: "I declare the defendant guilty
of violating the state's anti-boycott law." The penalty was a
fine of $500 and court costs, or 386 days at hard labor in the
County of Montgomery. Then Judge Carter announced
that he was giving a minimum penalty because of what I
had done to prevent violence. In the cases of the other Negroes charged with the same violation—the number had
now boiled down to 89—Judge Carter entered a contin-
uance until a final appeal was complete in my case.

In a few minutes several friends had come up to sign my
bond, and the lawyers had notified the judge that the case
would be appealed. Many people stood around the courtroom in tears. Others walked out with their heads bowed.
I came to the end of my trial with a feeling of sympathy for
Judge Carter in his dilemma. To convict me he had to face
the condemnation of the nation and world opinion; to ac-
quit me he had to face the condemnation of the local community and those voters who kept him in office. Throughout the proceedings he had treated me with great courtesy,
and he had rendered a verdict which he probably thought
was the best way out. After the trial he left town for a "welcomed rest."

I left the courtroom with my wife at my side and a host of
friends following. In front of the courthouse hundreds of
Negroes and whites, including television cameramen and
photographers, were waiting. As I waved my hand, they

shouted: "God bless you," and began to sing, "We ain't
gonna ride the buses no more."

Ordinarily, a person leaving a courtroom with a conviction behind him would wear a somber face. But I left with a
smile. I knew that I was a convicted criminal, but I was
proud of my crime. It was the crime of joining my people
in a nonviolent protest against injustice. It was the crime
of seeking to instill within my people a sense of dignity and
self-respect. It was the crime of desiring for my people the
unalienable rights of life, liberty, and the pursuit of happiness. It was above all the crime of seeking to convince my
people that noncoöperation with evil is just as much a moral
duty as is coöperation with good.

So ended another effort to halt the protest. Instead of
stopping the movement, the opposition's tactics had only
served to give it greater momentum, and to draw us closer
together. What the opposition failed to see was that our
mutual sufferings had wrapped us all in a single garment
of destiny. What happened to one happened to all.

On that cloudy afternoon in March, Judge Carter had
convicted more than Martin Luther King, Jr., Case No.
7399; he had convicted every Negro in Montgomery. It is
no wonder that the movement couldn't be stopped. It was
too large to be stopped. Its links were too well bound together in a powerfully effective chain. There is amazing
power in unity. Where there is true unity, every effort to
disunite only serves to strengthen the unity. This is what the
opposition failed to see.

The members of the opposition had also revealed that they
did not know the Negroes with whom they were dealing.
They thought they were dealing with a group who could
be cajoled or forced to do whatever the white man wanted
them to do. They were not aware that they were dealing with
Negroes who had been freed from fear. And so every move

they made proved to be a mistake. It could not be otherwise, because their methods were geared to the "old Negro," and they were dealing with a "new Negro."

4

FROM

Coming of Age in Mississippi

by Anne Moody
(1940–   )

By the time Anne Moody was in college, the Montgomery bus boycott was past history. The nonviolent approach to integration had led to sit-ins, and the effectiveness of organized protest, as opposed to individual effort, was brought home to people like Anne.

Born in Wilkinson County, Mississippi, Anne soon learned that it meant survival to ignore and accept the injustices around her. As a teen-ager, however, she found it increasingly difficult to remain silent. Finally, after a violent break with her family, Anne Moody left her home in Centreville to attend college. At Tougaloo in the late fifties she became very active in the civil-rights movement and for this reason can never return to Centreville again.

A WEEK before summer school ended. I was in town shopping with Rose, a girl from the dorm. We had planned to

split cab fare back to campus, but discovered we did not
have enough money. Cab fare out to Tougaloo was $2.50
and bus fare was thirty-five cents one way. We decided to
take the Trailways back. When we got to the station, I suggested to Rose that we use the white side. "I'm game if you
are," she said.

I walked in the white entrance. When I looked back, I
saw that Rose had not followed. I decided I would not go
back to see what had happened, because she would try and
talk me out of it. As I was buying my ticket, she walked
up behind me.

"Shit, Moody, I thought you were kidding," she said.

I didn't answer. I was noticing the reaction of the man
behind the counter. He stood looking at me as if he were
paralyzed.

"Make that two tickets, please," I said to him.

"Where is the other one to?" he said.

"Both to Tougaloo," I said.

As he was getting the tickets for us, another man had
gotten on the phone. He kept looking at us as he was talking. I think he was reporting to the police what was taking
place. The man that sold us the tickets acted as if that was
the last thing in the world he wanted to do. He slapped the
tickets down on the counter, and threw the change at me.
The change fell off the counter and rolled over the floor.
That bastard had the nerve to laugh as we picked it up.
Rose and I sat opposite each other, so we could see what
was happening throughout the terminal. The bus was to
leave at three-thirty, and we had gotten there about two-
forty-five. We had some time to wait. Rose had a watch. I
asked her to keep a check on the time.

People came in and stared. Some even laughed. Nothing
happened until a bunch of white soldiers sat with us and
started talking. The conversation had gone on for some

time when a Negro woman got off one of the incoming
buses. She saw us sitting there and walked right in. She
had about six small children with her. The little Negro
children started running around the station picking up
things from the counter and asking if they could buy them.
At that point the excitement started. A drunken white man
walked into the station behind the Negro lady with all the
children. He started cursing, calling us all kinds of niggers.

"Get them little dirty swines outta heah," he said, pulling one of the little boys to the door.

"Take your filthy hands off my child," the Negro woman
said. "What's going on here anyway?"

"They got a place for you folks, now why don't you
take them chilluns of yours and go on right over there?"
the drunkard said, pointing to the Negro side of the bus
station.

The lady looked at us. I guess she wanted us to say
something. Rose and I just sat there. Finally she realized a
sit-in or something was going on. She took her children
and hurried out of the door. Instead of going to the Negro
side, she went back on the bus. She looked as though she
was really angry with us.

After that the drunkard started yelling at us. I didn't get
too scared, but Rose was now shaking. She had begun to
smoke cigarettes one after the other. She looked at her
watch. "Moody, we have missed the bus," she said.

"What time is it?" I asked.

"It's almost four-thirty."

"They didn't even announce that the bus was loading,"
I said.

I walked over to the man at the ticket counter. "Has the
bus come in that's going to Tougaloo?" I asked him.

"One just left," he said.

"You didn't announce that the bus was in."

"Are you telling me how to do my job?" he said. "I hear you niggers at Tougaloo think you run Mississippi."

"When is the next bus?" I asked.

"Five-thirty," he said, very indignant.

I went back and told Rose that the next bus left at five-thirty. She wanted to leave, but I insisted that we stay. Just as I was trying to explain to her why we should not leave, the white drunk walked up behind her. He had what appeared to be a wine bottle in his hand.

"Talk to me, Rose," I said.

"What's going on?" Rose said, almost shouting.

"Nothing. Stop acting so damn scared and start talking," I said.

The drunk walked up behind her and held the bottle up as though he was going to hit her on the head. All the time, I was looking him straight in the face as if to say, "Would you, would you really hit her?" Rose knew someone was behind her. She wouldn't have been able to talk or act normal if someone in the station threatened to shoot her if she didn't. The drunkard saw that I was pleading with him. He cursed me, throwing the bottle on the floor and breaking it. At this point, more people got rallied up. They had now started shouting catcalls from every direction. Some bus drivers walked into the station. "What's wrong? What's going on heah?" one of them shouted. One took a chair and sat right in front of us. "Do you girls want to see a show?" he said. "Did you come here for a little entertainment?"

We didn't say anything.

"I guess you didn't. I'll put it on anyhow," he said. "Now here's how white folks entertain," putting his thumbs in his ears and wiggling his fingers, kicking his feet and making all kind of facial expressions. The rest of the whites in the bus station laughed and laughed at him. Some asked him to imitate a monkey, Martin Luther King, Medgar Evers. His performance went on for what seemed to be a good thirty minutes. When he finished, or rather got tired of, clowning, he said, "Now some of you other people give them what they really came for."

All this time the man was still on the phone talking to someone. We were sure he was talking to the police. Some of the other people that were sitting around in the bus station started shouting remarks. I guess they were taking the advice of the bus driver. Again Rose looked at her watch to report that we had missed the second bus. It was almost a quarter to seven.

We didn't know what to do. The place was getting more tense by the minute. People had now begun to crowd around us.

"Let's go, Moody," Rose began to plead with me. "If you don't I'll leave you here," she said.

I knew she meant it, and I didn't want to be left alone. The crowd was going to get violent any minute now.

"O.K., Rose, let's go," I said. "Don't turn your back to anyone, though."

We got up and walked backward to the door. The crowd followed us just three or four feet away. Some were threatening to kick us out—or throw us all the way to Tougaloo, and a lot of other possible and impossible things.

Rose and I hit the swinging doors with our backs at the same time. The doors closed immediately behind us. We were now outside the station not knowing what to do or where to run. We were afraid to leave. We were at the back of the station and thought the mob would be waiting for us if we ran around in front and tried to leave. Any moment now, those that had followed us would be on us again. We were standing there just going to pieces.

"Get in this here car," a Negro voice said.

I glanced to one side and saw that Rose was getting into the back seat. At that moment the mob was coming toward me through the doors. I just started moving backward until I fell into the car. The driver sped away.

After we had gotten blocks away from the station, I was still looking out of the back window to see who would follow. No one had. For the first time I looked to see who was driving the car and asked the driver who he was. He said he was a minister, that he worked at the bus station part-time. He asked us not to ever try and sit-in again without first planning it with an organization.

"You girls just can't go around doing things on your own," he said. He drove us all the way to campus, then made us feel bad by telling us he probably would get fired. He said he was on a thirty-minute break. That's a Negro preacher for you.

I had counted on graduating in the spring of 1963, but as it turned out, I couldn't because some of my credits still had to be cleared with Natchez College. A year before, this would have seemed like a terrible disaster, but now I hardly even felt disappointed. I had a good excuse to stay on campus for the summer and work with the Movement, and this was what I really wanted to do. I couldn't go home again anyway, and I couldn't go to New Orleans—I didn't have money enough for bus fare.

During my senior year at Tougaloo, my family hadn't sent me one penny. I had only the small amount of money I had earned at Maple Hill. I couldn't afford to eat at school or live in the dorms, so I had gotten permission to move off campus. I had to prove that I could finish school, even if I had to go hungry every day. I knew Raymond and Miss Pearl were just waiting to see me drop out. But something happened to me as I got more and more involved in the

Movement. It no longer seemed important to prove anything. I had found something outside myself that gave meaning to my life.

I had become very friendly with my social science professor, John Salter, who was in charge of NAACP activities on campus. All during the year, while the NAACP conducted a boycott of the downtown stores in Jackson, I had been one of Salter's most faithful canvassers and church speakers. During the last week of school he told me that sit-in demonstrations were about to start in Jackson and that he wanted me to be the spokesman for a team that would sit-in at Woolworth's lunch counter. The two other demonstrators would be classmates of mine, Memphis and Pearlena. Pearlena was a dedicated NAACP worker, but Memphis had not been very involved in the Movement on campus. It seemed that the organization had had a rough time finding students who were in a position to go to jail. I had nothing to lose one way or the other. Around ten o'clock the morning of the demonstrations, NAACP headquarters alerted the news services. As a result, the police department was also informed, but neither the policemen nor the newsmen knew exactly where or when the demonstrations would start. They stationed themselves along Capitol Street and waited.

To divert attention from the sit-in at Woolworth's, the picketing started at J. C. Penney's a good fifteen minutes before. The pickets were allowed to walk up and down in front of the store three or four times before they were arrested. At exactly 11 A.M., Pearlena, Memphis, and I entered Woolworth's from the rear entrance. We separated as soon as we stepped into the store, and made small purchases from various counters. Pearlena had given Memphis her watch. He was to let us know when it was 11:14. At 11:14 we were to join him near the lunch counter and at exactly 11:15 we were to take seats at it.

Seconds before 11:15 we were occupying three seats at the previously segregated Woolworth's lunch counter. In the beginning the waitresses seemed to ignore us, as if they really didn't know what was going on. Our waitress walked past us a couple of times before she noticed we had started to write our own orders down and realized we wanted service. She asked us what we wanted. We began to read to her from our order slips. She told us that we would be served at the back counter, which was for Negroes.

"We would like to be served here," I said.

The waitress started to repeat what she had said, then stopped in the middle of the sentence. She turned the lights out behind the counter, and she and the other waitresses almost ran to the back of the store, deserting all their white customers. I guess they thought that violence would start immediately after the whites at the counter realized what was going on. There were five or six other people at the counter. A couple of them just got up and walked away. A girl sitting next to me finished her banana split before leaving. A middle-aged white woman who had not yet been served rose from her seat and came over to us. "I'd like to stay here with you," she said, "but my husband is waiting."

The newsmen came in just as she was leaving. They must have discovered what was going on shortly after some of the people began to leave the store. One of the newsmen ran behind the woman who spoke to us and asked her to identify herself. She refused to give her name, but said she was a native of Vicksburg and a former resident of California. When asked why she had said what she had said to us, she replied, "I am in sympathy with the Negro movement." By this time a crowd of cameramen and reporters had gathered around us taking pictures and asking questions, such as Where were we from? Why did we sit-in? What organization sponsored it? Were we students? From what school? How were we classified?

I told them that we were all students at Tougaloo College, that we were represented by no particular organization, and that we planned to stay there even after the store closed. "All we want is service," was my reply to one of them. After they had finished probing for about twenty minutes, they were almost ready to leave.

At noon, students from a nearby white high school started pouring in to Woolworth's. When they first saw us they were sort of surprised. They didn't know how to react. A few started to heckle and the newsmen became interested again. Then the white students started chanting all kinds of anti-Negro slogans. We were called a little bit of everything. The rest of the seats except the three we were occupying had been roped off to prevent others from sitting down. A couple of the boys took one end of the rope and made it into a hangman's noose. Several attempts were made to put it around our necks. The crowds grew as more students and adults came in for lunch.

We kept our eyes straight forward and did not look at the crowd except for occasional glances to see what was going on. All of a sudden I saw a face I remembered—the drunkard from the bus station sit-in. My eyes lingered on him just long enough for us to recognize each other. Today he was drunk too, so I don't think he remembered where he had seen me before. He took out a knife, opened it, put it in his pocket, and then began to pace the floor. At this point, I told Memphis and Pearlena what was going on. Memphis suggested that we pray. We bowed our heads, and all hell broke loose. A man rushed forward, threw Memphis from his seat, and slapped my face. Then another man who worked in the store threw me against an adjoining counter.

Down on my knees on the floor, I saw Memphis lying near the lunch counter with blood running out of the corners of his mouth. As he tried to protect his face, the man who'd thrown him down kept kicking him against the head. If he had worn hard-soled shoes instead of sneakers, the first kick probably would have killed Memphis. Finally a man dressed in plain clothes identified himself as a police officer and arrested Memphis and his attacker.

Pearlena had been thrown to the floor. She and I got back on our stools after Memphis was arrested. There were some white Tougaloo teachers in the crowd. They asked Pearlena and me if we wanted to leave. They said that things were getting too rough. We didn't know what to do. While we were trying to make up our minds, we were joined by Joan Trumpauer. Now there were three of us and we were integrated. The crowd began to chant, "Communists, Communists, Communists." Some old man in the crowd ordered the students to take us off the stools.

"Which one should I get first?" a big husky boy said.

"That white nigger," the old man said.

The boy lifted Joan from the counter by her waist and carried her out of the store. Simultaneously, I was snatched from my stool by two high school students. I was dragged about thirty feet toward the door by my hair when someone made them turn me loose. As I was getting up off the floor, I saw Joan coming back inside. We started back to the center of the counter to join Pearlena. Lois Chaffee, a white Tougaloo faculty member, was now sitting next to her. So Joan and I just climbed across the rope at the front end of the counter and sat down. There were now four of us, two whites and two Negroes, all women. The mob started smearing us with ketchup, mustard, sugar, pies, and everything on the counter. Soon Joan and I were joined by John Salter, but the moment he sat down he was hit on the jaw with what appeared to be brass knuckles. Blood gushed from his face and someone threw salt into the open wound. Ed King, Tougaloo's chaplain, rushed to him.

At the other end of the counter, Lois and Pearlena were

joined by George Raymond, a CORE field worker and a student from Jackson State College. Then a Negro high school boy sat down next to me. The mob took spray paint from the counter and sprayed it on the new demonstrators. The high school student had on a white shirt; the word "nigger" was written on his back with red spray paint.

We sat there for three hours taking a beating when the manager decided to close the store because the mob had begun to go wild with stuff from other counters. He begged and begged everyone to leave. But even after fifteen minutes of begging, no one budged. They would not leave until we did. Then Dr. Beittel, the president of Tougaloo College, came running in. He said he had just heard what was happening.

About ninety policemen were standing outside the store; they had been watching the whole thing through the windows, but had not come in to stop the mob or do anything. President Beittel went outside and asked Captain Ray to come and escort us out. The captain refused, stating the manager had to invite him in before he could enter the premises, so Dr. Beittel himself brought us out. He had told the police that they had better protect us after we were outside the store. When we got outside, the policemen formed a single line that blocked the mob from us. However, they were allowed to throw at us everything they had collected. Within ten minutes, we were picked up by Reverend King in his station wagon and taken to the NAACP headquarters on Lynch Street.

After the sit-in, all I could think of was how sick Mississippi whites were. They believed so much in the segregated Southern way of life, they would kill to preserve it. I sat there in the NAACP office and thought of how many times they had killed when this way of life was threatened. I knew that the killing had just begun. "Many more will die before it is over with," I thought. Before the sit-in, I had always hated the whites in Mississippi. Now I knew it was impossible for me to hate sickness. The whites had a disease, an incurable disease in its final stage. What were our chances against such a disease? I thought of the students, the young Negroes who had just begun to protest, as young interns. When these young interns got older, I thought, they would be the best doctors in the world for social problems.

Before we were taken back to campus, I wanted to get my hair washed. It was stiff with dried mustard, ketchup and sugar. I stopped in at a beauty shop across the street from the NAACP office. I didn't have on any shoes because I had lost them when I was dragged across the floor at Woolworth's. My stockings were sticking to my legs from the mustard that had dried on them. The hairdresser took one look at me and said, "My land, you were in the sit-in huh?"

"Yes," I answered. "Do you have time to wash my hair and style it?"

"Right away," she said, and she meant right away. There were three other ladies already waiting, but they seemed glad to let me go ahead of them. The hairdresser was real nice. She even took my stockings off and washed my legs while my hair was drying.

There was a mass rally that night at the Pearl Street Church in Jackson, and the place was packed. People were standing two abreast in the aisles. Before the speakers began, all the sit-inners walked out on the stage and were introduced by Medgar Evers. People stood and applauded for what seemed like thirty minutes or more. Medgar told the audience that this was just the beginning of such demonstrations. He asked them to pledge themselves to unite in a massive offensive against segregation in Jackson, and throughout the state. The rally ended with "We Shall Overcome" and sent home hundreds of determined people. It seemed as though Mississippi Negroes were about to get together at last.

Before I demonstrated, I had written Mama. She wrote me back a letter, begging me not to take part in the sit-in. She even sent ten dollars for bus fare to New Orleans. I didn't have one penny, so I kept the money. Mama's letter made me mad. I had to live my life as I saw fit. I had made that decision when I left home. But it hurt to have my family prove to me how scared they were. It hurt me more than anything else—I knew the whites had already started the threats and intimidations. I was the first Negro from my hometown who had openly demonstrated, worked with the NAACP, or anything. When Negroes threatened to do anything in Centreville, they were either shot like Samuel O'Quinn or run out of town, like Reverend Dupree.

I didn't answer Mama's letter. Even if I had written one, she wouldn't have received it before she saw the news on TV or heard it on the radio. I waited to hear from her again. And I waited to hear in the news that someone in Centreville had been murdered. If so, I knew it would be a member of my family.

5

FROM

The Long Shadow of Little Rock

by Daisy Bates
(1919?–   )

Daisy Lee Gatson was born "in the little sawmill town" of Huttig, Arkansas. Huttig was a company town, and it was there that she felt the first sickening impact of racial discrimination. Miss Gatson (later Mrs. L. C. Bates) has been a determined worker for the civil-rights movement all her life. She and her husband moved to Little Rock in 1941 and started a newspaper, the State Press. *She was elected state president of the NAACP. It is not surprising, therefore, that she was a leader in the effort to integrate Central High School in Little Rock in 1957.*

Arkansas had been moving along—albeit slowly—in the direction set by the school-desegregation decision of the Supreme Court in 1954. The local school board of Little Rock had already proposed admittance of nine Negro students to the high school in the fall of 1957, and this proposal was met with tacit, if reluctant, acceptance by the community. On August 22, 1957, however, Governor Griffin of Georgia, addressing an Arkansas audience, lashed out at the Supreme Court decision and praised local segregation groups. Arkansas Governor Faubus joined with Griffin and whipped up the mob by surrounding Central High School with National Guardsmen, and announcing on television that "blood will run in the streets" if Negro students attempted to enter Central High.

On the following pages Daisy Bates describes the courage of the families, especially the children, willing to stand up against the racist South.

LITTLE ROCK was tense and solemn the day of September twenty-second before the volcano of hate finally erupted in a mighty explosion heard around the world. Except for the urgent, erratic pealing of church bells, the streets were ominously quiet. Hidden behind locked doors were the city's children, who usually were outside at this time, laughing, roller skating, playing ball, and jumping rope. Few strollers took advantage of the pleasant sunny weather; if they had no urgent business outdoors they remained indoors with their children, occupying themselves with the minute details of their personal lives. To anyone familiar with Little Rock on a sunny Sunday afternoon, the city seemed to have stopped breathing.

Some of the clergy had called for a city-wide day of prayer for peace, and many earnest men and women, both black and white, silently appealed to God for help and guidance. But many others, including ministers of God, screamed for action against what they deemed an affront to the Southern way of life, to God and the white people. Before the day ended Mrs. Margaret Jackson, head of the Mothers League, issued a statement calling for an all-out demonstration in front of the school the next morning.

Elizabeth Eckford came by my home after church. "Mrs. Bates," she asked, "now that the National Guard's gone, what's going to happen? Are we going in tomorrow? Will we have protection this time?"

"I'm sure you will, dear," I told her.

I explained to her that Chief of Police Marvin Potts was mobilizing his police forces, that the school board was meeting, and that by the day's end we should know the extent of the protection that would be given.

"Did you know," asked Elizabeth, "two white ministers and a lawyer visited all of our homes Friday and prayed with us?"

"Yes." I smiled. "I knew." The ministers had come to the *State Press* office earlier Friday to tell me, "We came to pray with you." I had just finished reading an article concerning the Reverend Wesley Pruden, pastor of the Broadmoor Baptist Church and a leader in the Capital Citizens Council. I had been thinking about the hundreds of ministers who had not spoken out against the mobsters who had been terrorizing the city in the last seventeen days. I had heard that many ministers were privately pro-integration, and I wished that these men were even half as vocal as Mr. Pruden.

Therefore I may have been a bit impatient when I replied to my visitors: "I don't need prayer. If you are really interested in doing something to help, go visit the homes of the nine children—pray with them—they are the ones who will have to face the mob."

The ministers were the Reverend Bert Cartwright, of the Methodist Church, and the Reverend William Campbell of the National Council of Churches, the Nashville minister who had been among those accompanying the children the first day. With them was C. C. Mercer, a Negro attorney.

Superintendent of Schools Blossom called me late that night and asked me to notify the children to meet the next morning at my house where they were to await further instructions as to how to get them to school. Assistant Chief of Police Gene Smith, I was told, would be in charge of the city police at the school.

On Monday morning, September 23, all nine children, accompanied by their parents, arrived at my home before eight o'clock. All but two parents had to leave for work immediately. The two who remained were Oscar Eckford, a night worker, and Mrs. Imogene Brown, an unemployed practical nurse.

Reporters came and went. They wanted to know whether the children were going to school. A few of the newspapermen called me aside, lowered their voices, and asked, "Mrs. Bates, are you really sending the children to Central? The mob there is really vicious now."

There were several radio outlets in our home and the children stationed themselves all over the house to listen. Radio commentators were broadcasting sidewalk interviews with men and women in the mob gathered in front of Central. A man was saying, "Just let those niggers show up! Just let 'em try!" Someone else said, "We won't stand for our schools being integrated. If we let 'em, next thing they'll be marrying our daughters."

None of us said anything, but all of us were watching the hands of the clock move closer to eight-thirty. The radios blared, but the children were strangely silent. Elizabeth sat alone, almost motionless. Carlotta and Ernest walked restlessly from room to room. The faces of all were solemn but determined.

Once when I entered the living room I saw Mrs. Brown

seated on the sofa, her hands clasped tightly in her lap, her eyes closed, her lips moving in prayer. Across the room Mr. Eckford sat with bowed head. For the first time I found that I was praying, too.

At last the call came from the police. They told us it would be safer to take a roundabout route to the school. They would meet us near Central and escort the children through a side entrance.

The white newsmen left my home for Central High. The Negro reporters remained, seating themselves around the kitchen table drinking coffee. They were: L. Alex Wilson, general manager and editor of the *Tri-State Defender,* of Memphis, Tennessee; James Hicks, managing editor of the *New York Amsterdam News;* Moses J. Newsome of the *Afro-American,* of Baltimore, Maryland; and Earl Davy, *State Press* photographer.

I told them they must take a different route from the one the children would take, but that if they were at the Sixteenth Street and Park Avenue entrance to Central, they would be able to see the nine enter the school.

We had two cars. I went in the first car with some of the children and C. C. Mercer. Frank Smith, field secretary of the NAACP, followed with the rest of the nine. To this day I cannot remember which of the nine were in our car. Nor can they.

As we approached the side entrance to the school, the main body of the mob was moving away from us. I got out of the car and told the children to go quickly. From the sidewalk I watched the police escort them through the door of the school. Someone in the mob saw them enter and yelled, "They're in! The niggers are in!"

The people on the fringes of the mob started moving toward us. A policeman rushed up to me. "Get back in the car, Mrs. Bates. Drive back the way you came, and fast!"

I tumbled into the car. Mr. Mercer was waiting at the wheel. The car radio was on and a hoarse-voiced announcer was saying: "The Negro children are being mobbed in front of the school." I knew the children were in the school and, for the moment, at least, safe. But who was being mobbed?

We sped back to the house to reassure Mrs. Brown and Mr. Eckford. Then I called the other parents at work to quiet their fears.

A series of false radio reports followed. Newscasters, broadcasting from the school grounds, reported that the children were being beaten and were running down the halls of the school, bloodstained; that the police were trying to get them out, but the nine children, hysterical with fright, had locked themselves in an empty classroom.

A young white lawyer, who was very close to Assistant Chief of Police Gene Smith, devised a plan by which he would keep me informed of the goings on inside the school. When I called him, he assured me that the reports were false. After each report I would check with him, then call the parents. Once Mr. Eckford screamed at me in exasperation, "Well, if it's not true why would they say such things on the air?"

"The children have barricaded themselves inside the school, the mob is breaking through the barricades, and the police are powerless to rescue the children," we heard one breathless newscaster announce. Again I called and demanded to know what was going on. I was told that the children were safe, but the police didn't know how much longer their forces could control the mob, which had now grown to over a thousand.

Later that day we learned that a white teen-age girl had been slipping in and out of the school, issuing false reports to the radio broadcasters. They had put her statements on the air without checking them. Gene Smith, Assistant

Chief of Police, had finally caught up with her and ordered her arrested.

One could say it was the answer to Mrs. Brown's prayer that the Negro reporters arrived at Central about five minutes ahead of us. Jimmy Hicks of the *Amsterdam News* later told me just what did happen that morning.

"We parked our car near the school and made a dash for the Sixteenth Street entrance. When the mob saw us, they yelled, 'Here they come!' and came rushing at us. The women screamed, 'Get the niggers! Get 'em!' About a thousand folk blocked the streets. One big burly guy swung at my head. I ducked. The blow landed on my shoulder, spinning me around. I ran between two parked cars which concealed me from the mob. Two men jumped on top of Earl Davy, dragging him into a bank of high grass. Others were kicking and beating him while the two held him. They took his press camera and threw it to the sidewalk and smashed it flat with their feet. Several men jumped on Alex Wilson, knocking him to the ground and kicking him in the stomach. As he was getting up, one of the mobsters hollered, 'Run, nigger!' Alex wouldn't run. The brute, with a brick in his hand, jumped on Alex's back, and raised the brick to crush Alex's skull.

"'The niggers are in the school! The niggers are in the school!'

"The man jumped off Alex's back, calling to the others, 'Come on! The niggers are in!' The mobsters beating Davy, Newsome, and Wilson all charged toward the school like a pack of wild animals.

"We probably saved you and the children, but I know you saved us. Some of the mob had spotted me between the cars and were advancing on me with sticks and clubs. And when they charged toward the school, we got the hell out of there. But you know, during all that beating, Alex never let go of his hat."

The frenzied mob rushed the police barricades. One man was heard to say, "So they sneaked them in behind our back. That's all we need. Let's go get our shotguns!" Hysterical women helped to break the barricades and then urged the men to go in and "get the niggers out!" Some of the women screamed for their children to "Come out! Don't stay in there with those niggers!" About fifty students rushed out, crying, "They're in! They're in!"

Around eleven-thirty, Gene Smith realized his police force was inadequate to hold the mob. He ordered the nine removed from the school. They were taken out through a delivery entrance in the rear of the school, placed in police cars and driven to their homes. When it was announced that the children had been removed, the reporters rushed to my home and asked me what was our next step. Would the nine return to Horace Mann, the all-Negro school? I said No, they were going to remain out of the school until the President of the United States guaranteed them protection within Central High School. This was interpreted by the reporters as my having requested troops.

The mob, thwarted in its attempt to put its hands on the Negro children, switched momentarily to another field of battle. They went after the "Yankee" reporters.

The entire *Life* magazine staff on the scene was beaten. Photographers Francis Miller and Gray Villet were slugged in the mouth. Writer Paul Welch was beaten in the face and cut on the neck. All three men were arrested for inciting a riot. After their release Mr. Miller said, in bitter sarcasm, that he was evidently arrested for striking a man's fist with his face.

Most of the citizens of Little Rock were stunned as they witnessed a savage rebirth of passion and racial hatred that had lain dormant since Reconstruction days. As dusk was falling, tension and fear grew. The mob spread throughout the city, venting its fury on any Negro in sight.

Two Negro women driving through the city were pulled from their car and beaten. Two Negro men in a truck were surrounded by the mob near the school and beaten, and their truck windows smashed with rocks. Mayor Woodrow Mann wired President Eisenhower for protection. The Justice Department called Harry Ashmore, editor of the *Arkansas Gazette,* and asked him to describe the situation. He said, "I'll give it to you in one sentence. The police have been routed, the mob is in the streets and we're close to a reign of terror."

That evening I sat in the semidarkened living room with L. C. [Mrs. Bates' husband] and reporters, watching the empty quiet street through our broken living-room window. The police car that had been assigned to guard our house was barely visible across the street. A cab stopped in front of the house. All of us stood up. I heard a soft click. L. C. had released the safety on his .45 automatic. Dr. G. P. Freeman, our next-door neighbor and dentist, was aimlessly running his hand along the barrel of a shotgun he held in his left hand. When Alex Wilson of the Memphis *Tri-State Defender* stepped from the cab, I breathed a sigh of relief. As he entered the house Alex said, "I had planned to return earlier, but the story of the mob was a little difficult to write." He took L. C.'s gun, saying, "I'll watch for a while." He took a seat in front of the window. I watched him place his light gray hat on the table near him. I thought, "What a guy! He took the brunt of the mob today, yet here he is holding a gun to help protect *us.*"

The radio commentator reported that teen-age mobs had taken to cars and were driving wildly through the streets throwing bottles and bricks into Negroes' homes and places of business. One of the white reporters jumped out of his seat. "Ye gods!" he demanded. "Aren't they *ever* going to stop? Such hate! I heard a woman say today, 'I hope they drag nine dead niggers from that school.' "

I left the room to call the parents of the pupils to see whether they had adequate protection. They reported that the city police were on the job. About 10:30 P. M. I returned to the living room. Brice Miller, reporter for the United Press International, was talking to L. C. I saw his photographer in the shadow across the street.

"What's up, Brice?" I asked.

"Oh, nothing. Just checking."

"Oh, come now," I said. "We've all heard the rumor that the mob would ride tonight, and this will probably be their first stop. Isn't that the reason your photographer is across the street?"

"Well, yes," he admitted.

"Where did you hear the rumor?"

"One of the segregationist students told me. She was so pleased to have a reporter hanging on her words. I, of course, notified the police and the FBI."

L. C. broke into the conversation. "Something's up—things are too quiet." He asked Brice Miller about the radio reports.

"Oh, they're just a bunch of wild kids getting in on the act. They're not the real dangerous ones," he guessed.

"Say, Freeman," said L. C., "maybe we should stand guard outside for a while."

L. C. got a shotgun from the closet and, with Dr. Freeman, went outside. I went into the kitchen to make coffee. Brice Miller followed. "Since I'm here," he said, "maybe you can give me the reaction of the parents to today's mob."

Just then L. C. rushed back into the house. "Something's up! A car just passed driving slow with its lights off and a bunch of tough-looking characters in it. And the police car outside is following it."

Miller plunged past L. C., calling his photographer. "Come on! This might be it." Not only his photographer but all the reporters except Alex Wilson followed him.

"Do you have plenty of ammunition for these guns?" Alex asked.

"Yes," L. C. said.

"Well, we'll be ready for them if they show up."

Dr. Freeman stood guard at the bedroom window, Alex Wilson at the living-room, and L. C. at the kitchen window. L. C. told me to turn out the lights and go downstairs. I turned out the lights and sat on the top step of the stairway. We heard the wail of sirens approaching us. The minutes seemed like hours as I sat in the darkened stairway waiting for something to happen.

"The police are back," said L. C. He opened the door and turned on the lights.

"Turn that light off!" commanded the policeman as he entered. "And stay away from the window." The policeman, a big, red-haired man, was tense with excitement. "We just stopped a motorcade of about one hundred cars, two blocks from here. When we followed that car that passed, we ran into the mob head on. We radioed for help and a whole group of city and Federal agents showed up. We found dynamite, guns, pistols, clubs, everything, in the cars. Some of the mob got away on foot, leaving their cars. We don't know what will happen tonight, so no one is to leave the house."

No one slept that night.

At about 2:30 A.M. the phone rang. I answered. A man's voice said, "We didn't get you last night, but we will. And you better not try to put those coons in our school!"

Just before dawn I went to the kitchen to make a fresh pot of coffee. L. C. was sitting by the window, his shotgun cradled in his arm. Dawn was breaking. I watched the sky turn from dull gray to pale pink as the sun's rays flashed across the horizon. The aroma of the coffee aroused Wilson and Freeman from their cramped sitting positions. They entered the kitchen looking tired and worn.

"And I thought I had it tough as a correspondent during the Second World War," said Alex.

"I'm going to stick to pulling teeth, myself," said Freeman.

The next day the children remained at home. A tense and weary city waited to hear from the White House.

The reporters sat around our living room, drinking coffee and arguing among themselves on what possible action the President might take.

That morning calls came into my home from NAACP people, from parents, business and professional people, all asking the same question. "Have you heard from the White House?"

Around 8:30 A.M. a city truck stopped in front of my house and a tall, husky Negro man approached the door and rang the bell. "Mrs. Bates, have you heard anything from Washington?"

"No, not directly," I said, "but the President issued a proclamation..."

Before I could explain what the proclamation said and what I hoped it meant, he exclaimed: "Proclamation be damned! We've had the Constitution since 1789 and I doubt whether those goons who took over our town yesterday can read. Last night they came into our neighborhood and rocked our homes, breaking windows, and all that. We've taken a lot because we didn't want to hurt the chances of Negro kids, but I doubt whether the Negroes are going to take much more without fighting back. I think I'll take the rest of the day off and check my shotgun and make sure it's in working condition." He walked away.

Just then another group of white reporters joined the others in my living room.

"Why aren't you at Central?" I asked them.

"Ha! Are you kidding?" one of them replied, speaking for the rest. "There's a mob of about five hundred out there in front of the school—jeering the city police standing in front of the barricades. It's a mean-looking bunch, too. We got out of there when we saw the police arrest two of them for carrying taped rubber hoses filled with lead."

"Are there any reporters out there now?"

"A few, but they're sticking close together."

In midafternoon the city was electrified by the news that President Eisenhower had federalized all ten thousand men of the Arkansas National Guard units. He had also authorized Charles E. Wilson, Secretary of Defense, to send in such regular United States troops as he deemed necessary " . . . to enforce any order of the United States District Court for the Eastern District of Arkansas for the removal of obstruction of Justice in the State of Arkansas with respect to matters relating to enrollment and attendance at public schools in the Little Rock School District." Under the authorization of this order, the Secretary of Defense ordered 1,000 paratroopers to Little Rock from Fort Campbell, Kentucky. The soldiers were part of the 101st Airborne "Screaming Eagle" Division of the 327th Infantry Regiment.

When the Negro and white paratroopers arrived at Camp Robinson, an Army Base in the suburb of North Little Rock, there was a general exodus of newsmen from our house. One reporter called back to me, "Come on, Mrs. Bates, aren't you going to see the troops enter the city?"

"No," I replied, "but thank God they're here."

After the newsmen were gone, I walked out onto the lawn. I heard the deep drone of big planes, and it sounded like music to my ears. I walked around the yard. I saw other women standing in their yards, looking upward, listening. I heard the subdued laughter of children and realized how long it had been since I'd heard that sound. Kept within doors in recent days, they now spilled out onto yards and driveways. From an open kitchen doorway Mrs. Anderson was heard singing, "Nobody knows the trouble I've seen . . ." A fear-paralyzed city had begun to stir again.

Around 6 P.M., the long line of trucks, jeeps, and staff cars entered the heart of the city to the wailing sound of sirens and the dramatic flashing of lights from the police cars escorting the caravan to Central High School. The "Battle of Little Rock" was on.

Some of the citizens watching the arrival of the troops cried with relief. Others cursed the Federal Government for "invading our city." One got the impression that the "Solid South" was no longer solid.

A young white reporter rushed to my house and grabbed me by the hands, swinging me around. "Daisy, they're here! The soldiers are here! Aren't you excited? Aren't you happy"

"Excited, yes, but not happy," I said after getting myself unwhirled. "Any time it takes eleven thousand five hundred soldiers to assure nine Negro children their constitutional right in a democratic society, I can't be happy."

"I think I understand how you feel," the reporter said. "You're thinking about all the other southern Negro children who'll have to 'hit the line ' someday."

"Yes, and I'm sure there will be many."

"What's the next move?" he asked. "Will the children be going back to Central tomorrow?"

I parried the question. I knew the parents would be on tenterhooks waiting to hear from me, and with the same question on their minds. I delayed calling them. I was awaiting a call from Superintendent Blossom. Finally, about

10 P.M., I called all the parents to tell them I had not heard from Mr. Blossom. I assumed that the mob would be at the school the next morning, and therefore decided that the children could not be sent to Central the next day, troops or not.

Shortly after midnight Mr. Blossom telephoned. "Mrs. Bates, I understand you instructed the children that they were not to go to Central in the morning."

"That is correct."

"But General Walker said that he is here to put the children in school. So you must have them at your house by eight-thirty in the morning." Major General Edwin A. Walker, chief of the Arkansas Military District, had been put in command of the 101st Airborne Division and newly federalized Arkansas militia.

"I can't," I said. "I can't reach them. We have an agreement that if I want them, I will call *before* midnight. In order to get some sleep and avoid the harassing calls, they take their phones off the hook after midnight." How I wish I had done the same, I thought wearily, as I listened to the Superintendent's urgent tones. "I suppose I could go to each home, but I can't go alone," I said.

"I'll call Hawkins and Christophe and ask them to accompany you," Mr. Blossom said. "You may expect them shortly." Edwin Hawkins was Principal of Dunbar Junior High School and L. M. Christophe was Principal of Horace Mann High School, both Negro schools.

At about 1 A.M. the three of us set out. Our first stop was some eight blocks away, the home of fifteen-year-old Gloria Ray. We knocked for what seemed ten minutes before we got an answer. The door opened about three inches exposing the muzzle of a shotgun. Behind it stood Gloria's father.

"What do you want now?" was his none-too-cordial greeting, as he looked straight at me. He forgot—I hoped that was the reason—to remove his finger from the trigger or at least to lower the gun.

My eyes were fixed on the muzzle, and I could sense that Hawkins and Christophe, standing behind me, were riveted in attention. In my most pleasant, friendliest voice, and trying to look at him instead of the gun, I said that the children were to be at my house by eight-thirty the next morning, and that those were the instructions of Superintendent Blossom.

"I don't care if the President of the United States gave you those instructions!" he said irritably. "I won't let Gloria go. She's faced two mobs and that's enough."

Both Mr. Christophe and Mr. Hawkins assured him that with the Federal troops there, the children would be safe. We all, of course, added that the decision was up to him. At this point I asked if he wouldn't mind lowering his gun. He did. I told him if he changed his mind to bring Gloria to my house in the morning. Somewhat shakily we made our way to the car.

"Good Lord," sighed Mr. Christophe, "are we going to have to go through this with all nine sets of parents?"

The children's homes were widely scattered over Little Rock, and so our tour took better than three hours. Our encounter with Mr. Ray impressed on our minds the need to identify ourselves immediately upon entering the grounds of each home. But the cautious parents still greeted us with gun in hand, although they were a little more calm than Mr. Ray, and accepted the change in plans without objection.

At eight twenty-five the next morning, all the children except Gloria had arrived. My phone rang. "What time are we to be there, Mrs. Bates?" It was Gloria.

"They're all here now."

"Wait for me!" she said. "I'll be right over!"

In less than ten minutes, Mr. Ray, shy and smiling, led Gloria into the house. He looked down at his daughter with pride. "Here, Daisy, she's yours. She's determined to go. Take her. You seem to have more influence over her than I have, anyhow."

No sooner had Gloria joined the group than I was called to the telephone. A school official wanted to know whether the children were there. "All nine," I answered. I was told that a convoy for them was on its way.

While we waited, reporters were asking the nine how they felt, and the children, tense and excited, found it difficult to be articulate about the significance of the troops' mission. Half an hour crawled by. Jeff, standing at the window, called out, "The Army's here! They're here!"

Jeeps were rolling down Twenty-eighth Street. Two passed our house and parked at the end of the block, while two remained at the other end of the block. Paratroopers quickly jumped out and stood across the width of the street at each end of the block—those at the western end standing at attention facing west, and those at the eastern end facing east.

An Army station wagon stopped in front of our house. While photographers, perched precariously on the tops of cars and rooftops, went into action, the paratrooper in charge of the detail leaped out of the station wagon and started up our driveway. As he approached, I heard Minnijean say gleefully, "Oh, look at them, they're so—so soldierly! It gives you goose pimples to look at them!" And then she added solemnly, "For the first time in my life, I feel like an American citizen."

The officer was at the door, and as I opened it, he saluted and said, his voice ringing through the sudden quiet of the living room where a number of friends and parents of the nine had gathered to witness this moment in history: "Mrs.

Bates, we're ready for the children. We will return them to your home at three-thirty o'clock."

I watched them follow him down the sidewalk. Another paratrooper held open the door of the station wagon, and they got in. Turning back into the room, my eyes none too dry, I saw the parents with tears of happiness in their eyes as they watched the group drive off.

Tense and dramatic events were taking place in and around the school while the Negro pupils were being transported by the troops of the 101st Airborne from my home to Central High.

Major General Edwin A. Walker, operation commander, was explaining to the student body, in the school auditorium, the duties and responsibilities of his troops.

" . . . You have nothing to fear from my soldiers and no one will interfere with your coming, going, or your peaceful pursuit of your studies. However, I would be less than honest if I failed to tell you that I intend to use all means necessary to prevent any interference with the execution of your school board's plan . . ."

A block from the school, a small group of hard-core segregationists ignored Major James Meyers' orders to disperse peacefully and return to their homes. The major repeated the command when the surly, angry crowd refused to disperse. He was forced to radio for additional help. About thirty soldiers answered the emergency call "on the double," wearing steel helmets, carrying bayonet fixed rifles, their gas masks in readiness, and "walkie-talkies" slung over their shoulders.

The soldiers lowered their rifles and moved slowly and deliberately into the crowd. The mob quickly gave way, shouting insults at the troops in the process. In a matter of minutes the streets, which for days had been littered with hate-filled

mobs, cigarette butts, half-eaten sandwiches, and used flash
bulbs, were strangely quiet.

At 9:22 A.M. the nine Negro pupils marched solemnly
through the doors of Central High School, surrounded by
twenty-two [Airborne troops] soldiers. An Army helicopter
circled overhead. Around the massive brick schoolhouse 350
paratroopers stood grimly at attention. Scores of reporters,
photographers, and TV cameramen made a mad dash for
telephones, typewriters, and TV studios, and within minutes
a world that had been holding its breath learned that the
nine pupils, protected by the might of the United States
military, had finally entered the "never-never land."

When classes ended that afternoon, the troops escorted the
pupils to my home. Here we held the first of many conferences that were to take place during the hectic months
ahead.

I looked into the face of each child, from the frail, ninety-
pound Thelma Mothershed with a cardiac condition, to the
well-built sturdy Ernest Green, oldest of them all. They sat
around the room, subdued and reflective—and under-
standably so. Too much had happened to them in these
frenzied weeks to be otherwise.

I asked if they had a rough day. Not especially, they said.
Some of the white pupils were friendly and had even invited
them to lunch. Some were indifferent, and only a few
showed open hostility.

Minnijean Brown reported that she had been invited by
her classmates to join the glee club.

"Then why the long faces?" I wanted to know.

"Well," Ernest spoke up, "you don't expect us to be jumping for joy, do you?"

Someone said, "But, Ernest, we *are* in Central, and that
shouldn't make us feel sad exactly."

"Sure we're in Central," Ernest shot back, somewhat impatiently. "But how did we get in? We got in, finally, because we were protected by paratroops. Some victory!" he said sarcastically.

"Are you sorry," someone asked him, "that the President sent the troops?"

"No," said Ernest. "I'm only sorry it had to be that way."

6

FROM

Go South to Sorrow

by Carl Rowan

(1925–   )

In 1890 Mississippi solved the problem of excluding the Negro from the ballot without contravening the Fifteenth Amendment to the United States Constitution. A suffrage amendment was written into the Mississippi constitution which imposed a poll tax of two dollars, excluded voters convicted of certain crimes, and also barred all those who could not read any section of the state constitution or understand it when read or give a reasonable interpretation of it. Isaiah T. Montgomery, the only Negro delegate to the Mississippi constitutional convention, said the poll tax and education requirements would disenfranchise 123,000 blacks and only 11,000 whites. By 1910 North Carolina, Alabama, Virginia, Georgia, and Oklahoma had followed suit, and the Negro was effectively disenfranchised in those states.

In a small town in Mississippi, newsman Carl Rowan interviewed an elderly man named Gus Courts in the late 1950s. When, some five years earlier, someone had asked Courts what he would like most to do, Courts replied, "To vote." In this selection from Go South to Sorrow *Courts tells Rowan what obstacles stood between him and first-class citizenship in Humphreys County, Mississippi.*

Carl Rowan, newspaperman, author, and later ambassador to Finland, was born in Tennessee. Although he spent many years writing for the Minneapolis Tribune, *it was to his native South that he returned to gather material for his books* South of Freedom *and* Go South to Sorrow.

"IN 1952 a few of us Negroes decided we wanted to be first-class citizens. We formed the 'Citizens League' and tried to pay our poll taxes.

"Sheriff Ike Shelton refused to let us pay. We consulted Dr. T. R. M. Howard at the Regional Council of Negro Leadership in Mound Bayou [an all-Negro town where Howard lived until 1956, when he left Mississippi under "pressure"]. Howard referred us to a white lawyer who helped us file an affidavit charging the sheriff with a federal offense. The sheriff was called before a federal grand jury in Oxford. Three or four of us Negroes were summoned up. Reverend George W. Lee was one of them.

"We got up to Oxford, but they compromised when the sheriff agreed to open the books and let Negroes pay their poll taxes, so we never were called. We came back, and the sheriff let every Negro in our Citizens League pay their poll tax. Reverend Lee printed literature, and we put it out, urging other Negroes to pay their poll tax. In 1953 and 1954 about four hundred Negroes paid their poll tax, and about ninety-five registered to vote.

"But when the Supreme Court ruled that segregation in public schools was unconstitutional, things tightened up. The whites formed a Citizens Council and Negroes who had registered began to get threats. Soon we noticed that just about every peckerwood in town had a list of the registered Negroes.

"One day a planter who I worked for for several years came to me with a list and took me off alone. He told me to get my name off.

"You mean I've got to take my name off after all this fighting to get it on?" I asked him.

"He said yes—but I refused.

"A little later he came to me [about July, 1954] and said: 'Gus, the Citizens Council wants to talk to you.'

"I was working for him at the time, I also was president of the NAACP.

"He takes me to the bank—right into the office of a vice president. About twelve or fifteen white men was sitting around.

" 'Courts, you're doing something the white citizens here disapprove of,' the banker said.

"I asked him what.

" 'Get it through your head, Courts. The white people here are not going to stand for any NAACP here. They're agitators and they're Communistic,' he tells me.

"I told him the NAACP was holding up for the law.

"I asked if it was against the law for us to vote, and he said no. 'But you tell me you're going to stop us?' I asked him.

" 'Yes, we'll force you out of your store. We'll see that you can't work anywhere. You can't buy anything.'

"He demanded the NAACP membership list, but I told him that, far as I could recall, there was only one member; me, the president.

"After this, they didn't rant or cut up. They talked real nice and let me go."

(In a telephone interview, the banker told me that "to the best of my knowledge, no Citizens Council meeting ever was held at the bank, and to the best of my knowledge, Courts never attended a Citizens Council meeting." He said he definitely is a member of the Citizens Council, as are "most of the substantial members of the community—I'd say ninety-five per cent of the white men." He said he had "talked to Courts" but denied efforts to prevent him from voting.

"How do you feel about Negroes voting?" I asked him.

"You know how I feel."

"No, how do you feel?"

"I'd rather not say."

Courts goes on with his story:

"A month after the bank meeting I was revisited by my employer. He asked me to talk to him in his car.

"He took out the list of registered Negroes and told me: 'Well, Gus, getting your name off ain't gonna help you none now. They see where your heart is.'

"I got out of his car and—I reckon I shouldn't have did this, but I did—I said, 'Damn the Citizens Council.'

"Three days after I said 'damn the Citizens Council,' I went to pay the rent on my store (I always paid in advance).

"The landlord refused to accept my rent. He gave me ten days to get out. I walked right out and went across the street where I rented a place from a Negro.

"I hadn't been there a week when another white member of the Citizens Council came into my store. He asked to talk to me and I got in his car.

"He held up the same list of voters—didn't say a word, just let me read the list. There was a 'v' behind my name. I said, 'What's that "v" for?'

"He said it meant that those with the 'v' were qualified to vote. I saw that they had whittled the ninety-five names down to about twenty-five. He says to me: 'What the Council wants me to find out is do you intend to vote.'

" 'Is it against the law?'

" 'No.'

" 'Then I intends to vote.'

" 'Get out,' he said to me. I started back to my store and he blew his horn and said: 'Have I threatened you?'

" 'No, sir.'

" 'Then I'd better not read anywhere that you said I did.' "

(I also contacted this man by telephone. He described Courts as "one of the biggest liars there is in the county— why, half the Nigras here wouldn't believe him on oath." He denied that he ever tried to pressure Courts out of voting. "I don't know that I ever talked to him," he said.

"Are you a member of the White Citizens Council?" I asked.

"I am. The best businessmen, farmers and lawyers, and some preachers are all members."

"Did the Citizens Council call Courts before it at a meeting at the bank?"

"Well, no. Some of the boys talked to him there, but that wasn't an official Council meeting. That was before the Council actually was officially formed. We didn't form the Council till July or August, 1954.")

Courts goes on:

"Meanwhile, Reverend Lee, the Negro minister who was influential in getting Negroes registered, not only refused to take his name off the list but was active trying to get other Negroes to stand firm."

(On the night of May 7, 1955, Reverend Lee was killed by two shotgun blasts fired from a passing car as he was driving home in Belzoni. Asked to investigate, the sheriff expressed uncertainty that he had been shot. He said the lead pellets in the Negro minister's neck and jaw "could have' been fillings from his teeth.")

Courts goes on:

"The day Reverend Lee was killed, a white man came to my store and said, 'You see what happened to Reverend Lee?'

" 'Yes, sir.'

" 'You know, that could happen to you.'

" 'You're right.'

" 'You know, the sheriff and the doctor both could be too late.'

"Then the white man walked away.

"I was a little uneasy now, especially knowing what they did to Reverend Lee. I guess everybody was a little bit more nervous when the Negro domestics—you know, the cooks and the nursemaids—came home with word that the first Negro to put a foot on the courthouse steps on election day would be shot.

"We twenty-two Negroes who had refused to take our names off the registration list called a meeting and drafted a letter to Mississippi Governor Hugh White, asking protection on election day.

"The governor should have sent our petition to the sheriff but instead it came back to the Citizens Council.

"Despite the threats, we twenty-two Negroes met and decided to go to vote together. We figured they was cowards— you know, they ain't gonna do nothing, 'less they catch a man off to hisself.

"We got to the poll and the whites were all lined up on both sides of the walk. But one white man stepped out and, in a real nice voice, said they was gonna let us vote.

"I felt so good. He told us to come to the side door and go in two at a time. Well, bless the Lord, they handed us a typewritten sheet of questions. Questions like, 'Are you a member of the Democratic Party of Mississippi?' and 'Do you believe in integration?'

"I refused to try to answer them. I said I already was a qualified voter. Four or five Negroes tried to answer them, but they were all disqualified. We all left.

"Griff Byrd, a retired Negro professor, said he figured they had beat us and that he would leave the group and go on home. He started down the street alone when suddenly a white guy jumped him and the professor saw a knife cut his clothes near the belly.

"The professor grabbed the knife and it cut his hand to the bone. They took the professor to the hospital and we got the police to question the white guy.

" 'Oh, I was trimming my nails and that nigger walked into me and cut hisself'—that's what the white guy said. That ended that.

"Things got shore enough hot after the professor was cut. I went to the two wholesale houses where I'd been buying my groceries all the time and they said Citizens Council members had told them not to sell to me. One house said it would sell if I paid cash, 'cause there would be no records. I paid cash, but the next week they said the Council people had been back and told them not to sell to me for cash.

"I drove over to Tchula, but as soon as I walked into the wholesale house, the man recognized me and said: 'I can't sell you a thing, Courts.'

"I contacted the drummer from the Greenwood wholesale house, but he said he couldn't sell to me.

"Well, sir, I had a friend in business who was dealing with a wholesale firm in another town. He said he would get me some groceries. He put in an order, but they were suspicious because it was so big. They refused him.

"I gave up on the store and rounded up some hands to go

chop cotton—but every time we got a job, a leader in the Citizens Council would show up and talk to the boss and we'd get fired.

"I put my cotton hands in my truck and drove over to Sunflower County. The Council man followed my truck and told the manager to fire me and my workers. The manager told him no, that I owed him a bit of money and was working off a debt.

"He then saw the main boss, who came out and said that he didn't want to get mixed up with the Citizens Council in Humphreys County and that he'd have to let me go.

"I went back to my store—no job, no groceries to sell, no nothing. My wife told me: 'Now see what a mess you got yourself in, all on account of this civil rights business. Now what you gonna do?'

"Before going to bed that night I got on my knees and prayed: 'Lord, if I'm wrong, show me a sign; but if I'm right, Lord, make a way for me.'

"Next morning we was eating breakfast when a white man banged on my door. He was a drummer from a wholesale house in Jackson. Said he'd opened a new route through Belzoni and had missed me every time through. He wanted to sell me some groceries.

"I told him about the Citizens Council, but he said he didn't care about all that nonsense—that he was just selling groceries to people with money. He gave me a week's credit, took my order and delivered me plenty of groceries.

"Well, I was stacking the groceries in my window when a salesman for a Belzoni wholesale firm passed by and almost fell over he was so amazed.

"That night I was visited by the manager of a local wholesale firm.

" 'Gus, I helped you all I could. But this Citizens Council —it's got you and me tied up,' the manager said to me.

" 'No, sir. They got you tied up—not me. I got groceries now.'

" 'You want to make some money, Gus?'

" 'I reckon I do. I been in the red all my life.'

" 'Gus, you go take your name off the registration books and resign your NAACP leadership and I've got authority to come and load your store with groceries. You can make all the money you want.'

" 'Mister, I'm not gonna sell my rights for no bowl of soup.'

" 'That doesn't sound like any bowl of soup to me, Gus.'

" 'Well, that's what it would be. I'd be selling out my rights—and I got children, mister. I'd be selling out their rights.'

"The wholesale man just laughed and left, shaking his head.

"Three days later, I went to the filling station to buy my kerosene. The manager says to me: 'You know, Gus, this Citizens Council is right straddle my neck for selling to you.'

"Right off, I didn't want him to think I was begging. I said: 'I didn't come to ask you for kerosene. I came to ask you to move your tank out of my store so I can get another one.'

"His face was kinda red, but he told a truck driver to go on over and fill my tank with kerosene. Then he told me he didn't like what the Council was doing.

" 'Gus,' he says to me, 'they're planning to get rid of you—I don't know how, and I don't want to know how. But I know they're planning to get rid of you.'

"About three days later, on Friday, November 25, I was standing in my store making change for a customer. Suddenly a gun fired. The woman buying groceries—Savannah Lutton was her name—ran out of the door. She ran back in screaming: 'Mr. Courts, them's white people out there shooting, Mr. Courts, Mr. Courts, ain't you shot?'

"I looked down and, Lord help me, my arm and my stomach was ableeding. We called for the sheriff but couldn't reach him. Chief of Police M. L. Nichols came. He told me to get over to the Belzoni hospital. I walked out of that store and told a friend of mine to take me to the hospital in Mound Bayou [the all-Negro town] . My wife tells me that a half-hour later the sheriff came into the store,   asking: 'What happened to Courts—where is he?'

" 'My husband's gone to Mound Bayou,' my wife told him.

"She said the sheriff turned angrily to the police chief and cursed him, demanding: 'Why didn't you bring him to the hospital? I've been waiting there with a doctor for half an hour.'

"I reckon if I'd gone to that hospital I wouldn't be alive today," Courts concluded. "The Lord was with me."

7

FROM
Letters to a Black Boy

by Bob Teague
(1929–   )

Bob Teague has made it, in terms of the white world in which he lives. He makes a salary which puts him in the top brackets as far as earning power is concerned. But even though certain executive positions are open to black men now, earning power is not spending power. Teague despairs that not more white-collar jobs are open to blacks, and he decries the fact that no matter how much money he (or any other black) earns, it cannot be spent with as much freedom as Mr. Charlie has.

Teague's form of protest is different from that of many other blacks. It is passive rather than active, negative rather than positive. He simply refuses to vote, and in the following letters to a black boy (who happens to be his son) explains his attitude.

292

Dear Adam,

Having explained that your daddy is not in the front lines
of the Black Revolution, I think a word may be in order
about the private little wars I fight with Mister Charlie
every day. Today I fought a major battle. The weapon of
the enemies was familiar, but extremely powerful in this
terrain—the office where I work. Ah, but they reckoned
without your daddy's derring-do.

Without explanation I was summoned to the fifty-second
floor. That's where the power structure of my company
holds its councils of war. Never before had I reconnoitered
that sanctified stronghold.

When I arrived, still wondering what kind of operation
this might be, I found a dozen Mister Charlies waiting in
ambush. More than that, they were clearly ready to annihi-
late the self I think I am; they were smiling.

The battle was joined with handshakes all around. There
wasn't a man in the trenches, including your daddy, earning less than forty thousand dollars a year. We were not
quite equals, however.

Then they told me. I had been chosen—I suppose by a
vote—to represent our company at a job-opportunity conference in Jersey City. There was a lot of unrest over there,
they said in a stuttering, roundabout way.

As a matter of fact, there is a lot of unrest everywhere.
Only three days ago, I ignored an invitation to attend a job-
opportunity conference at the White House. The telegram
was signed "Hubert H. Humphrey, Vice President."

"Our company is very pleased to be participating in a
conference like this," one of my adversaries said. "We think
there should be more conferences like this in a lot of places
where they are needed. Now. Where do you fit in? Well,
you'll be stationed at a booth with visual exhibits and equipment that show what our company is all about. There'll be

a lot of young fellows circulating among the various booths
set up by a dozen corporations. A lot of young fellows from
the minority groups, I might add. They'll be coming around
to ask questions that you should have no trouble answering."

There was a long, embarrassing cease-fire. One dozen
Charlies were waiting for my response. I couldn't help the
silence; I was too choked with rage to talk.

Finally, I felt controlled enough to try a probing coun-
terattack. Without four-letter words.

"Well, gentlemen," I said slowly, carefully, but a bit
too fiercely. "If you're *telling* me I have to go to this job-
opportunity conference, I'll go. Frankly, I need this job
I've got. But if you're *asking* me about going, then I say I
want nothing to do with it."

There was another ominous silence over the foxholes.
I looked at my bosses around the perimeter. Twelve good
men and true. Their smiles had been replaced by redden-
ing masks of astonishment. There was nothing about this
situation in the field manual.

As for me—I was just plain angry and scared. They could
wipe me out right there.

Dimly, in some barely accessible region of my mind, I
realized that I should have softened my answer. Not my
position, but my answer. I should have given them some in-
dication of my deep involvement with my job in their company, my sense of allegiance and belonging, my apprecia-
tion for their giving me a rare opportunity for self-expression
and self-fulfillment. It was also true that since joining the
company, I had never had a feeling—until that job-con-
ference summons—that I was being misused or exploited
in any way. Not for a moment.

These men had met me on my own terms. I had not been
hired to be a Negro reporter. As a matter of fact, I had been
hired before they knew the color of my skin. One of them

had admired some of my by-line writing in *The New York Times*, and called to offer me a job as a radio news writer. Furthermore, once I accepted the job, they treated me no differently from white writers hired about the same time.

All of us fledglings had been dumped into "the pool." Which meant writing half a dozen news scripts a day, or night, for other people to read on the air. It was the lowest rung in the business. We were told, in effect, that with luck, hard work, devotion to duty and to deadlines, we could work our way up to writing for television. After that, they said, with more luck, et cetera, we might work our way up to street reporter for radio or TV. And after that, with more et ceteras, we might wind up as broadcasters! Hallelujah! With maybe a five-minute news show of our own.

They had seemed to be in no hurry at all to advance me or anyone else in the pool. Which was frustrating at times. But I did have the feeling that my black skin, a handicap most of my life, might now work to my advantage. It would be poetic justice.

That is not how it worked out.

It took me the better part of a year to make the grade in radio writing, and advance to writing for television. There was a great deal I had to learn about editing film and video tape, mixing sound, mixing film and tape, interlocking film with separate sound tracks, projecting two reels of films at the same time, and much more. I learned by asking questions about the things I didn't understand. And by reading books about film and video tape and what makes television work.

Even with concentrated effort, however, it took about a year and a half to qualify as a full-time street reporter. Now I had to learn how to direct the shooting of film at the scene of news events, how to compete with other bird dogs in the street in mass interviews, and much more.

After two years and nine months, I got a nightly fifteen-minute newscast, having filled in occasionally on five-minute TV news shows beforehand. Now I had to learn how to speak all over again. That meant elocution lessons, breathing exercises, memory exercises and, again, much more. It was hard work. The hardest phase perhaps was learning to put together a compact yet comprehensive, understandable and entertaining news package. And supervising writers, production assistants, film editors and videotape editors working with me.

Then, after four and a half years with the company, I was promoted to half-hour newscasts. The hard work continued, and I found still more to learn.

In all that climb, I was never anything less than a general-assignment working stiff, never anything less than my colleagues. I was not fenced in or fenced out of news assignments, whether the subject was politics, murder, civil rights, disaster or beauty queens. When any assignment came up, if I was the man on deck, I covered it.

And there were times when I had reason to bitch and swear like everyone else about our common grievances—long periods of ridiculous nighttime hours, extra shifts on what was supposed to be a day off, and working with borrowed equipment in the office. It took me four and a half years to get a desk and a typewriter of my own.

All of this, disappointments as well as triumphs, had given me a sense of belonging. Also, a sense of having achieved a measure of fame and fortune on merit, not through somebody's charity. The money was damned good, too. And I was proud in the knowledge that my regular nightly appearances on the screen—talking about anything and everything—served to reinforce in literally millions of black people a belief that all black people harbor deep down: Anything they can do, we can do as well—if only they'll give us the same chance.

But all that is what I *should* have told that formidable array of company executives in refusing to go to Jersey City. During our tense confrontation, I suppose, none of those sentiments could break through my wall of resentment.

As the silence deepened in the room, I realized that it was too late now to retreat. I had told them flatly that I wanted no part of their so-called job-opportunity conference. And since retreat was out of the question, your daddy charged again.

"Furthermore," I said quietly, resigned to the worst, "I resent the whole idea right down to my toes. In the first place, I don't have any jobs to give. It seems to me that the people who do the hiring for this company are the ones to go. That's the only way to convince minorities that you mean business. Not just playing another game. It doesn't mean a thing to send a black example.

"And I resent being regarded as some kind of freak all of a sudden. To be trotted out on exhibit when it suits somebody else's purposes. I am not a freak. I am a man. I am a full-time employee of this company, and I'm doing a competent job. If I'm not, I should be fired."

Well, they didn't fire your daddy; and I have the feeling that nothing further will be said about my going to Jersey City or anywhere else. Except on regular news assignments.

As it always happens in your daddy's little combats, the world hasn't been changed. But I like to think that there are twelve more Charlies in the world who are beginning to understand this: Equal opportunity has nothing to do with conferences. What it's about is simply filling a job with the first capable man who comes along.

Dear Adam,
This is Election Day, my son. The bars are closed. The polls are open. And the Tall Lady has left us alone. She has gone to cast her vote, against my better judgment, and

you have settled down to an afternoon nap. Now I wish to explain why, as part of your daddy's madness, I would not vote if they paid me.

I do not share the white man's confidence in the democratic process at any level—voting, whether in clubs, Congress or courts. Because the question is never what is right, but what the greatest number says is right. And the greatest number is always white. They usually vote against me.

I realize that my position is perhaps unwise, and I am not necessarily recommending it. Your daddy, as they say in the ghettos, is simply telling it like it is.

My refusal to vote, in an age when black men are fighting and dying for the right to vote, is a slice of the black man's cake of ironies. But you see, by the time your daddy was old enough to vote, I had learned that in this country voting is a white man's charade. With its indirect as well as direct results.

It was by legislative voting that they gave us the runaway slave law, which allowed them to return my great-great-grandfather to his master.

It was also by voting that they deceived us with those so-called Civil Rights Acts that promise freedom now. These are nullified, it seems, by other votes on lower levels.

It was by voting on all levels that they came up with that inescapable maze of laws, codes, ordinances and gentlemen's agreements that deny black men more than accidental access to the fruits of the American dream.

It is by voting for judges who ignore justice, or voting for the hacks who appoint them, that they convict, jail and condemn my kinsmen, almost at whim, on the flimsy evidence of their blackness.

It is by the same kind of voting that they regularly excuse their own kind from the penalties legally due to them for denying and brutalizing my brothers.

And finally, it is by several kinds of voting that they interpret the Constitution to mean that it is perfectly natural
and fair to run this society on the premise that black men
are not quite equal and therefore should not be free.

So voting is not for me. It is too insulting and degrading
to support Mister Charlie's pretenses, to pretend that I am
fooled. I am proud to say that your daddy has never even
stooped to register. My self-respect forbids me to accept as
my due the crumbs of Mister Charlie's gaudy feast—the
piddling fallout from his election charades.

He calls them "the democratic process in action." But no
matter what promises he makes, regardless of what issues
he and his kinsmen in the great majority—the power structures—may or may not decide to vote on and regardless of
how the votes turn out, it all adds up to the same:

Voting is a wonderful civilized institution—if used with
integrity, justice, fair play. It *can* move mountains, create
better living and change the world. But somehow, in this
climate, it doesn't work unless you are white.

8

FROM
The Autobiography of Malcolm X

by Malcolm X
(1925–1965)

Malcolm X predicted he would not live long enough to read his published autobiography. Tragically, his prophecy came true. As he was addressing a group of followers on the eve of George Washington's birthday in 1965, the attention of the audience was diverted to the back of the hall. At the same time, at least three men in the front row stood up and fired simultaneously at Malcolm X. He died shortly thereafter.

Malcolm X (born Malcolm Little in Omaha, Nebraska) lost his father when he was quite young and often had to shift for himself. During his teens he alternated between dope peddling and pimping, and by the time he was twenty-one found himself in prison for armed robbery. While in jail he discovered the Black Muslim religion, and after his release became a devoted lieutenant to Elijah Muhammad.

Eventually, however, Malcolm X lost faith in both Muham-
mad personally and in the extremism of his doctrine. By this
time Malcolm had tempered his position enough to admit
that perhaps not all white men were "devils." The Black
Panther Party leaned heavily on his writings and speeches
for their own program.

THE Deep South white press generally blacked me out. But
they front-paged what I felt about Northern white and
black Freedom Riders going *South* to "demonstrate." I
called it "ridiculous"; their own Northern ghettoes, right
at home, had enough rats and roaches to kill to keep all of
the Freedom Riders busy. I said that ultra-liberal New York
had more integration problems than Mississippi. If the
Northern Freedom Riders wanted more to do, they could
work on the roots of such ghetto evils as the little children
out in the streets at midnight, with apartment keys on
strings around their necks to let themselves in, and their
mothers and fathers drunk, drug addicts, thieves, prostitutes. Or the Northern Freedom Riders could light some
fires under Northern city halls, unions, and major indus-
tries to give more jobs to Negroes to remove so many of
them from the relief and welfare rolls, which created lazi-
ness, and which deteriorated the ghettoes into steadily worse
places for humans to live. It was all—it *is* all—the absolute
truth; but what did I want to *say* it for? Snakes couldn't
have turned on me faster than the liberal.

Yes, I will pull off that liberal's halo that he spends such
efforts cultivating! The North's liberals have been for so
long pointing accusing fingers at the South and getting
away with it that they have fits when they are exposed as the
world's worst hypocrites.

I believe my own life *mirrors* this hypocrisy. I know
nothing about the South. I am a creation of the Northern

white man and of his hypocritical attitude toward the Negro.

The white Southerner was always given his due by Mr. Muhammad. The white Southerner, you can say one thing— he is honest. He bares his teeth to the black man; he tells the black man, to his face, that Southern whites never will accept phony "integration." The Southern white goes further, to tell the black man that he means to fight him every inch of the way—against even the so-called "tokenism." The advantage of this is the Southern black man never has been under any illusions about the opposition he is dealing with.

You can say for many Southern white people that, individually, they have been paternalistically helpful to many individual Negroes. But the Northern white man, he grins with his teeth, and his mouth has always been full of tricks and lies of "equality" and "integration." When one day all over America, a black hand touched the white man's shoulder, and the white man turned, and there stood the Negro saying "Me, too . . ." why, that Northern liberal shrank from that black man with as much guilt and dread as any Southern white man.

Actually, America's most dangerous and threatening black man is the one who has been kept sealed up by the Northerner in the black ghettoes—the Northern white power structure's system to keep talking democracy while keeping the black man out of sight somewhere, around the corner.

The word "integration" was invented by a Northern liberal. The word has no real meaning. I ask you: in the racial sense in which it's used so much today, whatever "integration" is supposed to mean, can it be precisely defined? The truth is that "integration" is an *image*, it's a foxy Northern liberal's smoke-screen that confuses the true wants of the American black man. Here in these fifty racist and neoracist states of North America, this word "integration" has millions of white people confused, and angry, believing wrongly that the black masses want to live mixed up with the white man. That is the case only with the relative handful of these "integration"-mad Negroes.

I'm talking about these "token-integrated" Negroes who flee from their poor, downtrodden black brothers—from their own self-hate, which is what they're really trying to escape. I'm talking about these Negroes you will see who can't get enough of nuzzling up to the white man. These "chosen few" Negroes are more white-minded, more anti-black, than even the white man is.

Human rights! Respect as *human beings!* That's what America's black masses want. That's the true problem. The black masses want not to be shrunk from as though they are plague-ridden. They want not to be walled up in slums, in the ghettoes, like animals. They want to live in an open, free society where they can walk with their heads up, like men, and women!

Few white people realize that many black people today dislike and avoid spending any more time than they must around white people. This "integration" image, as it is popularly interpreted, has millions of vain, self-exalted white people convinced that black people want to sleep in bed with them—and that's a lie! Or you can't *tell* the average white man that the Negro man's prime desire isn't to have a white woman—another lie! . . .

The black masses prefer the company of their own kind. Why, even these fancy, bourgeois Negroes—when they get back home from the fancy, "integrated" cocktail parties, what do they do but kick off their shoes and talk about those white liberals they just left as if the liberals were dogs. And the white liberals probably do the very same thing. I can't be sure about the whites, I am never around them in private—but the bourgeois Negroes know I'm not lying.

I'm telling it like it *is*! You *never* have to worry about me biting my tongue if something I know as truth is on my mind. Raw, naked truth exchanged between the black man and the white man is what a whole lot more of is needed in this country—to clear the air of the racial mirages, clichés, and lies that this country's very atmosphere has been filled with for four hundred years.

In many communities, especially small communities, white people have created a benevolent image of themselves as having had so much "good-will toward our Negroes," every time any "local Negro" begins suddenly letting the local whites know the truth—that the black people are sick of being hind-tit, second-class, disfranchised, that's when you hear, uttered so sadly, "Unfortunately now because of this, our whites of good-will are starting to turn against the Negroes. . . . It's so regrettable . . . progress *was* being made . . . but now our communications between the races have broken down!"

What are they talking about? There never was any *communication*. Until after World War II, there wasn't a single community in the entire United States where the white man heard from any local Negro "leaders" the truth of what Negroes felt about the conditions that the white community imposed upon Negroes.

You need some proof? Well, then, why was it that when Negroes did start revolting across America, virtually all of white America was caught up in surprise and even shock? I would hate to be general of an army as badly informed as the American white man has been about the Negro in this country.

This is the situation which permitted Negro combustion to slowly build up to the revolution-point, without the white man realizing it. All over America, the local Negro "leader," in order to survive as a "leader," kept reassuring

the local white man, in effect, "Everything's all right, everything's right in hand, boss!" When the "leader" wanted a
little something for his people: "Er, boss, some of the people
talking about we sure need a better school, boss." And if the
local Negroes hadn't been causing any "trouble," the "benevolent" white man might nod and give them a school, or
some jobs.

The white men belonging to the power structures in
thousands of communities across America know that I'm
right! They know that I am describing what has been the
true pattern of "communications" between the "local
whites of good-will" and the local Negroes. It has been a
pattern created by domineering, ego-ridden whites. Its
characteristic design permitted the white man to feel "noble"
about throwing crumbs to the black man, instead of feeling
guilty about the local community's system of cruelly exploited Negroes.

But I want to tell you something. This pattern, this
"system" that the white man created, of teaching Negroes
to hide the truth from him behind a façade of grinning,
"yessir-bossing," foot-shuffling and head-scratching—that
system has done the American white man more harm than
an invading army would to him.

Why do I say this? Because all this has steadily helped
this American white man to build up, deep in his psyche,
absolute conviction that he *is* "superior." In how many,
many communities have, thus, white men who didn't finish high school regarded condescendingly university-edu-
cated local Negro "leaders," principals of schools, teachers,
doctors, other professionals?

The white man's system has been imposed upon non-
white peoples all over the world. This is exactly the reason
why wherever people who are anything but white live in
this world today, the white man's governments are finding

themselves in deeper and deeper trouble and peril.

Let's just face truth. Facts! Whether or not the white man of the world is able to face truth, and facts, about the true reasons for his troubles—that's what essentially will determine whether or not *he* will now survive.

Today we are seeing this revolution of the non-white peoples, who just a few years ago would have frozen in horror if the mighty white nations so much as lifted an eyebrow. What it is, simply, is that black and brown and red and yellow peoples have, after hundreds of years of exploitation and imposed "inferiority" and general misuse, become, finally, do-or-die sick and tired of the white man's heel on their necks.

How can the white American government figure on selling "democracy" and "brotherhood" to non-white peoples —if they read and hear every day what's going on right here in America, and see the better-than-a-thousand-words photographs of the American white man denying "democracy" and "brotherhood" even to America's native-born non-whites? The world's non-whites know how this Negro here has loved the American white man, and slaved for him, tended to him, nursed him. This Negro has jumped into uniform and gone off and died when this America was attacked by enemies both white and non-white. Such a faithful, loyal non-white as *this*—and *still* America bombs him, and sets dogs on him, and turns fire hoses on him, and jails him by the thousands, and beats him bloody, and inflicts upon him all manner of other crimes.

Of course these things, known and refreshed every day for the rest of the world's non-whites, are a vital factor in these burnings of ambassadors' limousines, these stonings, defilings, and wreckings of embassies and legations, these shouts of "White man, go home!" these attacks on white Christian missionaries, and these bombings and tearing down of flags.

Is it clear why I have said that the American white man's malignant superiority complex has done him more harm than an invading army?

The American black man should be focusing his every effort toward building his *own* businesses, and decent homes for himself. As other ethnic groups have done, let the black people, wherever possible, however possible, patronize their own kind, hire their own kind, and start in those ways to build up the black race's ability to do for itself. That's the only way the American black man is ever going to get respect. One thing the white man never can give the black man is self-respect! The black man never can become independent and recognized as a human being who is truly equal with other human beings until he has what they have, and until he is doing for himself what others are doing for themselves.

The black man in the ghettoes, for instance, has to start self-correcting his own material, moral, and spiritual defects and evils. The black man needs to start his own program to get rid of drunkenness, drug addiction, prostitution. The black man in America has to lift up his own sense of values.

Only a few thousands of Negroes, relatively a very tiny number, are taking any part in "integration." Here, again, it is those few bourgeois Negroes, rushing to throw away their little money in the white man's luxury hotels, his swanky nightclubs, and big, fine, exclusive restaurants. The white people patronizing those places can afford it. But these Negroes you see in those places can't afford it, certainly most of them can't. Why, what does some Negro one installment payment away from disaster look like somewhere downtown out to dine, grinning at some head-waiter who has more money than the Negro? Those bourgeois Negroes out draping big tablecloth-sized napkins over their knees and ordering quail under glass and stewed snails—why, Negroes don't even *like* snails! What they're doing is proving they're integrated.

If you want to get right down to the real outcome of this so-called "integration," what you've got to arrive at is intermarriage.

I'm right *with* the Southern white man who believes that you can't have so-called "integration," at least not for long, without intermarriage increasing. And what good is this for anyone? Let's again face reality. In a world as color-hostile as this, man or woman, black or white, what do they want with a mate of the other race?

Certainly white people have served enough notice of their hostility to any blacks in their families and neighborhoods. And the way most Negroes feel today, a mixed couple probably finds that black families, black communities, are even more hostile than the white ones. So what's bound to face "integrated" marriages except being unwelcomed, unwanted, "misfits" in whichever world they try to live in? What we arrive at is that "integration," socially, is no good for either side. "Integration," ultimately, would destroy the white race . . . and destroy the black race.

The white man's "integrating" with black women has already changed the complexion and characteristics of the black race in America. What's been proved by the "blacks" whose complexions are "whiter" than many "white" people? I'm told that there are in America today between two and five million "white Negroes," who are "passing" in white society. Imagine their torture! Living in constant fear that some black person they've known might meet and expose them. Imagine every day living a lie. *Imagine* hearing their own white husbands, their own white wives, even their own white children, talking about "those Negroes."

I would doubt if anyone in America has heard Negroes more bitter against the white man than some of those I have heard. But I will tell you that, without any question, the *most* bitter anti-white diatribes that I have ever heard have come from "passing" Negroes, living as whites, among whites, exposed every day to what white people say among themselves regarding Negroes—things that a recognized Negro never would hear. Why, if there was a racial showdown, these Negroes "passing" within white circles would become the black side's most valuable "spy" and ally.

9

FROM

Seize the Time

by Bobby Seale

(1936–   )

In October, 1966, Huey Newton, Bobby Seale, and several followers set out a ten-point program which capsuled the aspirations of their revolutionary Black Panther Party. Protesting the injustices of a racist society, the platform demanded, among other things, freedom and self-determination, decent housing and education, an end to police brutality toward, and fair trials for, all black people. Word for word, the American Declaration of Independence was set down as the conclusion to their platform. It is a fact that, as we enter the decade during which we will celebrate the two hundredth anniversary of the American Revolution, 10 percent of this nation's people are still denied many of the freedoms and rights afforded other citizens because of the color of their skin.

The Black Panthers insist they are not a racist organiza-

310

tion. They assert they only want what is rightfully theirs under the Constitution of the United States. They have interpreted the second article of the Bill of Rights to mean they are entitled to defend their life, liberty, and property with guns. "We have never used our guns," says Chairman Bobby Seale, "to shoot up white people. We only defend ourselves against anybody, be they black, blue, green, or red, who attacks us unjustly."

ONE NIGHT Huey, Little Bobby, and I were patroling this pig in North Oakland. We had been patroling him for a couple of hours. We'd be about a block away from him wherever he'd go. Sometimes we'd stop and lose the pig, but ten, twenty minutes later he'd make it around again, he'd be back where he was, and we'd patrol him some more. Little Bobby had an M-1, I had a .45, and brother Huey had a shotgun and a law book on the back seat. Brother Huey was driving my old '54 Chevy. I guess we patroled for quite a while, then on Fifty-eighth Street we saw the pig stop up at the corner. We stopped at the corner, and he backed up and parked right in front of the stop sign at the corner of Fifty-eighth and Grove. I remember us saying we were tired of patroling this pig, "Let's go in." It was about 8:30 or 9:30 when we drove down the street and stopped next to the pig. We were stopped at the stop sign. I looked over at the pig. Naturally we were carrying guns in Oakland in those days. The shotgun barrel was sticking up. I was holding on to the shotgun while Huey drove. I was on the right hand side of the front seat and the shotgun was to my left, next to my left leg. It was standing straight up resting on its butt. I looked over at the pig, the pig looked back and looked over to me and to Little Bobby, who had his M-1 in the back seat between his legs, the barrel of it showed through the window, too.

Huey had completed his stop and he started off again and started turning right, right in front of the pig's car. As we were turning right, the pig flashed his lights on and he flashed his high beams on. Huey kept moving. He didn't stop and didn't speed up. See, those pigs don't shake Huey at all. I guess we drove no more than twenty feet when we could see the red light flashing. He was starting his engine up and pulling out of the spot where he was parked, making a right turn right behind us. Huey kept moving. He got ready to make a left turn right there at the next little corner. He made his left turn and said, "I'm not going to stop till he puts his damn siren on because a flashing red light really don't mean nothin', anything could be a flashing red light." Well, the pig cut his siren on as he was turning the corner following us and when he cut his siren on, Huey stopped. We'd been stopped by pigs a number of times, pigs who'd seen us with guns and didn't know what to do. We were down with it because Huey had put us together and knew how to handle the situation.

This pig surprised us because he stopped his car as soon as we stopped. He stopped his car about twenty-five feet in back of our car. Some pigs stop right up behind you, but he was twenty-five feet from us. He got out of his car and as soon as he did, and came walking from his door, we could hear this pig hollering, "What the goddam hell you niggers doing with them goddam guns? Who in the goddam hell you niggers think you are? Get out of that goddam car. Get out of that goddam car with them goddam guns."

Huey said, "You ain't putting nobody under arrest. Who the hell do you think you are?"

The pig snatched the door open. When he snatched it open he said, "I said get out of that goddam car and bring them goddam guns out of there."

Huey said, "Man, what the hell?" By this time the pig

came all the way up, his head inside the door, and he's reaching across Huey real fast. This all happened so fast. He was
grabbing hold of the barrel of the shotgun, and I tightened
up on it and pulled it away from him. At the same time I was
pulling the shotgun away from him, Huey grabbed the pig
by the collar, pushed his head back up against the roof of
the car, then shifted around and got his foot and kicked him
in the belly, shoving him all the way out of the car. The pig
fell backwards about ten feet from the car but as he was going out, no sooner had Huey finished putting his foot in
this pig's belly, kicking and pushing him out of the car—and
the pig was being propelled and off balance, away from the
car—than Huey was grabbing hold of the barrel of the shotgun. No sooner did Brother Huey's feet hit the ground, but
he was jacking a round off into the chamber, "Clack upp,"
and taking three quick steps.

The pig looked up and looked around, and Huey P. Newton was stand there saying, "Now, who in the hell do you
think you are, you big rednecked bastard, you rotten fascist
swine, you bigoted racist? You come into my car, trying to
brutalize my property away from me. Go for your gun and
you're a dead pig." The pig folded his hands up. By this
time I'd gotten out of the car on the other side, put the .45
in my hand, and pulled the hammer back. As soon as Huey
finished saying what he had to say, Little Bobby jumped
out on the back of our car and jacked a round off in the M-1.
The pig heard these clicks and looked back at Huey, and
the pig folded his hands up. In other words, he was taking
his hands away from his gun. Huey had said, "Go for your
gun and you're a dead pig. Don't you know by the Fourteenth Amendment of the U.S. Constitution that you can't
remove a person's property from them without due process of
law?" Huey was mad, loud, and articulate.

The pig began to walk and he kind of did a half-moon,

walking around and away from Huey, trying to walk back to his car. Huey just stepped back holding his gun on him and the pig came walking back to his car hollering, "They got guns. They got guns. They got guns." He got on his radio, "Niggers down here got guns. Get me some help down here. Niggers got guns, they got guns." This pig was scared.

Black people began to come out of their houses, wanting to know what was going on. Huey said, "Come on out, black people. Come on out and get to know about these racist dog swine who been controlling our community and occupying our community like a foreign troop. Come on out and we're going to show you about swine pigs." People got to coming out. It must have been around 9:30 because we were in the back of Merritt College and people in night school were coming out, and I guess seventy or eighty had gathered up there before the other pigs got there. They had about fifteen cars come down there—fifteen cars and pigs everywhere. So me and Huey and Little Bobby were there with our guns. The people were there. I think Little Bobby placed his gun right back on the back seat again. He was sitting in the seat and he shut the door and got back out. Huey and I had been warning Little Bobby about keeping in his possession the written permission he had, and to carry with him the written permission thing from his father to carry and keep the gun because he was still under eighteen at the time, and I think he didn't have it. He realized that he'd better lay the gun down.

Huey was talking to most of the people and running it down to the people about how racism was rotten. How these pigs were brutal and murderous racists. And every time Huey said something I'd say it right behind him, I'd say the same thing, I'd say, "That's right." And he would say, "Racist

dogs pigs occupy our community, come down here to brutalize and kill and murder us. I'm tired of it," and I'd say,
"That's right, racist dogs, pigs occupying our community
like a foreign troop that occupies territory. Black people are
tired of it." Every time Huey said something I'd say something. The pigs must have thought that we was crazy niggers. A pig walks up and says, "Let me see that weapon!"

Huey says, "Let you see my weapon? You haven't placed
me under arrest."

"Well, you just let me see the weapon, I have a right to see
the weapon."

Huey says, "Ain't you ever heard of the Fourteenth Amendment of the Constitution of the United States? Don't you
know you don't remove nobody's property without due process of law?" Huey got loud at those last words. "What's
the matter with you? You're supposed to be people enforc-
ing the law, and here you are, ready to violate my constitutional rights. You can't see my gun. You can't have my gun.
The only way you're gonna get it from me is to try to take it."

Then another pig walks up to me. "Come over here by
the car."

"I ain't going no goddam place. Who the hell you think
you are? You ain't placed me under arrest."

"But I have a right to take you over to the car."

"You don't have no right to move me from one spot to
another."

Huey P. Newton, the Minister of Defense, teaches us and
runs it down to us that whenever a cop moves a person from
one spot to another, then he's technically under arrest, and
if the cop states that you're not under arrest, or doesn't say
you're under arrest when you ask, then he has no right to ask
you to move from one spot to another.

"You just got through telling me I wasn't under arrest, so
I'm not moving nowhere, I'm staying right here."

"Well, you let me see that gun."

"I said you can't see my gun," and I ran down the Fourteenth Amendment of the Constitution just like Huey had run it down. The pigs were frustrated, mad, and didn't know what to do.

"Well, I got a right to look at the serial number."

"I already know what the serial number is," I said.

"I got to make sure it has a serial number." So I held my gun in my hand and he looked at it with his flashlight. "Hold it up, let me see."

"No, I ain't holding up nothing. You got a flashlight so you look at it from that distance right there, because you don't get near this gun." So I read the serial number, and I said, "There's the serial."

The pig took the serial number down and after that a police lieutenant came down, and he kept saying, "Well, if we charge him, we'll probably lose the case, just for them having guns, we'll probably lose the case because they turn around the Second Amendment of the Constitution about them having a right to carry guns as long as they ain't concealed."

Then one big fat pig says, "Well, we gotta find something. We gotta find something to do to them." He was looking down, he started looking the car over and he said that the license plate was being held on by a coat hanger. It was secure all right, but it was just put together with a coat hanger. "Let's give them a ticket for this here, this here license plate is not adequately secure." He asked Huey for some identification and Huey handed him his license. They said his license looked kind of old so they gave him a ticket for not having a good new license. Huey later went to court, pleaded not guilty on both counts, and beat both tickets.

The pigs jumped up and left the scene and the black

people were asking what was happening. While Huey was calling the pigs all kinds of names and stuff, a lot of the brothers said, "Right on time, Huey. Tell it. Right. Run it down, Huey." Huey talked to the people some more and a lot of them said they were going to come down and join the Black Panther Party. And we did get some of the older brothers and sisters and some young brothers and sisters out there to join. Even a number of white people had a chance to watch that.

Badge 206 was the cop. The cop who almost got his head blown away that night. I kept telling him he was acting a fool. Badge 206. Badge 206. We never forgot his badge. I remembered his badge, Huey remembered his badge, and Bobby Hutton remembered his badge. We put his number on the front page of our newspaper.